PENSIONS

IN CRISIS

A PENSION RIGHTS CENTER REPORT

PENSIONS

IN CRISIS

Why the System is Failing America and How You Can Protect Your Future

Karen Ferguson

and Kate Blackwell

Foreword by Teresa Heinz

ARCADE PUBLISHING • NEW YORK

First Edition

This book provides an overview of rules relating to private retirement plans. It is not intended to be a substitute for legal or other professional advice. If legal or other assistance is required, the reader should seek the services of a competent lawyer or other professional. Professional advice cannot be given without full knowledge of an individual's particular situation.

Library of Congress Cataloging-in-Publication Data

Ferguson, Karen.
    Pensions in crisis : why the system is failing America and how you
can protect your future / Karen Ferguson and Kate Blackwell. — 1st ed.
        p.   cm.
    ISBN 1–55970–296–6
    1. Pensions — United States.   2. Old age pensions — United States.
3. Retirement income — United States.   I. Blackwell, Kate.   II. Title.
    HD7125.F46   1995
    331. 25'2'0973 — dc20   94-41722

Published in the United States of America by Arcade Publishing, Inc., New York
Distributed by Little, Brown and Company

10 9 8 7 6 5 4 3 2 1

BP

Design by Jeffrey L. Ward

Printed in the United States of America

For Andrew, Leni, Diana, and Gregory

For Andrew, Leni, Diana, and Gregory

CONTENTS

FOREWORD

Pensions in Crisis tackles the critical problem of how Americans prepare for retirement. Written for the average citizen and policymaker alike, the book will guide and enrich the coming national debate on pension policy.

Many of the issues discussed in the book were issues that occupied John Heinz during his 12-year career in the United States Senate. He wanted to ensure that women would be treated more fairly by the private pension system, to eliminate pension inequities for all people, and to develop programs that would educate the public about the need for sources of income to supplement social security. To those ends, he worked on a bipartisan basis to enact the Retirement Equity Act of 1984 and Tax Reform Act of 1986 — laws that provided pensions to millions of working men and women, widows, divorced homemakers, and others previously denied pension benefits.

As chairman of the Senate Special Committee on Aging, John Heinz became convinced that instead of this nation's fragmented approach to pensions, we needed to have a single, coherent policy on retirement income, and he made every effort to stimulate debate on the various alternatives. His death in a plane crash in 1991 cut short his campaign to move Congress and the country toward adopting such a policy.

In July 1992, the Teresa and H. John Heinz III Foundation awarded a grant to the Pension Rights Center to undertake a comprehensive study of the private retirement system. It had become clear to me that unless the American public was informed of the many significant problems confronting our private pension system we risked seeing the congressional debate on retirement income being silenced.

This book is the result. It lays out the problems and the choices we face. A crisis is before us. It is time to confront and overcome it.

—Teresa Heinz

PREFACE

I hope when this letter is read that you'll realize I do need help. I don't have much time left. . . . I'm 75 years old. My income just will not stretch far enough to pay all the bills.

— Ettie Jo Gilmer
Gantt, Alabama

Ettie Jo Gilmer's cry for help is one of thousands the Pension Rights Center receives every year from people who didn't get the pension they'd been counting on. They learned too late that pension rules can deny people benefits or give them next to nothing. They feel cheated. Many, like Ettie Jo Gilmer, face poverty for the first time in their lives. They are desperate and have nowhere to turn.

Americans as a whole are not prepared for retirement. Social security is not enough to live on, a fact few people realize. It is practically impossible for anyone other than those in the highest income brackets to save enough to make a difference. Everyone needs another source of income, which makes pensions absolutely critical. But although they pay off handsomely to some, pensions provide little or nothing to everyone else. Two-thirds of the nearly 90 million Americans in the private workforce today aren't even *in* a pension plan.

The numbers tell the story: the system is in crisis. And it's getting worse, as more and more employers drop traditional plans and tell their employees to save for themselves through 401(k)s and other tax-sheltered savings arrangements. The savings myth is today's new twist on retirement. What employers don't say — and what the numbers do — is that those who will profit from these new savings plans are people wealthy enough to save without tax incentives.

Even though it threatens the quality of life for millions of Americans, the crisis is still a quiet one. Social security and government pensions have made the headlines; private pensions, by and large, have not. The media pick up on occasional scandals but important pension issues go totally unreported, and what *is* reported tends to distort, mislead, or falsely reassure. It is time to set the record straight.

Private pensions affect everyone. Everyone must pay for the multibillion-dollar tax subsidy granted to employers that offer plans. Everyone receives less from social security on the assumption that pensions will make up the difference. And everyone feels the economic impact of the more than $3 trillion in private pension funds, rightly called the "largest lump of money in the world." It helps determine the jobs we get, the goods we buy, even the fate of our communities.

To protect their pensions, people need to know how the system works; what rules they should be aware (and wary) of, what's happening to the money in pension funds, and how to make sure it's safe. Ettie Jo Gilmer didn't have that kind of information. She didn't even know she needed it — until she found that she didn't have enough to live on. Millions of people are making the same discovery. It can happen to anyone.

ACKNOWLEDGMENTS

Our gratitude goes first to all the people who have contacted the Pension Rights Center over the years, whose experiences inspired the writing of this book and provided much of its content. In particular, we are grateful to those who took the time to tell us their stories in detail and permitted us to retell them here. We also especially thank Teresa Heinz, president of the Teresa and H. John Heinz III Foundation, and Jeffrey Lewis, executive director of the foundation, for their generous support of the research and writing of this book.

The book could not have been written without the staff of the Pension Rights Center, whose research assistance, logistical help, and never-faltering moral support we appreciate more than we can say. We owe an enormous debt to attorney Cindy Hounsell, who not only helped us with the numbers but also kept us going through successive stages of the writing with her great good humor and commonsense about it all. Shaun O'Brien we thank for his steady hand on the notes and his willingness to spend endless hours helping us track down answers to our endless questions. We thank Barbara Johnson for cheerfully typing and proofing numerous drafts of the manuscript without ever making a mistake, and Linda Delavorias and Angela Rakis for their helpful research assistance. For substantive suggestions and review of chapters, we thank attorneys Marilyn Park, Pat Humphlett, Trip

Reid, and Ann Marie Marciarille. And we thank Ellen Matthews, the center's administrator, for arranging the cartoon permissions and holding the office together through all the chaos.

We want also to acknowledge all those who generously shared their pension expertise with us by reviewing specific chapters and making invaluable technical suggestions, though we point out that the book does not necessarily reflect their views. We thank Nancy Altman, Randy Barber, Phyllis Borzi, Ronald Dean, Teresa Ghilarducci, Daniel Halperin, Ian Lanoff, Jeffrey Lewis, Robert Monks, Anne Moss, Robert Nagle, Norman Stein, and Michele Varnhagen. We are particularly grateful to Harry Conaway and John Turner, who took the time to critique the entire manuscript.

For their help in guiding us through the morass of pension statistics, we thank Gordon Lester, John Woods, and especially Daniel Beller.

For their close reading and very helpful editorial suggestions, we thank Barbara Coleman and Heddy Reid.

We want to acknowledge Paul Edwards, Andrew Ferguson, and Karen Friedman for suggesting key concepts; Alice Hudders, Susan Lehman, and Margaret Scott for sharing their artistry; Felix Jakob for assisting in the title stage; John Ferguson and Sidney Willner for their wise counsel throughout; Timothy Bent of Arcade Publishing for his skilled attention to our prose; and Ralph Nader for first recognizing the importance of citizen involvement in pensions.

PART I

THE PENSION PATCHWORK

CHAPTER 1

An American Dream

"You'll be able to settle down on a farm . . . visit around the country or just take it easy . . . and know that you'll still be getting a regular monthly pension paid for entirely by the company."

—Studebaker pension plan booklet[1]

It was just before Christmas in 1963 when Bill Piatkowski found out that his job was gone. He walked into the machine shop at the Studebaker plant in South Bend, Indiana, just as he had every morning for 24 years, ready for somebody to crack a joke. But nobody was smiling that day. Then one of his coworkers told him. Studebaker was shutting down its South Bend operations and moving to Canada. Seven thousand men and women would be laid off over the next few months as Studebaker systematically closed its doors. Tall, lanky Bill Piatkowski was one of the last to leave: "They closed up the plant after I walked out the door." He was 42 years old.

The pain went deeper than job loss. Four thousand workers lost their pensions as well. People who were already retired or had reached age 60 and had worked for the company for at least 15 years kept their benefits, but the others got a pittance, or nothing. Bill Piatkowski got a grand total of $115. As one of his colleagues remarked, bitterly, the payments were an insult, worse than nothing.

The workers had thought that their pensions were safe, but they were wrong. Large chunks of promised benefits had never been funded. This would have posed no problem had the company stayed in business, but Studebaker's decision to close caught the plan by surprise. There was no safety net. The risk belonged to the workers.

"It was the pensions that really hurt." Bill Piatkowski recalled. "It was part of working for the company, you know. We all had these book-lets the company handed out telling us we could count on the pension. And we were so loyal in those days. We didn't question. I remember my wife didn't even *like* people who didn't drive a Studebaker."

The pension loss was grievous, but retirement still seemed a long way off to the Piatkowskis. They had three young daughters to raise and bills to pay. Harriet Piatkowski advised her husband to take the first job he could find, and he did. Two jobs and three years later, he was working as a machinist for South Bend Lathe Company, which had taken over the old Studebaker machine shop building. It was like coming home. He was literally going back through the same door he'd walked out of in 1963, working "fifty feet from where I worked under Studebaker."

He enjoyed working at South Bend Lathe. "Every machine opera-tor in the country learned on one of our lathes," he says proudly. He was a supervisor in the press division and often worked unpaid overtime. Then new management came in and business began to go downhill; orders were sent off to a company in Korea; lathes were not well made — "scrap," he says. He had worked for the company for more than nine years when the owners terminated the pension plan.

This time, unlike Studebaker, the company had enough money in the pension till to pay workers the benefits they had earned. The trouble was, the plan required that employees had to have worked ten years to earn anything. Nine years and three months didn't do it. Bill Piatkowski became a two-time loser.

But the genial machinist wasn't counted out yet. South Bend Lathe was still in operation, so he still had his job, and though there wasn't a pension plan anymore, in its place he now owned "shares" of the company that could be cashed in on retirement. This arrangement, known as an employee stock ownership plan (ESOP), carries a risk that traditional pension plans don't: the size of the benefit depends entirely on the profitability of the business.

When Bill Piatkowski first came under the South Bend Lathe ESOP, his stock was worth $525 per share. Seven years later, when he was laid off at age 62, a share was worth $47. Today the company is in bankruptcy and his "pension" is valueless.

Three strikes.

Today, Bill Piatkowski is a soft-spoken man of 73, rarely seen without his baseball cap. He is still working — at two jobs, in fact: ushering at University of Notre Dame basketball and hockey games, and serving as a security guard three nights a week at the *South Bend*

Tribune. Combined, they bring in around $7,500 a year. The rest of his income comes from his social security checks, totaling a little more than $8,000 a year — almost exactly the average social security benefit today for a retired full-career worker.[2] Harriet Piatkowski receives a social security spouse's benefit equal to half this amount.

Bill and Harriet Piatkowski are not big spenders. She makes most of their clothes. He built their house himself. "It's a good design. People come and look at it and ask me for the plan." But the Piatkowskis have very little in savings.

"When I got laid off [from South Bend Lathe], my wife said, 'It's all right, Bill. We've got $2,000 in the bank.' Sometimes she even saves half of my *Tribune* check and puts it in the bank. Of course, we take it out pretty quick."

Theirs is a familiar scenario. Most Americans go into retirement with very little in savings.[3]

What is life like at 73 without a pension? "Well," Bill Piatkowski says, "for a night on the town you take your wife to McDonald's and share a large order of fries."

He pauses, then adds, "And you wake up in the morning and just hope you can keep on working."

"The pension promise doesn't mean you're going to get one, you know," Harriet Piatkowski said recently. "Life is unfair. As long as we've got our health . . ."

But what would happen if her husband were no longer able to work? What if he should die? As a widow, Harriet Piatkowski's sole source of income would be her husband's social security. She would join the ranks of one of the poorest segments of the American population — older women living alone.[4]

What happened to the American Dream? Retiring to a farm or buying an RV? Settling down secure in the knowledge that a pension check will be arriving every month? Harriet and Bill Piatkowski can tell you what studies have shown: there are two classes of citizens in the United States when it comes to retirement, those *with* pensions, who can make ends meet, and those *without* pensions, who can't.[5]

A product of American enterprise and nineteenth-century paternalism, the private pension system has played a vital role in shaping the American way of retirement as it exists today. Pensions are the principal reason that the United States retirement system differs from that in other industrialized countries. Most Western European countries have publicly mandated programs designed to ensure that workers can meet basic expenses after they retire. The social security system in the United States, however, was deliberately structured to provide people with only a bare-bones level of support, merely a *floor* on which to build retirement income. In Spain, a full-career factory worker like Bill Piatkowski can count on retiring with approximately 90 percent of pay; in Sweden, with 85 percent; in France, with 70 percent; and in Germany, with 50 percent.[6] In the United States, by contrast, social security provides the average full-career worker with only 40 percent of what he or she earned while working.[7] American retirees are supposed to make up the rest through savings and pensions — the other two legs of the so-called three-legged stool of U.S. retirement income policy.[8] However, more and more Americans cannot balance their retirement on those three sources of income. Social security is not enough; savings aren't a significant source of income for most older Americans; and *only one-third of private sector retirees are receiving monthly pensions.*[9]

Drawing by Margaret Scott

The fact is, private pensions were never intended for everyone; they started as rewards for a favored few. The first company to award them was American Express in 1875, followed by the railroads and a handful of other firms. These early pensions served as a highly useful way of easing older workers out of the workforce without too much pain. They were bestowed as gifts from employers to loyal long-service employees. By 1930, most big companies, including AT&T, General Electric, and Du Pont, had pension plans.

The years after World War II were the heyday of private pension plans. The most popular ones promised benefits to retiring workers based on their rate of pay and years of work. The insurance companies and consultants that created and sold them touted their flexibility. They could fill the bill for all kinds of labor forces, from coal miners to chemical workers, from those whose physical labor wore them out young to those who could go on working to older ages. Best of all, employers could design plans that gave bigger rewards to certain employees, such as themselves, and none at all to others.

Labor leaders at the time were won over to the idea of private pensions, though not to employers' view of them as rewards. In 1948, an appeals court ruled that, like wages, pensions were a condition of employment that unions could insist on including in the bargaining process.[10] Union pressures for pensions increased after this decision.

During the 1950s, the number of companies offering private pension plans grew by leaps and bounds. The number of workers covered rose from 10 million in 1950 to 19 million in 1960.[11] Pension fund assets ballooned from $12 billion to $55 billion.[12] It wasn't until the early 1960s, and the Studebaker plan collapse, that people began to question private pension plans seriously, to wonder who they were really benefiting, and to ask why so many people were *not* getting them.

When Studebaker closed, it was the workers' devastating pension losses that made the headlines. Scores of journalists descended on South Bend to report the Studebaker story. The result was an avalanche of mail to Congress. Hundreds of thousands of letters recounted stories of pension losses similar to those in Indiana as well as other disturbing practices, such as older employees being fired just before retirement to keep them from getting pensions and outright theft of workers' pension money.[13]

A decade of study and debate passed before Congress acted. Business groups initially fought the government's efforts to regulate what private enterprise had created and nurtured. But pensions were now widely viewed as more than rewards for favored employees; they were part of the wage package, woven into the fabric of the country's retirement policy. Finally, on Labor Day in 1974, the Employee Retirement Income Security Act became law. ERISA, as this landmark legislation is called, was hailed by its principal sponsor, New York Senator Jacob Javits, as "the greatest development in the life of the American worker since Social Security."[14]

To prevent future "Studebakers," ERISA set up an insurance program for pension plans that closed down without enough money to pay benefits. The new law established requirements for the safe handling of pension monies, gave workers the right to earn a pension after ten years of work (instead of 20 or 30 years or a lifetime, as was commonly the case), and provided benefits for widows and widowers.

Passage of ERISA launched two decades of efforts to make the American private pension system fairer and more secure. Through a series of laws passed in the 1980s, Congress extended pension protection to millions more workers, among them lower-paid, shorter-service, and older employees, as well as to widowed and divorced homemakers. Other laws strengthened the pension insurance program and limited the ability of companies to use their plans to manipulate the tax system.

Each of these reforms, when originally proposed, raised a storm of protest from the business community, which claimed that it would be the final "nail in the coffin" of the private pension system: if employers couldn't structure pension plans in ways that served corporate interests, they would simply drop their plans. After all, companies were not required to provide pension plans for their workers; if they couldn't run their plans the way they wanted, they would just pick up their marbles and go home. The threat induced lawmakers to accept complicated compromises in the final provisions of the new laws, so that although they protected large numbers of people, the reforms left out many others.

At the same time that Congress was writing new legislation to make private pensions fairer for more people, government agencies were busy reinterpreting existing laws in ways that allowed companies to escape the new requirements. For example, the Internal Revenue Service and the Labor Department, responding to pressure from industry lobbyists, revised rules to permit companies to close their pension plans for the purpose of scooping out so-called surplus cash and then depositing it into corporate coffers. More than $20 billion was stripped from pension plans before Congress limited (but did not put an end to) the practice of pension raiding.

Another rule revision permitted employers to offer new do-it-yourself savings plans that provided generous tax breaks to those employees who could afford to use them. These new plans gave American retirement policy a radical new twist, making individual workers, not employers, responsible for putting money aside for retirement.

Meanwhile, during all the rule changes, money in private pension plans continued to accumulate, so that these huge funds now dominate the economic landscape of the country.

It has been over 30 years since Bill Piatkowski lost his job with Studebaker, and his pension along with it. Large sections of the old automobile factory in South Bend have now been razed and are covered by rubble. But at the union hall down the street, Studebaker retirees still meet to talk about old times and old friends. They also continue to campaign for legislation to provide modest benefits for pension losers around the country — 38,000 elderly people who, like themselves, lost their pensions before ERISA was passed and have not benefited from any of the reforms.

Who *has* benefited? Just how much better off will tomorrow's retirees be?

Twenty Years of Private Pension Reforms

The *Employee Retirement Income Security Act of 1974 (ERISA)* provided protection for people working for private employers who were paying into pension plans after the effective dates of the law's provisions:

- Most people working under defined benefit pension plans as of July 1, 1974, came under the new pension insurance program.
- The law's provisions requiring certain plan information to be disclosed to employees went into effect on January 1, 1975, as did its protections against fund mismanagement.
- New rules reducing the number of years of work required to earn benefits to ten, and giving retirees the chance to provide survivors benefits applied to most people working during or after 1976.

In 1982, Congress passed the *Tax Equity and Fiscal Responsibility Act (TEFRA)*. Under this law, plans in which 60 percent of the contributions or benefits go to company officers and owners have to pay at least minimum benefits to other employees after two or three years of employment. TEFRA affected people working during or after 1984.

The *Retirement Equity Act of 1984 (REA)* gave new rights to homemakers widowed or divorced after 1984 and provided new protections for workers who leave the job for a time and then return.

The *Omnibus Budget Reconciliation Act of 1986 (OBRA)* ended the practice of denying pension credit for years worked after age 65 and gave pension coverage to employees who started work at or after age 60.

In the *Tax Reform Act (TRA)* of 1986, Congress reduced the length of time most people need to work before earning benefits from ten to five years. The five-year rule applies to people working under plans established by a company for its employees after 1988. (The ten-year rule was kept for union-negotiated plans to which more than one company contributes.) The law also limits (but does not end) practices that allow companies to exclude employees from a plan and to take social security into account in figuring the dollar amount of pension benefits.

CHAPTER 2

Pension Tension

[T]his pension field is an esoteric and abstruse one, bordering on the mysterious or the occult. . . . And it is also truly an eye-glazing subject.

—Rhode Island Senator John Chafee[1]

For 25 years, Leslie Clark crisscrossed the globe as a flight attendant for Pan American World Airways, calling 16 different cities home. Hectic as it made her life, she loved her job. It expanded her world, and Pan Am, by its own definition, became her extended family. Company officials liked to talk about the ways the airline took care of its people — in particular, through its good health plan and pension benefits. For Leslie Clark, these protections, along with the free travel, were the main reasons she had taken the job.

Up until only a few years ago, this 52-year-old dynamo would have told you that she had her career — and her future — firmly in hand. Then in 1991 Pan Am went bankrupt, and her secure world fell apart. Thanks to ERISA, she didn't lose her defined benefit pension. The government pension insurance program set up in response to the Studebaker debacle will pay her a pension of $4,800 a year for life, if she waits until age 60 to start collecting benefits. In addition, she received a lump sum payout of $5,500 from a Pan Am defined contribution pension plan.

"It's not much after 25 years of flying," she says, ruefully. Still, she's happy to have gotten something out of her plans.

Her new employer, Delta Airlines, also offers a defined benefit plan. Under the plan, thanks to the reform legislation passed in the

1980s, she will have to work only five years, rather than ten, to earn a pension. Delta also has a tax-sheltered savings plan established as a result of rule changes in the past decade. She has been flying extra hours so as to be able to contribute the maximum amount to this plan, though she has no idea how much it will ultimately yield.

Leslie Clark holds a lot of pieces of the "pension patchwork," but after all is said and done, she is terrified that they will not provide the blanket of protection she will need to keep her warm in her old age. When she reads articles on how much money people need just to live modestly in retirement, she panics. "What happens," she asks, "when I'm too old to push a 200-pound bar cart up an aisle?"

Reprinted by permission of Tribune Media Services.

Despite her pension tension, Leslie Clark is more fortunate than many of her friends and a large majority of American workers: *only one-third of full-time private sector workers are participating in traditional pension and profit sharing plans.*[2]

She is also better off than the thirty-something baby boomers she meets at her exercise class. Although they stand a 50–50 chance of being covered by some kind of private retirement plan, they are less likely than Leslie Clark to be in a pension or profit sharing plan that is funded by their employers.[3] The odds are that they will be in a tax-sheltered savings plan instead, which means they will be contributing the money, or most of the money, themselves.

The percentage of the workforce in old-style pension and profit sharing plans is shrinking rapidly as more and more companies replace them with savings plans. Overall participation in traditional plans has dropped 30 percent in the past decade.[4] The shift is most noticeable in the small business sector, where tens of thousands of small companies have dropped their old-style pension plans and told their workers to save for themselves. Most large companies like Delta Airlines have not formally canceled their pension plans but, rather, are deemphasizing them. Instead of putting money into plans that include employees at all income levels, as in the past, companies are channeling new retirement dollars into savings plans to match contributions made by employees who are well enough off to put money in first.

You don't have to be an economist to figure out the problem here: most Americans live paycheck to paycheck and either can't afford to contribute anything to a savings plan or are able to put in only small amounts. Those people who are making significant contributions don't need a tax incentive to put money aside. They would have saved anyway.

If current trends continue, the gap between older Americans at the top of the income ladder and those at the bottom — already greater than in any other major industrialized country[5] — will widen further. By the time the last of the baby boomers retires, one out of every five Americans will be over age 65. Although some of them will live well, most are likely to spend their golden years like Bill and Harriet Piatkowski, sharing fries and dreading the day when they are no longer able to work.

Significantly, employers are not claiming that their new savings plans can provide adequate income for the majority of retirees. They say only that do-it-yourself arrangements are less complicated and less costly than pension plans, which is true. And besides, they say, their employees are not protesting the changeover. This is also true. Employees have proved conspicuously silent in defense of "old-fashioned" company-paid plans.

Leslie Clark is a good example of the reason for this silence. She was shocked by how small her Pan Am benefits were. They amounted to only *half* the amount she had counted on getting! She had not realized that, like most plans, Pan Am's was structured to give large amounts to people who worked for the company up until the end of their careers, while those who quit or lost their jobs earlier got tiny benefits. Had she been able to work for the company until retirement, her pension would have been around $9,600 a year.

She is also worried that the Delta pension plan won't come through. Since she has another two years to go before she earns a right to a benefit, she hasn't yet tried to figure out the amount she may get — the calculation seems too complicated. By contrast, the savings plan seems simple and straightforward: she puts the money in, Delta matches part of it with company stock, and she gets a tax break; then she crosses her fingers that the investment choices she has made are the right ones. She knows that she is too far along in her career to accumulate sizable sums in her account, but she likes the simplicity.

Millions of Americans have learned through experience that private pension plans, designed for an older industrial age of full-career workers, severely penalize today's highly mobile postindustrial workforce: job changers usually leave most, if not all, of their benefits behind forever. Added to that loss are rules that can seem cruelly unfair, unexpected cutbacks when plans are discontinued, benefits decimated by inflation, and the plundering of pension funds by unscrupulous trustees. It isn't hard to understand why many employees have turned against traditional plans. To be sure, there are still plenty of people who profit handsomely from these plans, but even winners are not protesting the shift from pensions to savings arrangements, possibly because they are aware that their benefits come at the expense of those who have lost out.

If the new savings plans can't do the job and employees are dissatisfied with old-style pensions, what direction should future retirement policy take in this country? All Americans have a stake in the answer to that question, not only because it will determine how people live when they grow old but also because it will affect how much they will have to pay in taxes to support the system.[6] Decisions about retirement income will have an impact on the entire economy as well, since the more than $3 trillion in private pension funds today constitutes the nation's largest single source of savings and investment capital.[7]

Despite their tremendous importance to individuals and the economy, pensions have been largely overlooked as a public policy issue. Occasionally, disclosure of a pension scandal or predictions of an impending catastrophe have made headlines, but as a general topic of public concern, the perception seems to be that pensions are "eyeglazing" — not something to read about over morning coffee.

In fact, pensions are of tremendous interest to a great many people, particularly those who have had personal encounters with the system. These individuals may be bewildered, frustrated, or angry, but they do not think that pensions are boring. Most are impatient for the public spotlight to be focused on retirement policy issues.

That is starting to happen. Labor Day 1994 marked the twentieth anniversary of ERISA. Forums and conferences on old-age income are being convened with increasing frequency; there are new calls for the formation of a national retirement income policy; a variety of legislative proposals are being introduced into Congress. However, all these activities will lead *nowhere* unless those individuals who have had firsthand experience with pensions take an active part in the public policy debates.

Until recently, most workers and retirees who have run up against the system have felt uncomfortable speaking up about their concerns. They feel very much alone, unaware that others have had similar experiences, or that many different kinds of problems exist. Most know only their own particular corner of the nation's vast private pension crazy quilt.

But the biggest obstacle keeping pension veterans — and everyone else — from becoming effective participants in retirement policy discussions is that they do not fully understand how plans work or why they are structured the way they are. They need to know the rules of the pension game.

The World of Private Retirement Plans

DEFINED BENEFIT PLANS

Leslie Clark had two pension plans at Pan Am and is currently covered by a plan at Delta. Her original Pan Am plan, like her Delta pension plan, was a *defined benefit plan*, which guaranteed her a fixed lifetime benefit starting at retirement age. Nearly 26 million people, three-fifths of the 43 million workers participating in company and union retirement plans, are in this kind of plan.[8]

Most defined benefit plans base the amount of benefits on the number of years people work and on their average earnings during their last several years under the plan. In certain defined benefit plans, such as those in the auto and steel industries, benefits consist of a specific dollar amount for each year worked.

Defined benefit plans require that the employer put in enough money to pay the fixed benefits specified in the plan, an amount determined by mathematical estimates as to how much the fund's investments will bring in, how many workers will forfeit benefits, how many will die without spouses, how old they will be when benefits begin, and how long retirees and their spouses will live. These estimates are made by plan consultants known as actuaries. If they guess wrong and too little money has been put in, the employer puts in more. If too much money has been put in, a company can decrease its contribution, go on a contribution holiday, or even take out the surplus.

Defined benefit plans allow employers to provide pension credit to employees for those years they worked before the company started the plan, and they are generally insured by the federal private pension insurance program.

Newer kinds of defined benefit plans include *cash balance plans* and *minimum balance plans*. These promise fixed benefits to longer-service workers and give employees who leave the plan early in their careers the amounts accumulated in their accounts plus interest.

Limits have been placed on the pensions that can be paid by defined benefit plans. However, high-level executives can receive much larger benefits from special *supplemental* or *top-hat plans*, which can provide unlimited benefits. These plans do not have the same tax advantages as other plans and are generally not protected if the company goes into bankruptcy.

The World of Private Retirement Plans

DEFINED CONTRIBUTION PLANS

Leslie Clark's second Pan Am pension plan and her Delta savings plan are *defined contribution plans*. The benefits paid by these plans are usually based on amounts put into an employee's account, plus investment earnings. They do not guarantee a fixed benefit amount. Defined contribution arrangements are the primary retirement plan for 17 million people, two-fifths of private sector workers participating in retirement plans. In addition, 15 million workers also participate in a defined contribution arrangement as a second plan.[9]

There are many different kinds of defined contribution plans. The Pan Am plan, in which the employer contributes a specified percentage of the employees' pay, was a *defined contribution pension plan*. In some cases, the employees also contribute to these pension plans.

Simplified employee pensions (SEPs) are another kind of defined contribution pension plan. Each year the employer decides what percentage of pay to contribute to employee accounts that are invested by financial institutions. *Target benefit plans* are defined contribution pension plans in which the employer's contributions are a fixed percentage of pay designed to produce a specified benefit, based on predictions of probable investment returns.

Profit sharing plans are a different kind of defined contribution arrangement. Employers can base contributions on a percentage of pay or a percentage of profits. In discretionary profit sharing plans, employers can decide from year to year whether to contribute.

Employee stock ownership plans (ESOPs) and *stock bonus plans* are defined contribution plans in which benefit payments are made in company stock. In tax-sheltered savings plans, such as *401(k) plans*, *salary reduction SEPs*, and *403(b) tax-sheltered annuities*, workers themselves are entirely or primarily responsible for making the contributions.

Keogh plans for self-employed persons can be either defined benefit or defined contribution plans. Also, *floor offset plans* combine both defined benefit and defined contribution features.

PART II

THE RULES OF THE GAME

INTRODUCTION

Winners and Losers

James D. Robinson III won at the pension game. Fired from his job as chief executive officer of the American Express Company in 1992, he is receiving $60,000 from the company's pension plans. That's $60,000 a month. After 22 years with the company, James Robinson's pensions total some $720,000 a year, and they are only part of his executive retirement package. Severance pay and stock bonus options raise that figure considerably.[1]

But highly paid corporate officers are not the only pension winners. Private pension plans also pay off well to many other employees, particularly those who spend most of their working lives with one company. Charles LaRue worked for 38 years for the Delco-Remy Company, a General Motors plant that makes electrical equipment in Anderson, Indiana. An assembly line worker, he retired in 1979 at age 59 with a pension of $7,200 a year plus good health benefits. His plan, negotiated by the United Auto Workers Union, bases benefits on a dollar amount multiplied by years worked. The plan also raises retirees' benefits periodically. Over 14 years, his benefit has been raised three times, so that today he gets $8,400 a year.

Certainly, Charles LaRue's benefit is not in the same ballpark as James Robinson's. Nonetheless, it's steady income every month for the rest of his life. Combined with social security, which he describes as "a pebble on the beach," his income is close to $16,000 a year. His wife, a retired nurse, also gets a small pension and social security, so although their income is "a far cry from what we had when we were working," the LaRues live comfortably.

Some 8 million Americans receive checks from private pension plans.[2] The total amount paid in 1991 was $137 billion.[3] The majority of pensioners, like James Robinson and Charles LaRue, receive their benefits from defined benefit plans. Payments from these plans can be substantial, since they can go as high as $120,000 a year and can be even higher for corporate officers such as James Robinson, who have special, executives-only plans. Most people get much less, of course. As Charles LaRue points out, "They have no intention to make you wealthy when they give you a pension," but, he is quick to add, "It can make all the difference in getting by."

A growing proportion of private sector pensioners are getting benefits from defined contribution plans. These plans can also provide big payoffs. If substantial contributions are made throughout an employee's career and investment earnings are good, the total amount

"I wish I'd known about that plan Hodgson is in. He still gets his pension on the first of each month even though he's dead."

Drawing by Handelsman. Copyright © 1980 by The New Yorker Magazine, Inc.

accumulated in one of these plans by retirement age can be extremely large. Since defined contribution plans usually make payments all at once instead of over a retiree's lifetime, they can produce sizable lump sum benefits, millions of dollars in some cases.

Then there are the losers of the pension game. They are generally modest citizens, traditionalists, people who did their best to follow the rules but lost out anyway — or were never allowed to play in the first place.

CHAPTER 3

It Just Isn't Fair!

The Plan does not include secretaries working for the company.

It was one of those chance things. Renee Cirrincioni, the secretary for a small company, was checking her correspondence file drawer and came across a copy of her company's pension plan. She knew that her employer had set up a plan several years earlier because she had greeted the pension consultants when they came to the office. Scanning the plan document, she was impressed by the generous benefits it provided. Then she read the words, "The Plan does not include secretaries working for the company."

At the time, she was 55 years old and had worked for the company for 14 years. She was the only secretary, and the only woman working there. All the other salaried employees were included in the plan, even though, except for the company president, none had been with the company as long as she had. The union workers had their own pension plan. It had never occurred to her that she would be left out.

Renee Cirrincioni put the plan back in the drawer. She never said a word to her boss about her exclusion, thinking that a protest might endanger her job. In 1993, at age 65, after 24 years with the company, she retired — without a pension. She still has trouble talking about what happened to her. "It just isn't fair!" is all she can say.

As Renee Cirrincioni discovered, the fact that an employer has a pension plan is no guarantee that all employees are included in it. There are many entirely legal ways to exclude people. They can, for example, be left out by name: "This plan does not cover Thomas Jones." Actuary Hank Garretson remembers a 70-year-old woman in a knitting mill in Pennsylvania, where she had worked since she was 12, who was written out of her pension plan when the new owner, "a young whipper-snapper from Harvard," decided that her benefits would be too costly. Another actuary, Paul Jackson, comments, "They can exclude everyone with red hair if they want to."

More commonly, people are left out of a pension plan by a specific exclusion. In Renee Cirrincioni's case, the exclusion was based on job category. "This plan does not include secretaries." As many as 10 percent of all workers left out of their companies' plans are excluded because of their job category.[1]

Although it is not common for only one employee to be left out, it does happen. According to actuary Richard Daskais, it's often the "girl" in the office, the secretary or the bookkeeper who, because of her long years of service and her age, would be entitled to a large pension. This kind of exclusion tends to turn up in plans designed to benefit an older, long-service owner of a small firm. Another consultant, Robert Richter, explains that owners of smaller firms set up plans basically as tax shelters and structure them so that they, along with company officers, end up with "the lion's share of the benefits." Hank Garretson puts it bluntly: "Most small employers see pension plans as their money. They ask, 'Why should we have to cover anyone else?' "

Women or employees in small companies are not the only ones denied pensions by job category exclusions. Richard Imperiale of Clinton Township, Michigan, was one of a group of warehouse workers who were excluded from the Kent-Moore Company plan. Kent-Moore had pension plans for its hourly union employees and for its salaried employees but none for the nonunion hourly warehouse workers. "To my knowledge," Richard Imperiale said, when he discovered the exclusion, "we eleven warehousepersons are the only full-time employees without any kind of retirement benefit throughout this corporation."

For the nearly ten years he worked for the Kent-Moore tool division, he protested this exclusion. Time and again, he was rebuffed by his superiors, who told him that the company did not want to encourage long-term employment among "warehousepersons." The management warned him to stop being a nuisance. Finally, after Richard Imperiale had left the company, Kent-Moore included the warehouse workers in a savings plan. It wasn't a pension plan, but it was better than nothing. "I do not know if the complaining I did had anything to do with this," he says now, "but I am very happy for my former coworkers."

Appeared in the *Wall Street Journal*. Used by permission of Cartoon Features Syndicate.

Workers usually find out about exclusions the hard way. Outraged, they want to know how they could possibly be legal. The explanation is that, historically, pensions have been considered a tool for business rather than a means of providing security to workers. The exclusion rule goes back to the 1920s, when the United States government granted tax-exempt status to pension plan trusts, allowing employers to take tax deductions for pension contributions at the time they make them and permitting employees to delay paying tax on their benefits until retirement, a tax advantage not granted to most other forms of income. As plans began to proliferate, however, policymakers became concerned that many of these nontaxed pension plans were being used as giant tax shelters for the bosses, who were also getting all the pension benefits while rank-and-file employees were getting little or nothing. President Franklin Roosevelt warned Congress in 1937 that the pension tax exemption "has been twisted into a means of tax avoidance."[2]

In 1942, Congress passed legislation limiting the extent to which private pension plans could discriminate in favor of higher-paid employees and company officers. The new law, as lawyer Nancy Altman has emphasized, was aimed at avoiding tax abuse and had little to do with providing retirement security to workers. It allowed a pension plan to qualify for tax-exempt status only if it included a certain percentage of the lower-paid employees: as low as 56 percent would do.[3] This non-discrimination formula did not alter the structure of private pension plans very much (though it prevented out-and-out tax avoidance for the rich). It did do something else, however, which smart pension consultants picked up on right away: it became a legal means for exclusion. If 56 percent of the employees had to be included, 44 percent could be left out.

Surprisingly, ERISA, the sweeping new pension law passed in 1974, did not override these coverage exclusion rules. Not until 1986 did Congress modify the coverage rules, following the testimony of 58-year-old bank clerk Madeline Sapienza, who told the Senate Special Committee on Aging that she had worked for a New York bank for 23 years and had never been included in the bank's pension plan.[4] Her testimony shocked members of Congress and the public. Most people had no idea that such pension exclusions were legal.

Former Pennsylvania Senator John Heinz, chairman of the Senate Special Committee on Aging, and Missouri Representative William Clay introduced legislation that would have made most exclusions illegal. Their bill, the Retirement Income Policy Act of 1985, would have required plans to cover *all* employees earning up to the social security wage base. Although other parts of the Heinz-Clay bill were adopted in the 1986 Tax Reform Act, lawmakers dropped the 100 percent coverage provision and settled for reducing the percentage of an employer's workforce that can be arbitrarily excluded from the pension plan from 44 down to 30 percent. Even more — up to 60 percent — can be excluded in certain circumstances.[5]

What is the rationale for pension exclusions? From the employers' view, private pension plans have never pretended to offer universal coverage, even to every employee within a single company. Pensions began as a way of taking care of only the employees the employer wanted to reward — those whom the boss believed were key to the business, or who had been loyal, or who had simply outlasted their usefulness. Many still perceive them this way. Any coverage beyond that, many employers argue, is simply icing on the cake.

A number of critics agree with Nancy Altman's assertion that the nondiscrimination rules are based on outdated views of pensions as "gifts" and have no role in a retirement income system designed to protect workers. Economist Emily Andrews calls coverage exclusions "inexplicable," noting that the only place where they might be justified is in large companies that operate several different lines of business and historically have had different kinds of plans.

In 1994, Connecticut Representative Barbara Kennelly introduced the Pension Reform Act, which would, among other things, require plans to cover 100 percent of an employer's workers in a separate line of business.[6] A similar provision was included in Ohio Senator Howard Metzenbaum's comprehensive Pension Bill of Rights Act of 1994.[7]

Even when a company plan includes every employee, employers can — and do — find other ways to deny people access to pensions. One primitive but often effective way is to pressure people to sign away, or waive, their rights.

Davine Jensen had been working as a full-time hygienist for eight years in a dentist's office in Tucson, Arizona, when her boss set up a pension plan. To her astonishment, the dentist informed her that he could not afford to include her in the plan. He asked her to sign a piece of paper agreeing to be excluded. Fearing that she would lose her job unless she agreed, she signed. Ten years later, she left her job without a pension.

A DIFFERENT ENDING

Helen Johnson's story began just like Davine Jensen's. She had been keeping the books for a year at a small tire company in Ithaca, New York, when the owner asked her to give up her right to be covered by the company's pension plan. She was 55 years old, and because the plan gave large benefits to older workers, the owner said that it would cost the firm too much to include her. Instead, he offered to pay her a $1,500 annual bonus.

Anxious to keep her job, she signed the waiver. When she turned 65 and retired, however, facing health problems and a bleak financial future, she challenged her former employer's action and won a settlement equal to the value of her pension.

Far more common than writing exclusions into the plan is American business's growing practice of hiring workers as consultants or temporary employees. These may be new employees *or* longtime permanent employees who find themselves suddenly transformed by a wave of the corporate wand into "contingent" workers.

Jimmie Ruth Daughtrey had worked for eight years as a computer specialist for Honeywell, Inc., in Atlanta, Georgia, when she was laid off and hired back as an "independent contractor." "It's a funny feeling," she remembered. "I found myself working in the same building where I'd been before. I did the same work. I even had the same schedule. But I was a consultant, with no pension, no health benefits, no nothing."

What especially rankled was that she found herself sitting next to younger, less experienced employees who hadn't been terminated. These young employees, she found out, hadn't worked long enough to acquire a vested right to a pension, as she had. The fair-haired grandmother with the broad Tennessee accent got mad. "I decided to file a lawsuit."[8] After five years in court, Honeywell finally agreed to a settlement.

The number of disenfranchised employees outside the umbrella of pensions and other benefits is growing at an astounding rate — almost 20 percent a year, according to Labor Department figures.[9] In January 1993, for example, the Bank of America in California "restructured" some 58 percent of its workforce from permanent employees into hourly or temporary workers with no benefits. The vast majority were women. Only 19 percent of Bank of America's workforce is now permanent.[10]

Employers defend the practice because it allows them, as they put it, "flexibility" in shifting their labor costs. "The ability to handle peak workloads without having to keep people around the rest of the time without much work to do, that's the driver," said Doug Miller, president of Norrell Services Inc., one of the country's largest temporary services.[11]

A number of economists have predicted that the contingency workforce is here to stay. It is a trend that former senator Howard Metzenbaum, for one, believes is "cutting the heart out of the American work force." "There are 34 million contingency workers today — over a quarter of our work force. Some say that they may outnumber full-time employees by the end of the decade. . . . It's the most important trend in business today, and it is fundamentally changing the relationship between Americans and their jobs." "Although so-called 'disposable' workers do cut costs," Senator Metzenbaum adds, "the costs don't disappear. They're shifted to the workers themselves and to the country."[12]

Richard Delaney of Oakland, California, international representative of the Office and Professional Employees International Union, has observed that a two-tier labor system is being created. The so-called contingency workforce is a "rapidly growing second-class workforce of Americans involuntarily relegated to jobs with no security, little or no benefits, and no dignity."[13]

Another way employers try to save on pension costs is by "leasing" their employees. According to figures compiled by the National Staff Leasing Association, more than a million Americans currently work under a leasing arrangement. Most companies that hire their employees this way are small firms, particularly doctors' and dentists' offices, but according to the *Wall Street Journal*, certain large corporations have also switched to leasing: Texas Instruments leases up to 15 percent of its employees.[14]

Under the Tax Equity and Fiscal Responsibility Act of 1982 (TEFRA), Congress attempted to curb this practice by providing that when the kind of work done by the leased employee has historically been performed under the direct supervision and control of the employer, the worker must generally be counted as an "employee" for pension purposes, unless the leasing company itself provides the worker with a pension plan meeting specified requirements and contributing at least 10 percent of pay.[15]

Yet another disturbing practice is for some employers with large numbers of lower-paid employees to require that workers contribute to the pension plan as a condition for becoming plan members. Since most lower-paid people can't afford to contribute, the money in the plan can be directed to the higher-paid.

Some employers go to extraordinary lengths to leave employees out of their pension plans. Margaret Hubbard began working in 1961 as assistant bookkeeper for a fledgling development company in Alexandria, Virginia. She stayed with the firm for 29 years, moving up to become corporate treasurer and director of customer relations. By the mid-1980s, she was the oldest woman employee with the longest time in the company, which by then employed 75 to 100 office personnel and 400 to 600 field personnel. She was the only one without a pension. Although she worked in the same office with the other staff, her employer had set up a completely new entity, an "investment company," that paid her salary and of which she was the only employee. For this reason, she was not eligible to participate in the regular company profit sharing plan. Whenever Margaret Hubbard reminded her employer that she was not covered by a pension, he would say, "Marge, you're family and we will take care of you!"

After she had worked for him for 27 years, her boss agreed, with great reluctance, she remembers, to give her a ten-year deferred annuity. It wasn't a pension, and it wasn't insured, but it was better than nothing. Eighteen months later, he cut her salary by two-thirds and asked her to retire. Seven months after that, she was notified that the company was being liquidated and that there was no money to pay her retirement benefit. The company then restructured itself, taking a new name but keeping the same offices, same equipment, and same employees. Her former boss told that her the "new" company had no liability for her retirement annuity. In 1992, Margaret Hubbard went before a congressional committee to tell her story. One result was that a lawyer volunteered to help her take her case to court. She filed suit and won back the annuity her boss had promised her.[16]

It is not enough for an employee to be covered by a pension plan, since all that means is that the employer's plan cannot specifically be designed to exclude him or her. A worker also has to become a member of the plan by meeting further requirements. Experts who talk about the number of *covered* workers often fail to mention that millions of those workers don't actually *participate* in their plans and therefore aren't earning any benefits.

For example, a 19-year-old hotel clerk might be covered by a plan but be too young actually to participate. If he leaves his job before age 21, the minimum age for membership in most plans, he will get no pension credit for the years he worked before that.[17] In addition, a new employee is not eligible to participate in most pension plans until he or she has worked at least a year.[18]

Plan membership can also be denied to unionized workers if their union has bargained in good faith with the employer about pensions — even if no agreement was reached or the union workers' own plan is inferior.

Finally, people can be excluded from participation in a plan if they work too few hours. The usual rule is 1,000 hours a year. This translates roughly to 20 hours a week or six months a year. A person can work full-time, but for several different employers, and because of the 1,000-hour rule not be covered by any pension. Forty-two percent of part-time workers in companies with plans cannot participate because they don't

work enough hours.[19] Those who work even slightly less than half-time, 19 hours a week instead of 20, are out of luck.

WHEN PART-TIME ISN'T PENSIONLESS

Major Clark worked as a messenger for a Virginia nonprofit organization but was told that because he was part-time, he was not a plan member. When he pointed out that although he was part-time he worked more than 1,000 hours a year, the organization admitted its mistake. He is now getting a pension.

For an increasing segment of the population, the half-time exclusion presents a serious obstacle to plan membership, since part-time work is their only option. Studies show that the steady expansion of part-time employment in this country is no longer largely a matter of people voluntarily choosing to work shorter hours. On the contrary, between 1969 and 1989, most of the growth in part-time jobs involved people who would have preferred full-time. Almost one-third of the people who held part-time jobs in 1988 did so involuntarily.[20]

Although companies are by no means required to exclude part-time workers from participation, most do. A survey of large and medium-sized firms by the Labor Department showed that in 1991, only 28 percent of part-time workers were covered by their companies' defined benefit pension plans.[21] Another 10 percent were covered by employer-financed defined contribution plans. Employers say that they are reluctant to contribute to pensions for part-timers because they are "marginal" workers of the here-today-gone-tomorrow variety, compared with the steady long-service workers they prefer to reward. Besides, they claim that part-timers' benefits, if they managed to earn any, would be minuscule, not worth the cost of keeping their names on the books.

But the 1,000-hour rule doesn't exclude only "marginal" workers from pensions. Seasonal employees spend their lifetimes working in industries where 1,000-hour-a-year jobs are hard to come by. Cannery workers, for example, may spend their lives working for many employers, all with pension plans, and never become eligible for a single plan.

Anticipating this problem, Congress directed the Department of Labor in 1974 to issue regulations protecting seasonal workers who regularly work fewer than 1,000 hours a year. Those regulations have never been issued. The National Senior Citizens Law Center sued to force the Labor Department to issue the regulations, but the court ruled that Congress intended to leave the matter up to the Labor Department's discretion.

Colorado Representative Patricia Schroeder has introduced legislation that would require employers to include employees working 500 hours in their plans. This change would be particularly helpful to women: 18 percent of women who work part-time put in between 500 and 999 hours, compared with only 2 percent of male part-time employees.[22]

Getting into a plan is one thing; getting something out of it is a different matter. Coverage and participation mark only the beginning of the process. Other requirements must be satisfied to get a benefit.

What to Do

How to Find Out if You Are in a Plan

If you have received a plan booklet or other summary of the plan, it is likely that you are in the plan. Pension law requires that plans provide a *summary plan description (SPD)* to all members. If you have not received an SPD but think that you may be a plan member, you can contact the Public Disclosure Room of the U.S. Department of Labor and ask for a copy of the plan's SPD.

If you have received a plan summary, read it to see what it says about who is covered and what the requirements are to become a plan participant. This section of the booklet may be headed "Who Is Eligible for the Plan." You can also ask the person running the plan, the plan administrator. Your personnel office or a union official should be able to tell you his or her name and address.

If you are told that you have been excluded because of your job category, talk to the company owner, the union, or your supervisor. Many owners simply follow the advice of a pension consultant in setting up a plan. Once an injustice is pointed out, some owners may be sympathetic — or at least embarrassed.

If you have been asked to give up pension coverage, ask to see a copy of the pension plan document. Employers cannot require employees to give up coverage unless there are specific provisions in the plan document permitting the exclusion of certain workers and authorizing waivers. These provisions must have been approved by the Internal Revenue Service (IRS). If the plan administrator refuses to give you a copy of the plan document, you can request it under the Freedom of Information Act from the Employee Plans Division at the IRS office for the area where the plan is located. *Note:* The one exception is that if the plan has 25 or fewer members and takes the position that you are not a participant, the IRS can deny your request.

If you think that you may be entitled to benefits or have other questions about coverage and participation rules, telephone the IRS's Employee Plans Technical and Actuarial Division.

CHAPTER 4

Stranded in Buckeye

> *Many contributions are made on behalf of participants*
> *who will not qualify for benefits.*
>
> —Form letter from U.S. Department of Labor

Requirements for earning a right to a pension have been eased over the years, but they can still create nightmares for the modern industrial cowboy. Listen to the ballad of Ernest Stump:

I was living and working construction in North Platte, Nebraska, when I heard there was a big construction job near Phoenix, Arizona. It was to be a 15-year job to build a five-unit nuclear generation plant at Wintersburg, Arizona. I made the trip down there and signed on and went to work May 9, 1979. We sold our home in North Platte and moved to Buckeye, Arizona.

After building three of the five nuclear generators, they canceled the last two. Through no fault of mine I was laid off October 14, 1986. Reason: Reduction in force. Which left me stranded in Buckeye, Arizona, with only eight years' work-related credits toward union retirement in Teamsters Local Union 83.

I applied for pension retirement October 21, 1986, and was told I was not eligible, because I had to have ten years' credit and I only had eight. I moved to Las Vegas, Nevada, and worked two and a half years with Teamsters Local Union 995. With the eight years in Local 83 and the two and a half years in Local 995, I would have ten and a half years' credit. I applied again December 1, 1991, for a pension. Again I was told I was not eligible, that the two and a half years in Local 995 did not count.

Now I want to know why. What happens to the money I contributed to the Union toward a pension? The eight years worked? I feel I have been wronged and cheated out of what is due me. I await an answer to this inquiry.

Ernest Stump
Henderson, NV

The trap Ernest Stump fell into had to do with *vesting rules.* All plans have them. They are rules that require people to work a certain number of years under the plan — usually five or ten — before they can be assured of any benefit. More than 6.5 million workers, about one-quarter of the people covered by defined benefit pension plans, are in plans that typically require ten years of work in order to earn a benefit.[1] These plans, set up under collective bargaining agreements between a union and groups of employers within one industry or craft, usually in a certain geographic area, are jointly run by the union and the employers. They are prevalent in mining, construction, trucking, and other fields in which people typically go from job to job within the same industry.

Also referred to as Taft-Hartley plans, multiemployer plans can be good for workers so long as they can consistently find jobs with employers that pay into the same plan. But these jobs may not be available. When they are scarce, it may take a worker 20 or 30 years to accumulate ten years' worth of union jobs. Many never do. *Half of workers in defined benefit multiemployer plans are not vested.*[2] Although many of these workers will eventually vest as they get older, many others will not: the union jobs just aren't there.

Here's how the ten-year rule struck down Emily Mills of Otsego, Michigan. She was one year short of vesting in her union plan when employees at the grocery store where she had worked for nine years voted to drop their union affiliation. That ended their membership in the union-negotiated plan. Although her employer had been contributing 46 cents for every hour she worked, Mills lost her entire pension. "It stinks," she says. "That's nine years of money that I earned. That was part of my benefit package."

Even people in single employer plans, most of which require only five years to lock in a benefit, can run into problems. *More than a third of workers in single employer defined benefit plans are not vested.*[3] Current figures show that about 55 percent of participants in their fifties in all plans are vested. The vesting rate is much lower — 33 percent —for workers under age 30.[4]

Some multiemployer plans give vesting credit to union members who have worked under other plans within the same industry, but these *reciprocity agreements* are often very limited. For example, many trucking industry plans give this credit only to workers who have a total of 20 years under the plans and work in the industry until they are at least 50 years old.

Glenn Mullett, a West Virginia welder, wrestled with the vesting problem for 28 years. Having worked construction since 1965, always at jobs with pension coverage, he didn't acquire a vested interest in a pension until 1993. Over those years, contributions were made for him into eight separate pension funds in West Virginia, Pennsylvania, and Ohio. Figuring that between 5 and 8 percent of his wages went into pension contributions, he said that it added up to about $20,000. His comment: "This situation is a travesty. Having to work ten years under the same plan is a form of servitude. It's an unjust windfall for the union." Luckily, Mullett, now 54, was able to keep working. Despite having had 13 different employers during the previous year, he has finally vested in one plan, Plumbers and Pipefitters Local Union #83 Pension Fund in Wheeling, West Virginia. It didn't take him ten years; it took 28.

Thousands of people have protested their losses under vesting rules, asking, like Ernest Stump, "What happens to the money I contributed?" The answer is that all pension plans, especially multi-employer plans, operate like a lottery. Money is put in for everybody, but only some will draw benefits — those lucky enough to satisfy all the plan's requirements. This forfeiture principle operates not only in defined benefit plans but also in defined contribution pension and profit sharing plans in which workers have individual accounts.

Why are plans set up this way? Why not let workers accumulate benefits for every year they work under the plan? The simple answer is that pension plans would then lose some of their usefulness for company owners. The promise of a pension at retirement keeps younger workers in the workforce and loyal to the company, or to the union that negotiated their pension plan. Pension plans that encourage mobility by eliminating or lowering vesting rules, so that changing jobs carried no penalty, would be counterproductive to many company owners as well as to some union leaders. They would also alter the lottery principle, which allows plans to pay very large benefits to some workers with money contributed by those who lost out.

Until the enactment of ERISA in 1974, plans could require workers to keep working until age 65 in order to receive any benefits at all. As Congress learned during hearings on the pension law, there were instances of workers being fired just before they reached retirement age. A study done for the Senate Labor Subcommittee in 1972 found that 23 percent of plan participants had to work until retirement age to receive any benefits. Some 79 percent of the plans required more than ten years to vest.[5]

As part of ERISA, Congress required plans to vest members after no more than ten years. This reflected the view that "pensions are not gratuities, like a gold watch, bestowed as a gift by the employer on retirement [but] savings which the worker has earned in the form of deferred payment for his labors."[6]

Eight years later, Congress lowered vesting requirements even further for small "top-heavy" plans, found primarily in medical, legal, and other professional firms. These plans had been providing the lion's share of benefits — more than 60 percent — to the firms' "key employees," that is, the doctors, dentists, and lawyers, while little or nothing trickled down to the medical assistants, nurses, secretaries, receptionists, and other support staff.[7] Congress required these plans to vest all employees after no more than three years. In the Tax Reform Act of 1986, Congress reduced vesting to no more than five years for all single employer plans, beginning with the 1989 plan year.[8]

For people at the beginning of their careers, the new vesting rules are a major improvement. An estimated 76 percent of participants in single employer plans can expect to vest under the new five-year rule, as compared with 53 percent before the 1986 law took effect.[9] Representative Barbara Kennelly estimated that in 1993, approximately 1.9 million additional workers were entitled to pensions, thanks to the relaxed vesting rules.[10] Unfortunately, people who left their jobs before the five-year rule went into effect in 1989 were not helped. Nor were the millions who work under multiemployer plans. Multiemployer plans were allowed to retain ten-year vesting rules at the urging of the construction trades unions, whose leaders worried about losing jobs to nonunion contractors.

Glenn Mullett, who for years has been campaigning for a change in the law, points out that the ten-year rule might make sense if workers could work full-time in the geographic area assigned to their local union, "but these days most of us just don't have that choice." He refers to the thousands of "travelers," people who go from job to job, union plan to union plan, and never lock in the right to a pension. Others manage to vest a small benefit in one plan but lose large sums in the other plans they've worked under for less than ten years. "The 'suitcase' people are hurting big time," says Mullett.

John Wantz, a World War II veteran and master plasterer from

Taneytown, Maryland, did construction work under three local union pension plans for 30 years. When he retired at age 65, he was told that he hadn't earned a pension under any of the locals. In one, he was told he was short only a quarter of a year to vest. No reciprocity agreement had ever been set up among any of the three locals he'd worked under, though he had been assured that one would be. He was very angry, especially when he found that friends had been treated the same way. "I feel that as taxpaying veterans of the Armed Forces of these United States of America, we should at least be given a logical answer to our situation . . . whether benefits expected through work performed under union rules exist or, if not, why not?" John Wantz protested that he had, in fact, followed the rules. Finally, his last plan agreed to pay him a small benefit for six of his 30 years' work.

In 1990, Secretary of Labor Elizabeth Dole recommended that Congress enact legislation reducing vesting requirements in multi-employer plans from ten years to five. She estimated that 1.1 million workers would benefit from the change. This proposal was included in tax legislation that passed the House and Senate in 1992 but was vetoed by President George Bush. More recently, five-year vesting for multi-employer plans was included in Representative Barbara Kennelly's proposed Pension Reform Act of 1994 and in Senator Howard Metzenbaum's Pension Bill of Rights Act of 1994.

In Glenn Mullett's view, however, even five-year vesting isn't the answer. "The five-year solution won't work. There ought to be one rule: the money follows the man."

Clearly, vesting rules still penalize millions. Joan Kuriansky, then executive director of the Older Women's League, told the Senate Labor Subcommittee that "even with the improvement in access to pensions through a reduced vesting period, there remains a large gap," particularly for women. She pointed to Bureau of Labor Statistics figures showing that although half of all men in the United States have been on their jobs 5.1 years, the median time for women is 3.7 years.[11]

As workers get older, although their job tenure tends to be longer, a significant gender difference still remains. For example, in the 50 to 59 age group, 20 percent of women will work less than five years on a job, contrasted with 14 percent of men.[12] The Urban Institute estimates that if three-year vesting were adopted for all plans, a million more women would be collecting benefits by the year 2020 than under the current five-year rule.[13] The Pension Portability Improvement Act of 1993 introduced by Florida Representative Sam Gibbons would reduce vesting to three years for all plans.[14]

Restrictive vesting rules are rarely found in pension plans in other countries. In the Netherlands, workers vest after one year of plan participation (although participation may not begin until age 25); they vest after two years in the United Kingdom (where workers may participate at age 19), and after two years in Ontario, Canada. Japan has no legislated vesting rules, but Japanese pension plans generally provide rapid vesting.[15]

Many people join Glenn Mullett in asking whether vesting rules of any sort make sense in a country with a highly mobile workforce such as ours. Ewa Bielski, former chair of the Citizens' Commission on Pension Policy, agrees with him: "Pensions should have day-one vesting. That way everyone will be equally expensive. There should be no financial incentive to get rid of workers to save on pension costs."

Business groups point out that if there were immediate vesting, benefits for many workers would be extremely small, and most would be cashed out and spent long before retirement. These payments would also reduce the amounts payable to longer-service workers. Ewa Bielski counters, "There should be no cashing out. The money should be put away and forgotten. Even small amounts will grow when invested until retirement age. Everyone needs a pension. Why should some people get benefits at the expense of others?"

PEANUTS reprinted by permission of UFS, Inc.

So arcane are pension rules that people cannot feel secure even if they have worked five years or even ten years for employers paying into the same plan. Some of those years still may not count. For example, plans can disregard years worked before age 18 for vesting purposes, and most do. Although this rule may not seem to be of great consequence, other ways of figuring vesting credit can make a difference to people.

Plans typically require that employees work 1,000 hours in a year for that year to count toward vesting.[16] All hours for which a worker is paid by the employer count, including holidays, sick leave, vacations, and jury duty. But it can sometimes be extremely difficult to prove that someone has worked the required number of hours. This is partic-ularly true in multiemployer plans in which workers are sent out to many different jobs from a union hiring hall. James Thomas was told at age 67 that despite 40 years of union labor for construction com-panies in the Washington, D.C., area, he wouldn't receive a dime of his benefit. Although he was certain that his employers had paid in for his 1,000 hours in the required number of years, the plan's records didn't show it.

WINNING BY THE RULES

When Richard Pennington, a member of a machinists multi-employer plan in Brooklyn, New York, left his plan to move to Connecticut, he was assured verbally by the plan administrator that he had vested. Despite that assurance, when he inquired about his benefit several years later, the plan trustees denied him his pension because he was 16 hours short of the ten years he needed.

Pennington found out that the trustees had failed to credit his paid vacation during his last year of work. Counting those hours, he had the time he needed to win his benefit. He got his pension.

Even 1,000 hours may not be enough if a plan uses an alternative way of defining a "year." Plans using an *elapsed time* method of measur-ing service can require that employees be working on the fifth (or tenth) anniversary of the date they were hired in order to vest. This rule was not included in the law; it is allowed under a government regulation adopted at the urging of large employers and unions. Since an elapsed time approach can provide less protection to many workers, the rule gives an extra year of vesting credit to people on leaves of absence or who are disabled or laid off. However, employees who are fired or quit before the last day of their fifth or tenth years are out of luck in an elapsed time plan.

Frank Fowler was let go by Stemco, a subsidiary of Colt Industries in Pittsburgh, after nine years and nine months of work. His plan had a ten-year vesting requirement and used the elapsed time method of measuring service. Had his plan used the 1,000-hour rule, or had he been laid off or given a leave of absence instead of being fixed, he would have received a benefit. "But why should they have done that?" Fowler asks bitterly. "They saved all that money by leaving me high and dry." Now he has a serious kidney problem that makes it impossible for him to go back to work, and he owes thousands of dollars in medical bills. He doesn't see any way out.

If people are away from jobs for long periods before they vest, plans can cancel the earlier years for vesting purposes. Leaving the plan for five or more years can cause a worker to lose all credit for years worked before the *break in service*. People in multiemployer plans requiring ten years for vesting may be able to take off more time without losing credit, as long as their time away from the job is shorter than the time worked before the break. This rule applies only to years worked after 1984. Before that, break-in-service rules were far more restrictive. Prior to 1976, for example, even one day off work could result in the forfeiture of all early years. Between 1976 and 1985, the rule was that all years could

---

WHEN NO IS NOT THE ANSWER

John Sherwood, a Maryland journalist, was laid off from his newspaper just short of the five years he needed to vest. He had worked 1,000 hours in the fifth year, but the plan administrator told him that he would get nothing because he was not working on the last day of his fifth year and his plan used the elapsed time method of counting vesting credits.

He didn't think that sounded right and decided to do some checking. When he inquired further, he learned about the special provision of the elapsed time rule requiring plans to give workers an extra year of vesting credit if they are laid off. The administrator of his plan hadn't known about the rule. John Sherwood got his pension.

be lost if the time away from work was as long as or longer than the period worked before the break.

These old break-in-service rules caused a great deal of grief and confusion. Thomas Piosky of Queens, New York, worked as a bartender and restaurant employee for 38 years, but his union pension plan did not credit him for the three years he worked at the Blue Moon diner. Because of this three-year gap, Piosky never made the required years of continuous employment under the plan to earn a right to a pension. Now living only on his monthly social security check of $592, he told Newhouse News Service, "The last two weeks of the month, I'm dead."[17]

Since 1985, the law has said that one year of time off to care for a newborn or newly adopted child may not be counted toward a break in service. Military service in times of war or national emergency is also not counted toward a break in service. Part-time work is not counted as a break if the employee works at least 501 hours during the year. Vicki Gottlich, staff attorney with the National Senior Citizens Law Center, has suggested that an "eldercare year," in which someone takes time out to care for an aging relative, should also be exempt from break-in-service rules.[18]

Some plans have dropped break-in-service rules, recognizing that work interruptions often occur for family reasons beyond an employee's control. Many people think that Congress should abolish break-in-service rules altogether.

After workers have vested in their pensions, they cannot ordinarily have their benefits taken away. But as so often happens with pension rules, exceptions exist. For example, pensioners who go back to work after they retire — often because they can't stretch their pension checks to make ends meet — can find their benefits suspended.

Suspension-of-benefits rules particularly affect people receiving special early retirement benefits from multiemployer plans. Those who go back to work in the same industry in the same part of the country for even one day can have their benefits stopped until they reach age 65. This is true even though the company they go back to work for does not pay into the pension plan. Retirees must be notified of this rule, but they often overlook it in the fine print of plan documents.

Retirees over the age of 65 in single employer plans can have their benefits suspended if they go back to work for their former employers, as can retirees in multiemployer plans. However, these suspensions last only for the length of time a retiree works more than 40 hours a month; pension payments resume as soon as the retirees' hours drop below 40.

Once workers become participants in their plans and gain the right to a benefit, the next step is to find out how much those benefits will be. Pension arithmetic can be daunting — and surprisingly different from what people expect.

What to Do

How to Find Out if You Will
Get Benefits from a Plan

A *summary plan description* explains how long it takes to vest under your plan and how years and hours are counted for vesting credit. For most people, however, a surer way to check vesting status is to request an *individual benefit statement.* These statements are available from the plan administrators of all single employer plans and some multiemployer plans.[19] If your plan administrator does not respond to your written request for an individual benefit statement within 30 days, contact the nearest field office of the U. S. Department of Labor's Pension and Welfare Benefits Administration.

The individual benefit statement will tell you whether or not you are vested. If you are told that you are not entitled to a benefit and you have close to ten or five years in the plan, always check out the basis on which your credits have been calculated. Plan administrators sometimes make mistakes.

If you have vested under your plan and then leave the company, the plan administrator is supposed to give you a statement telling you that you are vested and the amount of benefits you can count on receiving at age 65. A copy of this information will be provided to you when you apply for your social security benefits.

Workers who lose their jobs in large layoffs, or whose plans are terminated, may earn the right to a pension with fewer years of work than the vesting provisions require *if* their plans have sufficient funds to pay benefits. If this is your situation, you should contact the plan administrator or, if the company is in bankruptcy, the Pension Benefit Guaranty Corporation.

Also, you may be vested under your plan after two or three years if it is "top-heavy," meaning that 60 percent of the benefits or contributions are going to company owners and officers, or as soon as you become a plan member if you are in a simplified employee pension (SEP) or a plan for an educational organization. In some cases, employees working to age 65 vest regardless of years of service.

CHAPTER 5

Change for a Cup
of Coffee

*As a result of your Prudential service, you have a vested
pension benefit which will provide a monthly income of
$.47.*

To make sure that the letter wasn't a practical joke, Kathleen Durkin
phoned the benefits office of her former employer, the Prudential
Insurance Company. Now living in Scottsdale, Arizona, she had worked
for the company for ten years and expected her pension to provide a nice
addition to her retirement income. After all, Prudential is one of the
largest companies in the country. But a retirement technician at the
company confirmed it: at age 65, she would be entitled to a pension of
exactly 47 cents a month.

Her first reaction was to laugh. How could such a large, well-
heeled company like "The Rock" pay such a puny pension? Durkin was
lucky enough to have other resources for retirement, but she remembered colleagues from her Prudential days, hardworking women who
had little or no savings. For them, a pension of 47 cents a month
wouldn't be laughable; it would be disastrous.

"I am not dependent upon 'The Rock' for my retirement," Kathleen Durkin says indignantly, "but a lot of other women are." She
decided to take another look at the way her plan calculated its benefits.

What she learned was that, like many pension plans, Prudential's
was designed to provide very good retirement benefits to certain employees, namely, those with high earnings and many years of service,
while giving only token benefits — "change for a cup of coffee" — to

people who worked for low pay or part-time and who left the company before the end of their careers. Even more astonishing was that her plan subtracted from her pension an amount based on her social security benefit. Although few people receive as little as Kathleen Durkin, many receive very small pensions, often far smaller than they expected.

How much do people get from private pension plans? *Half of all private sector pensioners receive less than $4,482 a year.* Even among recently retired people, half get less than $5,844.[1] The statistics teach us two things. First, private pensions tend to give very little to the majority of people who get them. Second, there are striking differences between the benefits received by retired men and women. Newly retired women workers receive much less than half of what men get.[2] The gap between the amounts received by women and men has widened over the past decade.[3]

	ALL RETIREES		NEW RETIREES	
	Median	Average	Median	Average
Men	$5,640	$7,415	$7,200	$9,764
Women	2,172	3,683	2,586	4,331

African-American women receive the smallest pensions of all — half get less than $1,908 a year. What does this mean? Esther Champion of Baltimore, Maryland, who spent 50 years in the workforce, has a pension income of $1,750 a year. Not surprisingly, she is still working. A tall, poised woman of 74, Esther Champion tells a story that follows a pattern familiar to women of all races. During the early years of her marriage, while her son was young, she worked stints in factories — one that made parachutes, another that produced makeup compacts — followed by clerical work at *Reader's Digest*, jobs that were not covered by pension plans. At age 40, she landed a job with *Consumer Reports* in the customer service department. She was ecstatic. Not only was the work interesting, but she also got pension coverage.

She worked full-time at *Consumer Reports* for 20 years. Then in 1980, when she was 60 years old, her department was dissolved and she lost her job. Next came the news that her pension amounted to only $96.17 a month. Her relatively low salary over the years and the fact that she was under 65 when she stopped working lowered her pension considerably. A formula that factored in her social security benefit took another bite.[4] "We were assured pensions," she says wryly, "but we didn't know how much we were going to get after 20 years of service. . . . I'm lucky because I am healthy and can work. If I did not have work or became disabled, I would be in desperate straits. For too many women like myself, retirement is not an option."[5]

Women's pensions typically amount to only 37 percent of men's. Why the difference? For one thing, women's earnings are lower (71 percent of men's). Their time on particular jobs is less (by 1.4 years), and they spend less total time in the workforce. These factors alone would reduce women's pensions, compared with men's, but they are given even greater force by the way plans are designed. Instead of simply multiplying the years someone has worked under a plan by a straight percentage of pay or profits, most plans use formulas that give considerably more weight to higher earnings and to years worked later in a career. For women, with their typically lower wage history and shorter job tenure, the effect of this weighting can deliver a quadruple whammy. As Representative Patricia Schroeder has noted, what happens to them is "the result of discrimination throughout their lives which strikes its cruelest blow at the end."

In many cases, these pension formulas can be very complex, but there is nothing complicated about their purpose: to provide disproportionately large retirement benefits to company owners and officers at the lowest possible cost to the company. The tax advantages of pension plans and their usefulness in "managing" a workforce are not sufficient to persuade many employers, particularly small business owners, to set up plans. Something more is needed. What could be a better inducement than very large benefits for themselves at relatively little cost?

Over the years, policymakers have accepted this rationale, passing laws that curbed extreme abuses but also allowed skewed payoffs. Workers whose benefits are unexpectedly small, like Kathleen Durkin and Esther Champion, may be disappointed, but, employers argue, at least they are getting something rather than nothing. After all, the employer doesn't have to have a plan.

There are a great many complicated methods for figuring the dollar amount of a pension. With all their complexity, however, most benefit rules fall into two broad categories: rules favoring *older employees*, and rules favoring those who are *higher paid*.

Reprinted with special permission of King Features Syndicate.

Plan formulas are typically geared to reward employees who end their careers working for a particular company. As actuary Donald Grubbs observed, "It's often the case that a worker earns half his benefit in the first 30 years and the last half in the last 10 years."[6]

By far the largest proportion of pension plan participants (70 percent of all those in defined benefit plans) are in plans that base pensions on earnings.[7] The majority of these plans use *final pay* formulas, which calculate benefits using employees' earnings at the time they stop working or retire under the plan.[8] Final pay benefits are usually determined by averaging employees' pay for their last three or five years of work.

Since salary increases and inflation usually result in workers earning their highest salaries during their later years of work, final pay formulas mean that someone like Kathleen Durkin, who left a plan early in her career, will have a pension based on years when earnings are lower and get a very small benefit. People who retire while working under a plan get much more from that plan because their pay is higher at that point than people who worked under the plan earlier in their career.

A typical formula for a defined benefit final pay plan provides an annual pension equal to 1 or 1.5 percent of final pay, multiplied by the number of years the employee worked under the plan. Someone with a final salary of $25,000 who worked for 30 years under a 1 percent formula, for example, can wind up with a pension of $7,500 a year.[9]

An alternative to a final pay formula is a career average approach. Plans using it base benefits on the employee's earnings throughout his or her work life. Although it doesn't penalize those who leave early in their careers, this approach tends to provide lower benefits to those working under the plan until retirement age. A decreasing number of workers (14 percent overall) are in plans that use this approach.[10]

Twenty-three percent of defined benefit plan participants are in plans that use *flat benefit* formulas to determine benefits.[11] Typically these are union-negotiated plans and are most prevalent in the automobile and steel industries. Under flat benefit formulas, plans multiply the number of years someone has worked by a set dollar amount. This amount is either identical for all workers or the same for all employees in particular job categories. A plan using a flat benefit formula might pay $20 a month for each year of service, yielding a pension of $600 a month to a worker after 30 years. The 1991 average in plans using this formula was $23.50 a month per year of service, an increase of $3.50 a month per year of service over the 1989 average.[12]

Unions ordinarily bargain for increases in these flat amounts each time a contract is renewed. These raises can be retroactively applied to all the years someone has worked under a plan. But the higher benefits go to only those people working under the plan when the new contract goes into effect; those who have left do not benefit from the increases.

Although workers are unlikely to object to plans that establish pension rates based on earnings or contract terms at the time someone leaves a plan, they may protest other formulas, called *backloading*, that give greater dollar values to years worked at the end, or the "back," of a person's career. Under some backloading formulas, years worked immediately before retirement age are worth 133 percent more than early years.

A less extreme type of backloading formula is the one used by the United Mineworkers of America pension plan. It provides that the first ten years of work are worth $20 a month in benefits, the next ten years $20.50 a month, the third ten years $21 a month, and all years worked after the thirtieth year $21.50 a month. A person retiring with 40 years of credited service would have a pension of $830 a month under this plan, and another person who worked ten years under each of four different plans with this formula would get $200 under each plan, or a total of $800 a month.[13]

Fractional rule formulas are another kind of formula giving bigger benefits to people working under plans at older ages. These formulas adjust employees' basic benefits by dividing the number of years they worked under the plan by the number of years they *would have worked* if they had stayed until age 65. The fractional rule can be devastating for people who work under it early in their careers. Take someone who changes jobs at age 35 after ten years with a company and is making $30,000 when she leaves. If the pension is 1 percent of final salary times years of service, she might expect a pension of $3,000 a year at retirement age. The fractional rule, however, discounts that amount by 10/40, reducing it to around $750 a year. Someone else, also leaving the plan after ten years with final pay of $30,000 but at age 55, would be discounted by only 10/20 and receive a benefit of $1,500. Someone leaving at age 65 after ten years would not be discounted at all and would receive the full $3,000.

It is possible, under one variation of the fractional rule, for a person who works under a plan between the ages of 55 and 65 to be paid benefits four times the amount paid to someone who worked for the same salary between ages 25 and 35. Thus, an employer can set up a plan when he or she is age 55 and retire ten years later with a healthy pension. If the employer then stops the plan, younger workers end up with minuscule benefits. It is no coincidence that fractional rule plans are found predominantly in smaller companies and are often set up when the owner is within sight of retirement. There are, however, big employers using a fractional rule formula. These include Anheuser-Busch, Minnesota Mining & Manufacturing, and USX Texas Oil & Gas unit.[14]

Until recently, benefit formulas that provided a higher scale of benefits to older workers were found only in defined benefit plans. However, Internal Revenue Service rules now permit this kind of age weighting for profit sharing plans. Lawyer Victoria Quesada views the new rules as "one of the greatest threats to the fairness of the pension system that we have seen in recent years." She points out that these rules allow small business owners to allocate up to 85 percent of a plan's contributions to themselves. Although age weighting may encourage more small businesses to set up plans, these rules make it impossible for employees working under those plans at younger ages to earn adequate pensions. It also aggravates the problem of discrimination against older workers, since larger contributions for them make it less likely that they will be hired, or more likely that they will be fired.[15]

Most defined benefit plans use *early retirement* formulas that severely reduce benefits for people who retire early. Early retirement penalties can reduce a pension collected at age 55, instead of age 65, by more than half; a standard reduction is 6 percent a year.[16] Although this is understandable, since benefits will be paid for ten additional years, the early retirement penalty can come as a shock to participants. In some instances it can force people in stressful or dangerous jobs to continue working long after it is advisable or even safe for them to do so.

Mildred Hollis, a nurse administrator at Yale-New Haven Hospital in Connecticut, is concerned about the effects of early retirement reductions on lower-paid hardworking health professionals such as nurses and physicians' assistants. She describes the dilemma of a nurse who, when she turned 55, after working for more than 30 years, began thinking about slowing down. She found out that if she took early retirement, she would get less than half of the pension she would receive if she worked until she was 65 — too little for her to live on. Her only option, she concluded, was to keep working full-time until age 65.

Some plans offer special *early-out options* that allow people to retire early without penalty when they meet certain requirements of age and length of service. For example, a 55-and-out provision grants a full pension to workers whose age and years of service add up to 55. A significant number of larger pension plans, particularly in manufacturing, where there are strong unions, offer generous early retirement packages. Early-out benefits are valued by employees and employers alike. For workers, they lock in sizable pensions at a relatively early age. For employers, they provide a painless way of easing older workers out of the company or, when times are tight, reducing their total workforce.

Again, however, there is a catch for anyone counting on these early-out benefits. They are vulnerable. If something happens to the company before a worker meets the requirements — for example, if it closes a plant just a few months before a worker becomes eligible for an early-out benefit — the special benefits disappear. After nearly a lifetime with one company, a worker can lose his or her job and hundreds of thousands of dollars in pension benefits.

Someone can also lose the early-out pension even though he keeps his job. That's what happened to Richard Nichols. He was 51 and four years from a sizable early retirement pension at the Owens Illinois division in Bay City, Virginia, where he had worked for 31

years. His division was sold to Great Northern Nekoosa. He continued in the same job but was no longer under the Owens Illinois plan.
He was told that if he took early retirement at 55, as he'd intended, his
pension would be half of what he had counted on — about $12,000 a
year instead of $22,000 — a total loss over ten years of $100,000. For
workers who get nothing out of pension plans, these kinds of losses
may seem less significant, but for people who count on a certain
benefit only to see it snatched out from under them, the loss can be
overwhelming. "It's the worst thing that ever happened to me," says
Nichols.[17]

A HAPPIER ENDING

Diane Hill's story had a happier ending. She had worked for
General Motors for 27 years, nearly long enough to qualify for
GM's special "30-and-out" pension. But on January 1, 1985, the
company transferred her, along with thousands of its data process-
ing employees, to its EDS subsidiary, which it had just purchased
from Ross Perot. At the same time, the company changed the
pension plan so that time worked for EDS didn't count toward
qualifying for the 30-and-out pension.

Diane Hill went to Michigan Senator Carl Levin, who asked the
Internal Revenue Service to review what had happened. Senator
Levin pointed out that in August 1984, Congress had strengthened
the pension law to prevent companies from changing eligibility
rules for early-out pensions just as an employee was about to
qualify.[18] The IRS persuaded GM to agree that time worked for its
EDS subsidiary counted toward qualifying for the 30-year special
benefit. Diane Hill worked the three years she needed to get the
benefit, although the years she worked after the change did not
count in figuring the amount she received.

Rules benefiting older employees are not the only formulas that
can cut into people's pensions. Others, called *integration*, penalize
moderate-and-lower-income workers. Here's how they work.

Mary Green figures she lost nearly a quarter of the pension she had
counted on because her job was eliminated and she was forced to retire
at age 60, a year and a half short of the full early-out benefit offered by
her Quaker State Oil Company plan. To add insult to injury, the plan

took away another $1,800 from her annual pension. She was told that her benefit was being reduced to "integrate" it with her social security benefit. What, she wanted to know, did social security have to do with her pension? The people in the benefits office at Quaker State were not helpful. "You could never get an understandable answer," she says, though they assured her that what they were doing was legal. "It may be legal," she replied, "but it's morally wrong."[19]

Mary Green had spent more than 18 years working for Quaker State in Oil City, Pennsylvania, running a successful multistate training program for car dealers, supervising as many as 100 clerks, and helping to double the company's oil gallonage. She thought that she deserved better from her company and set out to discover why Quaker State was allowed to factor social security into her pension. She learned that integrating pension benefits with social security allowed her company to provide larger benefits to higher-paid employees at the expense of those who were lower on the salary scale. More than half of all workers in defined benefit plans have integrated pensions.[20]

There are two ways of integrating pensions. The Quaker State plan approach was to subtract, or offset, part of employees' social security benefits from their pension benefits. The other method is to say that pension benefits earned on salaries above a specified dollar amount are worth more than benefits earned on salaries below that amount. This is called an excess formula. The salary cutoff is usually the social security wage base, which is $61,200 in 1995. Only about 6 percent of employees earn above this figure.[21]

One of the largest corporate plans in the United States, the General Electric Retirement Plan, uses the excess method. The plan provides that benefits earned on the first $18,000 a year of pay are worth 1.45 percent of pay multiplied by an employee's work years, whereas benefits earned on wages or salary above that amount are worth 1.9 percent of pay. Under this formula, someone earning $20,000 a year at retirement who worked 30 years would get a pension of $8,970 a year, or 45 percent of preretirement pay. Someone earning $150,000 a year who worked 30 years would get $83,070 a year, or 55 percent of pay.

Plan consultants often recommend the GE approach over the Quaker State approach on the grounds that it's harder for employees to understand, making them less likely to protest! Either way, the less salary an employee makes, the less she or he will get from the pension plan if it "integrates."

Because Mary Green earned the reasonably good salary of $34,512 a year, she was hurt less than the clerks she supervised. Integration formulas wipe out proportionally more of a lower-paid employee's pension than a higher-paid person's. This is true despite low earners' greater need to add to their social security.

The rationale for integration goes back to 1942, when business groups convinced Congress that pensions and social security should be considered as an integrated whole. Since social security replaces a higher percentage of salary for lower-paid employees, their argument went, private pensions should go the other way and replace a higher percentage for higher-paid employees. Pensions that favored the higher-paid were seen to even out this "tilt" in social security.

Employers also justify integration by pointing out that when they put money into private pension plans *and* social security, they are contributing to two forms of retirement for their workers. Since their contributions to social security are comparatively larger for lower-wage workers — in percentages if not in amounts — they believe that they ought to get credit for these amounts and subtract them from pensions.

To most workers today, integration doesn't make sense. In the first place, the income-replacement theory works only for full-career employees. Applying it to shorter-service workers can leave them with appallingly small benefits. Nor is it accurate to gauge the total retirement income of higher-paid people by looking only at social security and pensions. Almost anyone who earns over $100,000 in salary has additional income from other assets, including significant amounts of tax-sheltered savings. These assets more than compensate for any weighting of social security in favor of the lower-paid. As for the double contribution to retirement, critics of integration point out that the money employers pay into the social security fund is not a contribution but a tax, part of the cost that every employer pays to do business.

Some integration supporters worry that some people's combined social security and pension benefits might equal more than 100 percent of their preretirement earnings. In reality, "overpensioning" is likely only in the case of someone who works a lifetime for the same company at very low pay. It can be argued with some justice that this person needs to start out retirement with a little more, since inflation will quickly erode the value of what is likely to be a very small pension. Actuary Edward Burrows suggests that a better approach is to "cap" pensions in the occasional instance in which retirees receive more than they were paid before retirement.

When you come right down to it, the real purpose of integration is to keep employers' costs down and to allow them to offer a larger pension share to favored management-level employees. If integration were not allowed, either higher-level employees would get smaller benefits or the company would have to put more money into the pension plan.

Nancy Altman points out that "when viewed from a worker security perspective, the integration rules clearly constitute bad policy. The current rationale for the favorable tax treatment of private pensions is that it is an inducement to employers to provide rank-and-file workers with supplemental pensions. The integration rules operate in a manner contrary to this goal."[22]

Integration astonishes people when they first learn about it. When one United States congressman heard testimony that integration had wiped out one employee's entire benefit, he whispered to an aide in consternation, "Can they *do* this?" The aide assured the congressman that they could.

That was in the days when the law allowed employers to subtract as much as 83⅓ percent of social security from pensions, although most employers settled for taking off 50 percent. Many people ended up like Margery Boley, who, after 20 years as a sales clerk for J. C. Penney Company in Columbus, Ohio, received a letter saying, "There is no benefit payable to you from the pension plan because the social security retirement benefit, as estimated under the plan formula, is sufficient to meet the Plan's income goal." Pension integration had caused her pension to completely disappear.

Marge Boley did what Mary Green was to do some ten years later. She went to Washington to testify before a congressional committee. Thanks to her testimony, the Tax Reform Act of 1986 added provisions to prevent this kind of vanishing act.[23] Under the 1986 law, an offset plan like Mary Green's at Quaker State can still subtract social security from a pension, but it cannot ultimately reduce a benefit by more than half. In a GE-type excess plan, the percentage of pay (or contributions) provided on higher earnings can be no more than double the percentage on lower earnings.

Although the 1986 law gave integration a new name — "permitted disparity" — and ensured that people can no longer lose everything, they can still lose considerable amounts. Half of their social security benefits can be subtracted from their pensions. And millions of workers who worked prior to the law's effective date of 1988 have years that can still be completely "integrated out," leaving them with minuscule benefits.[24]

Most workers agree with Mary Green, who told a Senate Labor Subcommittee that integration should be outlawed completely. "Why do you allow it?" she asked. "You should stop it." A person's social security benefits "should have no bearing whatsoever on a pension from a corporation. Social security is separate. . . . The law needs to be changed."[25]

Representative Barbara Kennelly called for an end to the practice by the year 2000 as part of her proposed Pension Reform Act of 1994.[26] In the interim, she proposed making the permitted-disparity rules applicable to all years a person has worked, not just to years after 1988. Kennelly calls the concept behind integration "outdated and unfair, particularly to women." The proposal, strongly supported by women's and retiree groups, is viewed with horror by the pension industry, but it is neither new nor radical. In 1974, as part of ERISA, both the Senate and the House of Representatives passed legislation eliminating future pension integration. The practice was reinstated only after an intensive lobbying effort that resulted in an after-the-fact technical amendment.

A PROTEST THAT WORKED

In some instances, angry employees have protested integration, and their employers have agreed to drop the practice. Lee Miller was a wireman for Baltimore Gas & Electric Company for 32 years. His plan was better than most: instead of subtracting 50 percent of social security benefits from the pension benefit, as most plans did before the 1986 Tax Reform Act, it subtracted only 15 percent. Nevertheless, Miller and his coworkers were outraged. They challenged the company on the issue and the Baltimore Gas & Electric plan eventually dropped its offset.

Employees need to look closely at their plans to make sure that employers aren't taking away more than they are entitled to under current integration rules. This happened to Yvonne Simmons, whose pension from the Rockwell Corporation was integrated down to $272.81 a month. Her pension should have been twice that amount, but Rockwell had used an incorrect figure for the social security benefit.

Plans typically use estimates of employees' social security benefits based on the assumption that they have worked continuously. For people who drop out of the workforce for periods of time, these estimates will be considerably higher than their actual social security benefits. Plan administrators are required to notify people when they retire of their right to have their pensions recalculated based on their actual social security payments. But it is up to the retiree to ask that this be done.[27]

Although formulas skewed to older and higher-paid employees are the most common sources of disappointment, there are many other rules that can also cause people to get benefits that are far less than they expected. Among them are rules that subtract workers' compensation payments from a pension or give less or sometimes no credit for certain early years worked — for example, before 1976 or, in the case of workers who change unions, before an employer started contributing to a multi-employer plan. Some employees are shocked to find that their employers never made contributions for them (which can happen with discretionary profit sharing plans). Or they discover that leaving a plan at a young age can mean that their lump sum payments are extremely small and, in some instances, if less than $3,500, cannot be repaid if they return to work. Most commonly, however, employees are disappointed because they have relied on benefit estimates provided by the plan without realizing that the plans can be stopped or changed at any time, freezing their benefits at current rather than projected levels.

Finally, there are people like Raymond Jansson, who took early retirement from Unisys after having been told in writing three different times what his benefit would be. Four months into retirement, he was notified that a mistake had been made. His benefit would be $2,800 a year less. He says that he would not have retired had he known that the benefit would be that small. He's filing a lawsuit and is determined to fight. "I'll take it all the way to the Supreme Court," he says.

What to Do

HOW TO FIND OUT HOW MUCH YOUR PENSION WILL BE

By law, your *individual benefit statement* must indicate whether you are vested and how much your annual pension would be at age 65 if you left the company as of the date of the statement (or if your employer stopped the plan). This is called your accrued benefit.

You should ask your plan administrator how much your benefit would be if you are married when you collect your pension, since your pension is likely to be automatically reduced to provide half of your benefit for your widow or widower, unless your spouse agrees to give up this protection. Ask how much your benefit would be if you decided to take early retirement. If your plan permits lump sum payments, you should ask what that amount would be.

If you have any questions about how your pension was calculated, ask to be shown what formula was used to figure your benefit. Be suspicious of projections of what your benefit would be if you continued to work until retirement age. These can be very misleading, since the company can change its method for calculating future benefits (or stop or freeze the plan) at any time, go out of business, or lay you off. Benefit projections mask the effects of formulas that reduce benefits for people leaving plans before retirement age.

Check whether the pension amount shown on the individual benefit statement is in addition to your social security benefits. Some statements include the social security payment as part of the total pension benefit. If your plan subtracts part of your social security from your pension, find out exactly how much social security will be offset. You can check the reasonableness of the plan's estimates by getting your *personal earnings and benefit estimate statement* free from the Social Security Administration.

Don't hesitate to ask questions about benefit amounts. Make sure that all the information you get from the pension plan is in writing and signed by a plan official.

CHAPTER 6

Eaten Alive

This plan does not provide adjustments for inflation.

At age 90, Howard Kaufman has learned everything there is to know about pensions and the cost of living. Back in 1968 when he retired from the Packaging Corporation of America, where he made paper boxes for 35 years, he received a modest pension of $74.83 a month. Now inflation has reduced that pension to less than a fourth of its original value. Today $74.83 will buy what $17.45 could buy in 1968.

"I worked for peanuts and I get peanuts for a pension," he says philosophically from his home in Dalton, Ohio. "It's pretty rough, though, when I have to compete to buy groceries with fellows who're retiring now with $600 to $700 a month for a pension."

Howard Kaufman has never gotten a cost-of-living adjustment (COLA). Without a COLA, even given a low 4 percent inflation rate, a pension's value will be sliced in half over 17 years, which is the typical retiree's life expectancy. If you reach 90, your pension can be eaten alive by inflation.

Most people who retire from jobs in private industry find themselves in Kaufman's situation. *Fewer than one out of five private sector pensioners has ever received a cost-of-living increase.*[1] Even among those who have been retired 20 years or more, only one-fourth have ever gotten an adjustment.[2] Indeed, the trend seems to be in the opposite direction. The number of plans granting COLAs has dropped dramatically in recent years. In 1983, more than half of private sector participants were in defined benefit plans that had provided at least one increase in the preceding five years.[3] By 1991, that number had shrunk to 11 percent.[4] Most of these increases were either one-time ad hoc adjustments provided at the whim of employers or "13th checks," extra monthly checks awarded by multiemployer plan trustees at the end of the year. Only 5 percent of participants are in plans that automatically provide inflation adjustments.[5]

The other bad news is that when increases come, they are usually much lower than the actual rise in the cost of living. Among the plans with built-in annual raises, the average increase is less than 3 percent.[6] During the 1980s, the consumer price index rose an average of 5.5 percent a year. Among those getting occasional raises, AT&T retirees saw their benefits increase by less than 10 percent between 1985 and 1988, whereas the consumer price index went up a total of 18.3 percent in that period. Of course, those workers were fortunate; during that time, three-quarters of all pensioners received no increase at all.[7]

Plans that do give cost-of-living raises usually restrict them to people who work at least until early retirement age, which is normally 55. Retirees who have left the plan earlier to take other jobs or been forced out because of disability or job termination generally get no benefit increases. Marvin L. Curland's job was terminated when he was 51 and had worked at General Dynamics in Norwich, Connecticut, for 23 years. He got a pension of $189.75 a month at age 65, but his plan gives COLAs only to retirees who worked until age 55. This means that someone with only ten years of service who was able to work until retirement gets inflation adjustments; Curland, who gave many more years of service, doesn't.

Today, after 20 years of inflation erosion, his pension has been whittled down to one-third of its original value. "What gets me," Curland says, "is they still send me letters addressed to 'Dear Retiree' when they treat me as someone less than a full-fledged retiree!"

Why do so few plans provide COLAs or grant only limited increases to select groups of employees? Employers give varying responses. For many, the reason is as simple as the fact that their competitors don't give COLAs. Why should they? Predictably, most say that cost is the main consideration.[8]

Actuary Donald Grubbs estimates that to keep pace with a 4 percent cost-of-living increase, a company would have to increase its pension outlays by 33 percent in the long run. If inflation grew to 8 percent,

Grubbs says, the cost of a plan would go up at least 77 percent.[9] However, he goes on to point out that the costs of COLAs "are not unpredictable or erratic costs. The expected increases can be projected and funded for." They can also be limited to a specified percentage, say, between 2 and 5 percent of total costs per year.

Effect of Inflation on the Purchasing Power of the Dollar

COMPARED TO THE AMOUNT THAT COULD BE PURCHASED BY $1.00 IN JANUARY OF	THE AMOUNT THAT COULD BE PURCHASED BY $1.00 IN JANUARY 1995 WAS
1995	$1.0000
1994	0.9727
1993	0.9488
1992	0.9188
1991	0.8955
1990	0.8476
1989	0.8057
1988	0.7698
1987	0.7399
1986	0.7292
1985	0.7019
1984	0.6780
1983	0.6507
1982	0.6274
1981	0.5788
1980	0.5176
1979	0.4544
1978	0.4158
1977	0.3892
1976	0.3699
1975	0.3466
1974	0.3100
1973	0.2834
1972	0.2735
1971	0.2648
1970	0.2515
1969	0.2369
1968	0.2269
1967	0.2189
1966	0.2116
1965	0.2076

The purchasing power of a dollar declined to $0.2076 during the 30 years from 1965 to 1994. In other words, goods that cost $1.00 in 1995 would have cost about $0.21 in 1965. To determine the purchasing power of any other amount, multiply the amount by the factor shown. For example, to determine the purchasing power of $100 in 1965, multiply .2076 × $100 = $20.76.

Prepared by Donald S. Grubbs, Jr.

Convincing a company to provide COLAs is an uphill battle even when a plan has more than enough money for them. Helen Quirini, a 73-year-old retired General Electric pieceworker, has fought long and hard for COLAs. In 1991, the $23.2 billion GE fund had $5.8 billion more than it needed to pay promised benefits, but when GE retirees asked that those "surplus" funds be used to increase retirees' fixed benefits, the company at first refused. "They cried crocodile tears about how they were saving the money for future employees." Helen Quirini recalls. "Then we discovered they weren't even contributing to the fund. They haven't contributed a penny to the pension fund since 1988!"

From her home in Schenectady, New York, Quirini coordinated nationwide picketing and local rallies to pressure GE into increasing the pensions of GE retirees. The company eventually granted a 5 percent increase in 1991 to pensioners who had retired before July 1, 1988.

An important factor in Helen Quirini's COLA campaign was the strong support of her union, the International Union of Electronic, Electrical, Salaried, Machine, and Furniture Workers (IUE). Pensioners like her, in plans negotiated by unions, stand a somewhat better chance of getting COLAs. That chance increases when they are in unions in which retirees are allowed to vote for union officers. But there is a limit to what unions can do. In a 1971 case, the Supreme Court ruled that retirees were not "employees" protected by the National Labor Relations Act; therefore, unions could not demand that companies bargain about retirees' benefits. What this means, according to Millie Hedrich of the United Electrical, Radio and Machine Workers of America, is that the only benefit increase retirees can expect, if any, is "what the company decides to give them."

Lack of inflation protection is "the most overlooked aspect of the private pension system," says actuary Edward Burrows. He advocates giving employees the choice of trading their fixed pensions for benefits that are smaller but are indexed for inflation over their lifetimes. His approach is similar to that developed by the Teachers' Insurance Annuity Association–College Retirement Equities Fund (TIAA–CREF), the defined contribution pension plan for people working in colleges and universities. TIAA offers a "graded benefit" that allows participants to reinvest enough money early in retirement to provide income that keeps pace with inflation. This strategy is popular with those who can afford it. The problem is, few can. Retirees choosing the graded benefit will get only about half their preretirement income.

Another alternative, suggested by economist Alicia Munnell, now

Assistant Secretary of the Treasury for Economic Policy, is that the government explore issuing index bonds, which could be sold to pension plans. These bonds would fully protect pensioners from the ravages of inflation. They are similar to index bonds that have been issued by governments in a number of other countries, including Great Britain, Brazil, Israel, and France.[10]

Germany and Ontario, Canada require pension indexing to keep pace with inflation. Ontario has passed legislation requiring the indexing of all pension benefits earned in the future to an amount equal to the consumer price index minus 1 percent.

Reprinted by permission of the Tribune Media Services.

The same inflation that eats away at the pensions of retirees also erodes the benefits of active workers who change jobs, sometimes even more cruelly. Because most pensions are not portable, benefits are frozen on the day someone leaves the plan. They are not subject to any cost-of-living increases from then on. Nor do they reflect later increases in workers' wages. Look at what inflation did to California engineer Jack Andressen's pension. When he left IBM in 1979 at age 48, he had earned a monthly pension of $708, payable at age 65. Today, that pension is worth less than $400 in 1979 dollars. He may be able to earn benefits under another plan to add to the frozen one, but it isn't likely that he can make up for the inflation loss.

Since American workers change jobs on average five to six times in their careers, the portability of pensions (or lack thereof) has emerged as a critical issue facing the private pension system. Donald Grubbs believes that the "[f]ailure to adjust the benefits of terminated vested participants for inflation has an even more damaging effect than the failure to adjust the pensions of retired employees, since younger employees have more years for the pension to shrink."[11] Economist John Turner ranks these losses due to inflation second only to those caused by workers cashing out benefits before retirement.[12]

Pension consultants have developed new designer plans aimed at balancing the interests of employees who stay with a company for their whole careers and the interests of those who change jobs. The best known of these is the cash balance plan, which specifies the amount of the employer contribution and the rate of interest on that contribution. First used by the Bank of America in 1985, cash balance plans covered a mere 3 percent of pension participants in 1991 but are proving particularly popular with labor-intensive employers such as banks, universities, and hospitals. Bank tellers and other employees working in positions with high turnover rates can take the amounts accumulated in their cash balance accounts when they leave the company; longer-service employees earn defined benefits.

Another innovative approach has been adopted by the Xerox Corporation. Developed by pension consultants Robert Paul and Dale Grant, the Xerox minimum balance plan provides roughly equivalent benefits for those who leave early and those who stay for a full career.

These new plans are still few and far between. They are growing in popularity, however, and they are not without risk. Herb Whitehouse, former secretary to the board of directors' employee benefits committee of the Chase Manhattan Bank plan, cautions that in a cash balance plan, employees are particularly vulnerable to changes in interest rates. For the shorter-service worker, poor investment returns over an extended period of time can mean smaller accumulations in the employee's individual account; a longer-service worker "may be dead in the water" if she leaves her plan when the market is down.

These new plans, though superficially simpler than traditional defined benefit plans, are almost never as generous. Paul Nordine, a vice president at Bank of America, told *Institutional Investor* magazine that the bank's "cash balance plan may provide something like two-thirds the benefit levels of the defined benefit plan it replaced."[13]

Most people who change jobs are still stuck with frozen benefits, and many of them are pushing for reform. The Institute of Electrical and Electronics Engineers (IEEE) has taken the lead in developing legislation that would allow employees to transfer vested pensions from one plan to another or into an individual retirement account should the second job have no pension plan. The Pension Portability Improvement Act of 1993 was introduced into Congress by Representative Sam Gibbons.

This initiative is strongly supported by the American Nurses Association and the Older Women's League, among others. It also has its critics, who point out that workers would come out ahead only if their old plan's estimate of future investment returns turned out to be lower than what workers actually got under the new plan. In fact, plan interest rate estimates often *are* wrong. The issue is whether employees should have the right to decide, in any case, whether they would be better off staying with the plan or transferring their money. Advocates such as Vin O'Neill of the IEEE believe that "the choice should be theirs."

The question most frequently asked about the Pension Portability Act is what would happen to an underfunded defined benefit plan if a large number of workers were to leave it at the same time. By definition, an underfunded plan does not have enough money to pay all promised benefits, and a large withdrawal of benefits could mean that the plan would become bankrupt. A possible solution to this problem, adopted in Great Britain, gives employers the choice of either allowing workers to transfer their vested pension money out of the plan or indexing the plan for inflation. If an employer chooses the indexing approach, the pension must be adjusted each year from the time the worker leaves the plan to the time he or she reaches age 65 by an amount equal to 5 percent annually or the retail price index, whichever is smaller. (The retail price index is similar to the U.S. consumer price index.)[14] A 1987 Congressional Budget Office study suggested this approach.[15]

Most plans in the Netherlands voluntarily index the vested benefits of active workers who have left the plan and grant any cost-of-living adjustments for current workers to former workers with vested benefits, reflecting not only inflation but also wage growth.[16]

What to Do

How to Campaign for Cost-of-Living Adjustments

Check your *summary plan description* (or ask your plan administrator, employer, or plan trustee) to see whether your plan offers *automatic* COLAs after retirement. If not, find out whether the plan has ever provided an *ad hoc* COLA (or a 13th check) in the past and, if it has, how much of an increase was given and when it was paid.

If your plan does not provide adequate inflation adjustments, consider organizing your own COLA campaign. This will require some detective work. First, find out how inflation has reduced the dollar value of your pension by looking at the table on page 65. Second, contact retirees you know from other companies in your community and accumulate examples of plans that give COLAs. Third, check to see whether your plan can afford an increase by looking at the *Schedule B* attached to the plan's detailed financial statement. You can request *Form 5500* or *Form 5500 C/R* from the plan administrator or call the U.S. Department of Labor's Public Disclosure Room. If you discover that in item 8 of the form (at the top of page 2) the "value of assets" is greater than the "accrued liability," it means that the plan's consultant considers it to be "overfunded." This means that an increase could be given without any additional company contributions.

Armed with this information, you and other retirees should meet with company officials or plan trustees, or write them a letter. Either way, you should present your need for a COLA as effectively as possible. Explain your personal financial needs, stress your role in building the company, point to the practices of other companies, and, if relevant, point to the plan's ability to afford the increase. A surprising number of company and union officials are simply unaware that the dollars paid to someone who retired 20 years ago are worth less than a third of their original value. If you can persuade retiree, community, or religious groups to support your campaign with letters, that will help, as will a rally to which you invite the local media.

CHAPTER 7

A Piece of the Pie

"[T]he great mass of women are still only a man or a misstep away from penury in retirement.

—Barbara Presley Noble, New York Times[1]

Marjory Pentecost is a survivor. A small, sprightly woman from Arlington, Virginia, she was married to a Methodist minister for 31 years. Then one day he told her that he was leaving her, that he wanted "to be free." The emotional blow was devastating, but so was the financial: she was penniless. For the first time in her life, she found herself "in the welfare system," dependent on food stamps and subsidized housing.

Now 73, she has managed to rebuild her life with support from her daughters, but her ordeal is still vivid in her mind. Why, after all those years of marriage, did divorce reduce her to poverty? The main reason, she came to realize, was the pension. Her lawyer had forgotten to include her husband's pension in the divorce agreement.[2]

For most couples, including Marjory Pentecost and her former husband, the pension is their second largest asset, the largest being the family house. The consequences of not getting a share can be earthshaking. Yet until recently, many divorced women discovered that their right to share in a husband's pension expired with their marriage. Lack of pension income has emerged as one of the biggest reasons that poverty rates among divorced and separated older women are so extraordinarily high. According to Brandeis University economics professor James Schulz, *more than one in every four divorced and separated women age 62 and over have incomes below the poverty level.*[3]

A majority of these women (65 percent) live on social security payments alone.[4] Employer-sponsored pension plans provide barely 2 percent of the income of older women, and the amounts are insignificant. In 1990, half of all older women receiving any pension money were getting only $269 a month. The median private pension income for men over 65 was $591 a month.[5]

"The numbers are frightening," says Professor Schulz, who cites the following grim statistics:

- Half of all women over age 65 who live alone have total incomes of less than $9,500 a year.
- Divorced and never married women over 65 are five times more likely to be poor than their married contemporaries.
- Almost four times more widows live in poverty than do married women the same age.

Ann Zinni, a 63-year-old political activist from Broward County, Florida, who recently separated from her husband, summed up the situation tersely: "Older women have to stay in unhappy marriages if they want to eat."

"The view of a pension as jointly-earned and jointly-owned marital property is a relatively new one," says Anne Moss, a lawyer who specializes in pensions and divorce. Although some state divorce courts began dividing pensions in the 1970s, many private pension plan administrators simply refused to pay benefits to divorced spouses. Not until 1984 did federal law require private pension plans to comply with court orders directing them to make payments to divorced spouses.

As often happens in the pension area, the law was changed because one person was outraged and decided to protest. In this case, it was Millicent Goode, a homemaker from Baltimore, Maryland, whose husband filed for divorce after 30 years of marriage. A Maryland court awarded her half of her husband's $1,200-a-month pension from Bethlehem Steel Company, but the plan refused to pay, claiming that federal law did not allow plans to honor state court decrees awarding pensions as marital property.

"I know I earned a share of my husband's pension and was awarded one-half of it as 'marital property' under state law and by court order," she told Congress. "I do not think a company should be able to use their interpretation of federal law to strip me of my right."[6]

Less than a year later, Congress passed the Retirement Equity Act of 1984, amending ERISA to require pension plans to honor court orders dividing pensions. Although most changes in the law come too late to help people who have already been hurt, Millicent Goode was luckier than most. Because of the new law, she was able to get her pension share.

But the law does not protect people automatically. Marjory Pentecost didn't get her share because her lawyer, apparently unaware of the new provisions, did not ask for a court order specifically including the pension in the divorce settlement. Without such an order, called a qualified domestic relations order (QDRO), spelling out how, to whom, and when the pension should be paid, plans don't have to pay the divorced spouse a dime. When Marjory Pentecost went to church authorities and explained the omission, their answer, in effect, was, "Sorry."

Vicki Gottlich, a staff attorney for the National Senior Citizens Law Center, notes, "A lot of women don't get their pension benefits because either their lawyers don't know about the law or the language they use is incorrect."[7] The QDRO must conform exactly to the legal requirements for such an order, or the divorced spouse loses out.

The court order not only must call for a division of pension benefits but also must specifically provide for widow's benefits in case the former husband dies. Judy Horstman, the former wife of a General Motors employee, had a divorce settlement that provided her with half of her ex-husband's sizable pension, to be paid when he eventually retired, and also a "joint and survivor annuity" payable if he died after retirement. Because her ex-husband died while still employed by GM, one year after the divorce, she got nothing from the pension plan. Her attorney had neglected to specify that a "preretirement survivor annuity" should be included in the QDRO.

Many people going through divorce cannot afford a lawyer and rely on simplified do-it-yourself arrangements. This can have unfortunate consequences, as Bonnie Wright discovered. After 30 years of marriage and five children, she and her husband Earl agreed to divorce. Since they had very little property, they used a form provided by the clerk of the local court. Earl Wright could not read, so he asked the clerk to fill in the information for him. He gave his wife his life insurance and health benefits, but his pension, earned after 25 years as an operating engineer, was not mentioned on the form. He died a month after the divorce. His plan specifically provided that his widow would get half of his benefits, but when Bonnie Wright applied for the benefit, the trustees told her that since she was divorced, she was not a widow. Without a QDRO, they would not pay her. From her home in Dongola, Illinois, she wrote, "What am I to do? I am destitute."

Women's and retiree groups are now urging Congress to change the law to require that pensions be automatically divided at divorce, unless the parties agree otherwise or a court orders that benefits not be paid. The division would be based on the number of years a covered employee was married. This approach has been adopted by the Foreign Service Retirement System.

In September 1992, the Congressional Symposium on Women and Retirement recommended that Congress enact legislation requiring the automatic sharing of private pensions. Representative Barbara Kennelly included such a provision in her Pension Reform Act of 1994. Senator Howard Metzenbaum has a similar provision in his Pension Bill of Rights Act of 1994.

"Wait a minute...you haven't said anything about the retirement plan."

Copyright © 1994. Reprinted courtesy of Bunny Hoest and Parade Magazine.

While divorce can be a sure road to poverty, staying married provides no guarantee of security where pensions are concerned. Rita Cevasco of Northport, New York, was widowed at the age of 57. A homemaker, she was left with two children still in college and large medical bills from her husband's cancer treatment. Her husband had earned a six-figure salary and worked 25 years for the same company. As his widow, she received a total income of $3,800 a year.

"Because my husband's pension was integrated with social security, and he was 58 when he passed away [too young to be eligible for a full retirement benefit], my pension comes to $318 a month. One cannot live on $318 a month."[8]

Widows are inevitably shocked by how little they get from their husbands' pensions. Half of all widows receiving benefits from private pension plans get less than $3,000 a year. These tiny widow's benefits are due to pension formulas that give spouses only half of what the retiree would have been entitled to had he lived.[9]

"The pension fund allotment of $356 per month reduces me to poverty and desperation," wrote Helen Shelly of Bluffton, Ohio, in a letter to her husband's union pension fund. Also widowed at 57, she found that "with no profession beyond homemaking, my opportunities for employment in the current economy are non-existent." Like many widows, Helen Shelly felt not only impoverished but also insulted by the pittance she was getting from her husband's pension plan. "The terms of the pension fund do not recognize my contribution to our family . . . [and] do not fulfill Ralph's intention to care for his family."

Anne Moss ascribes the pathetic size of most widow's benefits to the fact that "there is only one pie." "For widows to get a piece," Moss points out, "it means the couple must get less while he lives, to pay for the benefit if he dies. Then the widow gets half of that."

Of course, plans *can* offer survivors better pensions than the law requires, and some do. A number of plans, especially larger ones, offer 75 percent of a spouse's benefit to the widow or widower. A few even offer 100 percent basic survivor pensions. But these are a minority.

Some couples decide to take the risk and waive the widow's benefit protection in order to get the full benefit while the husband is alive. This is almost always a mistake. When Mary Souza and her 65-year-old electrician husband made that decision, they believed that they had no choice. "Based on the figures given to us then," she said, "we felt we needed to take the full pension to cover our expenses." A year later, he died suddenly. That was 1973, and Mary Souza hadn't worked outside the home since 1941, when her first child was born. She was 56, ineligible for social security until she turned 60. They had put aside $10,000 in savings, which she managed to live on with the help of an occasional part-time job and subsidized housing. When she became eligible for social security, it was based on her husband's work record and came to a little over $500 a month. To this day, that remains her total income.

The worst part, she said later, was that suddenly her own contribution seemed worthless. All those years spent keeping house for the family, leading a Girl Scout troop, volunteering at church and for the Heart Fund, "didn't seem to have counted for anything."[10]

In 1973, when the Souzas made their fateful decision, most couples did not even have a choice whether to elect a survivor's benefit: the majority of plans didn't offer them. In 1974, ERISA required private pension plans to provide survivor's benefits for spouses whose husbands died after reaching retirement age, beginning in 1976. But there were two loopholes in the law. One was that the widow's protection could be given up by the husband without the wife's knowledge.

Ruth Godbold was married for 30 years to a maintenance man for the Union Camp paper mill in Franklin, Virginia. In August 1981, her husband was diagnosed as having cancer; a month later, he was dead. "When I was straightening out Will's papers, I found out . . . that he signed away my right to get a pension," she told a congressional committee. "Neither I nor my three girls could believe it. We thought something must have gone wrong."[11]

The other flaw in the law was that if the employee died before reaching the plan's early retirement age, the surviving wife lost her right to widow's benefits even if he hadn't signed it away. Some of the most dramatic testimony ever heard in a congressional proceeding came from Patricia Tice of Potomac, Maryland. "I originally agreed to testify because I thought I could benefit from the pending legislation," she said, "but unfortunately, the legislative process has moved too slowly for me. . . . My husband died this morning." She told the shocked committee that her husband had been 50 years old and had worked for the IBM Corporation for 24 years when he was stricken with cancer. "Art was a model employee," she said, whose work with Apollo XV had earned him the right to have his name placed "among those that have been immortalized on microfilm in a capsule on the moon." When it became clear that he might not get well, Tice asked IBM what would happen to her husband's pension in the event of his death. "I found out I wouldn't end up with a dime of Art's pension unless he lived to age 55."[12]

Thanks in large part to Pat Tice's testimony, Congress changed the law in 1984. The Retirement Equity Act provides that once a worker becomes vested under a plan, the plan must automatically offer survivor's protection, unless both husband and wife sign a notarized consent waiving this benefit. The new law applies only to people widowed after 1984, however, leaving many widows below the poverty line.

ONE WIDOW'S PROTEST

Margaret Silva's husband died of a heart attack in 1982, after working for the FMC Corporation in San Jose, California, for 33 years. He was ten months short of his fifty-fifth birthday, and the company told her that she would get no pension. She filed a lawsuit and picketed the company until FMC agreed to set up a special fund for her and other FMC widows who would not benefit from the new 1984 law.

There are still loopholes in the law to be closed. One involves certain profit sharing and other individual account plans, such as 401(k) savings plans. When a worker leaves one of these plans, all the money can be paid to him or her without the agreement of the spouse, even though all the money in the worker's account would have gone to the spouse had the worker died while under the plan. Lump sum payments to workers can also be made without spousal consent by defined benefit plans when the total value of an individual's cash-out is less than $3,500.

Spousal protection also disappears if a mate leaves a plan and the pension is rolled over into an individual retirement account (IRA). Even though the husband's or wife's consent is required for the rollover, once the money is in the IRA, the "owner" can do with it whatever he or she wants, including cashing it in without the spouse's knowledge or agreement.

Former Older Women's League executive director Joan Kuriansky believes that the time has come for Congress to close these loopholes and guarantee that survivor's benefits be the same for both the retiree and the widow or widower, regardless of who dies first. "Why should widows have to live on half as much as the husband would have if he survived?" she asks.

According to Robert Myers, former chief actuary of the Social Security Administration, this protection could be provided at no additional cost. The benefit the couple receives would be reduced slightly more than at present, and then the survivor, whether retiree or spouse, would get 75 percent of that amount. The 1992 Congressional Symposium on Women and Retirement recommended the enactment of legislation to increase the benefit level of the survivor annuity to at least two-thirds of the initial benefit.[13]

What to Do

GETTING A PENSION BENEFIT AFTER A DIVORCE

If you are considering divorce and your husband or wife has earned a pension or other retirement benefit, check to make sure that the courts in your state divide pensions. Most courts divide pensions and also award surviving spouse's benefits. Although circumstances differ, pensions are typically divided based on the amounts earned during the period of marriage that the worker was covered by the plan.

You should ask for a pension share while the worker or retiree is living *and* for survivor's benefits whether the worker dies *before* or *after* retirement. As an alternative, you may want to trade these benefits for other property of equivalent value. If at all possible, use a lawyer to make sure that the court order or court-approved settlement meets all the requirements for a QDRO. Guidance may be available from the pension plan. A QDRO must include the following information:

- Your name and address and the employee's name and address;
- The name of the plan;
- The amount you are to be paid, or how it is to be figured;
- The form of payment you are to receive, that is, lifetime monthly payment, widow's pension, or lump sum; and
- The date payments are to start and stop.[14]

GETTING WIDOW'S OR WIDOWER'S BENEFITS

Ordinarily, if you have not agreed to give up survivor's benefit protection and are married to someone who was working under a defined benefit or defined contribution pension plan after 1984, a 50 percent benefit will be paid at the death of your spouse if he or she had a vested right to benefits, whether the death occurs before or after retirement age.

If the employee is in a profit sharing or other defined contribution plan that makes lump sum payments, it is likely that the amount accumulated in the employee's account will go to you if he or she dies while working under the plan and you have not agreed to another arrangement. However, if the employee changes jobs or retires and withdraws the money, you will lose the survivor's protection.

CHAPTER 8

The Pension
Piggy Bank

All our money is down the tubes.

The call from Dot Harkness's boss came at midnight. He had never called that late before, and his voice was shaking. "The profit sharing money is gone," he told her. "All our money is down the tubes."

"I was just sick," she recalls. "I remember that night I felt numb. Later, I became bitter."

The mother of three grown sons and a lifelong skier on the slopes towering over her hometown of Park City, Utah, Dot Harkness had thought that she could handle most situations. This one was different. The profit sharing plan run by the doctor's office where she was a receptionist had held $29,000 in her account. It was all she had for her retirement. She had even borrowed against it. Now what?

It turned out that the doctor had put all the employees' profit sharing money into a single investment, a land speculation deal that went bust. Dot Harkness's first thought was, "This can't have happened." She was wrong. Her second reaction was, "There has got to be a law." She was right.

In ERISA, Congress set standards for the management of pension and profit sharing funds. One of these, the *prudence rule*, requires that the funds be held "in trust" for employees and that those managing pension money act "prudently." In other words, the doctor who had appointed himself plan trustee was required to keep the money separate from his other accounts and to invest it wisely and carefully. Putting all the plan's money into a single speculative investment was, under any standards, imprudent.

The law is one thing; enforcing it is another. Dot Harkness said, "I went to five attorneys before I found one who agreed to write letters to the doctor. The doctor just ignored the letters. I called an attorney in Seattle who wrote my former boss, but the only person who answered was the [doctor's] accountant."

Finally, after her story had appeared in newspapers around the country, a Salt Lake City pension attorney offered to take the case to court for her. It took five years of worry and strain, but the case was finally settled, with the doctor agreeing to pay $80,000 back into the plan. Eventually, Dot Harkness received $29,000 — everything she was owed — out of which she paid her attorney's fees.

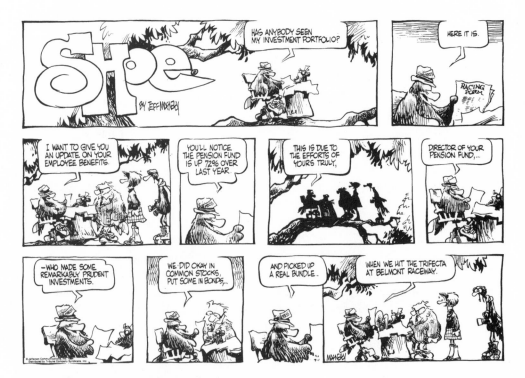

Reprinted by permission of Tribune Media Services.

Clifford Berrien's experience involved another provision in the pension law. Trustees must not only invest money prudently, they must also invest it "solely in the interests" of the people whose money is in the plan. This *conflict of interest rule* means that they cannot use the money to further their own interests, those of their relatives, or those of the people providing services to the plan.

In 1988, Clifford Berrien was thinking about retiring. A courtly man of 65, he enjoyed his ties to the community, forged over 23 years as a pharmacist with the Dart Drug chain in Washington, D.C. At that time, Dart had just gone through a leveraged buyout by two company directors, who were also trustees of the profit sharing plan. The money seemed safe enough at first; employees continued receiving statements that showed plenty of money still left in the plan. What they didn't know was that the company had stopped funding the plan and that the barrel was actually nearly empty.

Berrien got his first inkling that there was trouble when he called the plan administrator to ask for an account statement. When he had checked a year earlier, there had been $58,000 in his account. Now he was told that he had only half that amount. In addition, the plan administrator said that there could be no withdrawals. Astonished, Berrien spoke to some of his colleagues, one of whom said that he too had tried to withdraw his money from the plan but was told that there was nothing there!

A worried Berrien called his daughter, a lawyer in New York. She contacted friends and, eventually, the Labor Department. Other distraught Dart employees wrote to the department asking for an investigation. Finally, the Labor Department agreed to take a look. What it found ended up as front-page news, with the Dart Drug employees' profit sharing plan at the center of the drama. As part of their buyout, the plan's trustees, Stephen J. Hansbrough and Alvin F. Towle, who were also company officers and directors, had transferred $3.7 million from the old plan, which had covered Clifford Berrien and 1,373 other Dart employees, to a newly created one. They then invested money from the "new" plan in shares of the company's junior preferred stock at $100 per share, convertible to common stock at a rate of approximately $3 per share. At the same time, they purchased over 3 million shares of the company's common stock paying 33 cents per share, thus taking control of the company. Finally, they sold over 2.4 million shares at $1 per share to Dart employees. In effect, the plan was being used as a form of bank. It became an extra source of capital for them. This scheme drained the employees' profit sharing plan of some $3.5 million.

Meanwhile, Dart Drug went bankrupt, and all the employees lost their jobs. "We were told we could just get in line with the other creditors," Clifford Berrien remembers. "At that point, we didn't know whether or not we would ever see a penny of our pensions. Frankly, it looked pretty hopeless."

This was a plan involving millions of dollars, big enough for the Labor Department to go to court against the trustees. The lawsuit took nearly four years. In the end, Herbert Haft, the billionaire former owner of Dart, agreed to put $2.7 million back into the plan. Employees got between 80 and 90 percent of their retirement money. Clifford Berrien received $47,000 as a lump sum. As for the trustees who had bilked the profit sharing plan, after one paid a small restitution, a pittance of $100,000, they went free. "A slap on the wrist," says Berrien.

Each month the Labor Department reports new cases of trustees who have not been able to resist using pension funds as their personal piggy banks. Although there are laws on the books that make it a crime to steal or mismanage pension and profit sharing funds, the fact remains that control over the money is left in the hands of company owners and officers or, in the case of multiemployer plans, company and union officials. These funds can be a great temptation.

There is more than $3 trillion in private retirement plans today. Most pension money is well managed and most trustees don't play around with the money, but many do. A few engage in outright theft. More commonly, an owner will dip into the plan for quick cash to help a company through hard times. Then there are those trustees, like Dot Harkness's boss, who just can't resist a "sure thing" investment opportunity.

In 1994, the Labor Department's Pension and Welfare Benefits Administration (PWBA) opened more than 2,300 civil investigations of pension and profit sharing plan trustees suspected of misusing the participants' money and closed almost 3,500 civil cases, recovering nearly $150 million in plan assets.[1] Most of the cases involved questionable investments and "prohibited transactions," unlawful deals between plan trustees and people who have close connections with plan trustees, such as an employer, union official, relative, or someone providing services to the plan, such as a consultant, investment adviser, accountant, or actuary.

Criminal violations are less frequently investigated, but they do occur. There were 141 criminal indictments in pension cases in 1994, as compared with only 41 in 1993. In some cases, plan trustees received jail terms, paid fines of up to $10,000, or both. Some $6.8 million was ordered restored to plans as a result of criminal prosecutions.[2] In addition to La-

A SAMPLING OF CASES FROM LABOR DEPARTMENT FILES

• Billy James "Bill" Lowery, trustee of the International Brotherhood of Electrical Workers Local 175 pension, health, and welfare plans in Chattanooga, Tennessee, pleaded guilty to embezzling $117,403.06 from the plans. He was sentenced to one year in jail and three years of supervised release. (1993)

• Trustees of the Derio Oldsmobile, Inc., pension and profit sharing plans and the owner of the company were charged with misusing more than $626,000 in plan assets. The complaint filed in federal court in New Jersey alleged that the defendants had transferred all plan assets to the company's corporate account for the purpose of propping up the company, an auto dealership. (1993)

• Investment manager Robert A. White of Jersey City, New Jersey, embezzled approximately $200,000 from the assets of the Quentzel retirement plan and used the funds to purchase securities. He was sentenced to two years and six months in prison and three years probation. (1992)

• Charles, James, and Virgil Manke, owners of Manke Lumber Company of Tacoma, Washington, and trustees of the company's profit sharing plan, improperly loaned approximately $600,000 to William H. Scats, Jr., who provided insurance brokerage services to the company and the plan. The Mankes were ordered to pay some $649,000 to the plan out of company profits made possible by the improper loan. (1993)

• Officers of the retirement board of Public Service Company of New Hampshire improperly invested pension assets in highly risky uncovered options trading. A court ordered the officers to repay nearly $23 million as restitution. (1991)

bor Department investigations, the Internal Revenue Service assesses civil penalties against "parties in interest" who have engaged in prohibited transactions. The IRS is also in charge of enforcing funding laws.

Violations of the law show up in two ways: through Labor Department review of the reports that plan administrators are required to file with the government, and through complaints from plan participants who suspect that something is amiss. Plans with over 100 participants are required to file annual financial reports called Form 5500s and to undergo audits. Administrators of smaller plans need to file reports only every three years and are not audited. Theoretically, these reports and audits provide the basis of government oversight.

Reports are no good, however, if nobody reads them. The Labor Department candidly admits that each year its 328 investigators can check less than 1 percent of the nation's private pension plans. Deputy Assistant Secretary of Labor Alan Lebowitz told the *Philadelphia Inquirer* in 1992 that with their staff at that time, it would take 500 years to review all the nation's pension plans.[3] When plans *are* checked out by government enforcers, a troubling number of violations turn up. More than a third of the plans audited in 1989 were found to have violations, up from about one-fourth in each of the previous three years.[4]

The Labor Department concentrates its attention on the 8 percent of all pension plans[5] that contain roughly 86 percent of all pension assets.[6] That means that thousands of small plans don't get so much as a once-over from government regulators. Some 650,000 small pension plans constitute 92 percent of all plans that exist today.[7] They hold 14 percent of all pension assets and cover about 8.5 million people (11 percent of all people in all private plans),[8] but they are basically free of government oversight, and their trustees are basically free to do as they please, since complaints of possible theft or other violations from small plan members are routinely pushed onto the government's back burner. The smaller the plan, the less likelihood of government scrutiny. A federal field investigator told *Money* magazine that agents are instructed to spend no more than 10 percent of their time on plans with fewer than 50 participants.[9] As a result, many complaints are never investigated or are investigated too late to recover plundered funds. Years sometimes pass after complaints have been filed, years during which anxious complainants are typically told nothing about the status of their complaints.

Most frustrating of all, the government may elect to take no action even when there is proof of wrongdoing. Officials maintain that the resources just aren't there to prosecute abuses in plans with only a few members. If the employer doesn't voluntarily right the wrong, the matter is at an end, and the employees' money is lost. As one member of a plundered small plan angrily put it, "Small plans aren't protected. The administrator has total discretion to do whatever he likes with the funds."

For people like John and Ann Dullea, the frustrations can be overwhelming. As Ann Dullea put it, "We're lost in the system. Nobody listens. Nobody does anything. The watchdogs aren't there." John Dullea discovered that his employer, the owner of a small farming business in Georgetown, Minnesota, had set up a defined benefit pension plan that he kept hidden from the employees and used for his own exclusive benefit: the plan serves as a tax shelter for his company and, to date, has paid a pension only to him.

John Dullea notified the Labor Department but it never investigated or even telephoned the employer on his behalf. The Internal Revenue Service wasn't interested either — the amount involved was only $1 million. Finally, a private lawyer agreed to take on the case and Dullea filed suit. That was back in 1985. The case is still being litigated. Having run out of money to pay lawyers, Dullea is now representing himself. Fired from his job for looking into his pension fund, he now works as a trucker to support his wife and seven children.

It's not so much the loss of retirement money that angers the Dulleas as the fact that they've been unable to get any help. "This is the most disillusioning thing," said Ann Dullea. "I didn't think anything could be so awful."

JUST IN TIME

Duane Doblar, 63, worked for Erie Sheet Steel Corporation in Cleveland, Ohio, for 33 years, until the company folded in 1987. He was counting on his $200,000 share of the profit sharing plan to provide for a mentally retarded son. He received less than half of that.

Labor Department field investigators began looking into the matter in February 1988, found violations, and recommended that the department's lawyers in Washington go to court to recover the money. But nothing happened. The case was "too small," Doblar was told. Not to him, it wasn't!

He learned that a lawsuit had to be filed within three years of the claimed wrongdoing. He began telephoning everyone he could think of — senators, his representative in Congress, the Labor Department's inspector general's office. He refused to give up. Six hours before the last possible moment, the Labor Department filed suit. It charged the majority owner of the company, Jay Friedman, and his son, Perry Friedman, with giving themselves interest-free loans, selling a building owned by the plan for $50,000 less than value, and using plan assets to pay off a company debt.

Sometimes, even when small plans are reviewed, it's hard for government investigators to identify problems because reports are outdated. Given that small plans file less detailed financial statements, and file them less often, this is not surprising. Small plan administrators are also not required to include either a list of plan investments or an accountant's report, as large plan administrators must do. Lastly, most small plans are not protected by the federal pension insurance program, so when abuses occur, the consequences for individuals are usually ruinous. Roughly one-third of pension and profit sharing money is in uninsured defined contribution plans.

A number of people believe that to ensure the detection and reporting of abuses in small plans, stronger measures are needed. Raymond Maria, former acting inspector general of the Labor Department, has recommended a compliance audit by an independent public accountant every three years. As an alternative, the assets of small plans could be invested solely in federally insured institutions — beyond the reach of employers and others for whom the money may be too tempting.

Since large plans get more scrutiny than small ones, the Department of Labor is more likely to prosecute large plan fraud cases, especially if a significant amount of money is involved and if a private lawsuit has already been brought. This is what happened when John Hayes and other members of the Masters, Mates, and Pilots Union profit sharing plan discovered to their horror that the value of their pension fund assets, worth approximately $30 million in November 1984, had dropped to about $9.5 million by early 1986. Investigation showed that money had been invested in businesses in which fund managers had hidden interests. One investment was a pornographic cable-TV channel; another, a burned-out vessel that was supposed to be transformed into a cruise ship. In mid-1986, John Hayes and other plan members sued the trustees and the investment company for violating ERISA. Several months later, the Labor Department joined the suit. The case was eventually settled for $27 million.

Cases involving labor racketeering are also candidates for special government attention. They go to the Office of the Inspector General of the Labor Department. A study of 168 plans undertaken by the inspector general's office in 1989 uncovered $18.7 million in misused pension funds.[10] At that rate, the office projected, there would be about $4 billion worth of fraud throughout the system.

The variety of ways in which trustees and consultants bilk pension funds was chronicled by the New York State Organized Crime Task Force in its 1989 report to Governor Mario Cuomo. The report found:

Corrupt trustees embezzle funds by simply withdrawing money in their own or fictitious names. They make "loans" to themselves, friends, and organized crime associates, without expectation of repayment. They fraudulently pay for nonexistent goods and services, or pay money to ineligible "beneficiaries." They steer contracts for benefit plan services (for example, medical, dental and legal benefits) to companies controlled by fellow racketeers or to legitimate companies willing to pay kickbacks to obtain these lucrative contracts.[11]

Even in large plans, complaints and inquiries from individual plan participants, rather than government vigilance, often tip off federal oversight officials to abuses. One startling case was brought to the attention of the Labor Department by rank-and-file Teamsters Union members. It involved the well-known brokerage house Shearson Lehman Hutton, along with two smaller investment firms, three brokers, and several pension fund trustees. These brokers and trustees were responsible for managing $560 million belonging to several Teamsters Union pension and welfare plans in Utica, New York. In May 1989, following complaints from plan members and an investigation, the Labor Department filed a civil lawsuit. The suit charged that the brokers bought stocks and placed them in a holding account for several days. Losing trades were assigned to pension fund accounts, and profitable trades went into the accounts of friends, relatives, and other customers, including some plan trustees.

Another case involved the Bank of Alaska. Laborers Union members Chris White and Sam Goodman spent months in the recorder of deeds' office in Fairbanks, investigating real estate investments made by their union's $74 million pension fund. They discovered that the National Bank of Alaska, which was paid to manage the fund, had loaned some of the money to companies owned in part by two of its directors. Such "self-dealing" is prohibited by ERISA, and the union members petitioned the Labor Department to stop the bankers from "treating our pension funds as their private money machines." After the Labor Department filed suit, the bank quickly agreed to buy back the loans. The Internal Revenue Service then assessed penalties on the individuals who had received the loans. White and Goodman learned too late that if they had contacted the Intelligence Division of the IRS at the time they furnished the government with information, they could have collected an informant's reward of up to 10 percent of the amount collected.[12]

Raymond Maria told Congress in 1989 that the basic cause of

mismanagement of pension funds, large and small, was lack of deterrence. He warned that "the nation's pension and welfare plans are vulnerable to fraud and corruption because of a flawed enforcement strategy . . . that relies too much on civil remedies and not enough on criminal prosecutions." He pointed out that in most cases, the Labor Department's policy is to seek voluntary settlement, with the guilty parties returning the monies to the fund. Only in extreme cases will an individual be barred from continuing to serve as plan trustee. If actual theft is involved, the Labor Department can refer the case to the Justice Department for criminal proceedings, but until recently, such referrals have been relatively rare. Charles Lerner, director of the Department of Labor's pension law enforcement division, told the *Los Angeles Times* that "although investigators often cooperate in criminal cases, their first priority is to restore money to pension plans — and that civil solutions accomplish that faster."[13]

Raymond Maria disagrees with these tactics, which he believes reassure plan managers who play around that in the unlikely event they are caught, the worst penalty they will suffer will be a civil fine. This, he says, does nothing more than "increase the cost of doing business." Should wrongdoers be convicted of a criminal act, maximum penalties for pension fraud are currently $10,000 or five years imprisonment, or both. It has been more than 20 years since those penalties were established.

Stricter enforcement laws would be unnecessary were it not for the fundamental conflict that lies at the very heart of pension fund management: control remains with the people who put the money in. Because of ERISA, it is doubtful that an American employer could get away with pension theft on the grand scale of the British publishing mogul Robert Maxwell. Over the years, Maxwell bilked his employees' pension funds of hundreds of millions of dollars, a grisly deed that went undiscovered until shortly after his sudden, mysterious death. Nonetheless, American fund managers and employers continue to abscond with significant amounts of pension money, at least in part, because it lies within easy reach.

Whether or not theft or self-dealing goes on, employees' benefits depend on how well the pension fund has been managed. A plan administrator's investment practices are critical. This is particularly true for defined contribution plans, in which benefit amounts consist entirely of contributions plus investment earnings. In defined benefit plans, investment earnings do not directly affect benefits, but the plan will be more likely to improve benefits if the money has been invested wisely. As a rule, a 1 percent increase in the rate of return of a pension fund can result in a 20 percent increase in benefits.

Whether it is the plan's performance or acts of fraud or imprudence that impoverish pension funds, strict vigilance by plan members can mean all the difference in the world to the John Dulleas, Clifford Berriens, and Dot Harknesses of the pension world.

Copyright © 1994. Reprinted courtesy of Bunny Hoest and King Features Syndicate, Inc.

What to Do

HOW TO PROTECT YOUR PENSION MONEY

Start with the plan's *summary annual report* (SAR), which is usually a one-page summary of the plan's finances that you should get automatically. It will give you an idea of whether the plan's investments have lost money, whether administrative expenses are especially high, whether there have been financial arrangements with people closely connected to the plan, or whether money loaned by the plan has been paid back on time.

If the SAR raises questions, the next step is to look at the plan's detailed financial statement, *Form 5500*, filed with the government. In the case of most plans covering 100 or more people, it is accompanied by an accountant's report and list of investments. For small plans, there is a shorter *Form 5500 C/R*.

Plan administrators are required to provide copies of Form 5500 or 5500 C/R within 30 days of being requested to do so in writing. A reasonable copying fee may be charged. You can also get copies from the Department of Labor's Public Disclosure Room. What to look for:

- Are plan expenses reasonable? Are unrealistically large amounts being spent on the salaries of the people running the plan or on plan consultants, lawyers, or investment managers? What about rent or travel expenses?
- Have the plan administrators reported any investments with or loans to people with close ties to the plan, such as company or union officials, trustees, their relatives, or individuals providing services to the plan? These transactions are legal only when expressly permitted by law or by a specific Labor Department ruling.
- What about the types of investments? Does the plan have different kinds of investments: stocks, bonds, money market funds, real estate? Is too much money tied up in one type of investment, making the plan too vulnerable to a downturn?

Bring any questionable items or other discoveries to the attention of the nearest field office of the Labor Department's Pension and Welfare Benefits Administration.

CHAPTER 9

Nowhere to Turn

Most people [who are wrongly denied benefits] give up in frustration or they die in the interim.

—Former New Jersey Representative
William Hughes

Andrew Nunnally lost his job at a Baltimore, Maryland, casket company in September 1982. The company was sold for the fifth time since he'd begun working there, and the new owner let all the union employees go. He knocked on every door he knew of, but jobs in his line of work were scarce, especially union jobs. He was 62 years old. He had been working for casket makers in Baltimore for 45 years. He didn't want to stop.

He was comforted by the thought that if he did have to retire, at least he had his pension. He'd been a member of his multiemployer plan since it started back in 1954. Because of changes in company ownership, he knew that some of his work had been considered "covered," some not. Still, 28 years was a long time. He was sure that his retirement money was safe.

Then he received a letter from his pension plan administrator telling him that he lacked *one month* of employment under the plan to be eligible for a pension. He couldn't believe it. "It is really beyond my comprehension that I am being told I will have to find work with a company which has a contract with the [union] for at least one month," he wrote to a supervisor for the plan.

Again he tried to get a union job in order to fulfill the "one month" stipulation, but the jobs weren't there. In February 1983, he wrote to the pension plan trustees: "If you can find work for me, to still be in the [plan], anywhere, please let me know and I will be glad to do so."

He appealed his case to the plan trustees and was turned down. Eventually, through a friend, he found another job, though it paid just $7 a week more than his unemployment check, and it wasn't covered by the union plan.

Bewildered and frustrated, Andrew Nunnally would have given up the pension fight at that point had it not been for his wife, Frances, who by this time had retired from her job at a credit company. Even with their combined social security and her pension, their finances were tight. Their small row house was paid for, but property taxes were high, and their supplemental health insurance was expensive. Although his pension would be only $250 a month, they needed all the help they could get. They also believed that the plan trustees were wrong: he *had* worked enough time to vest. But how to prove it?

Frances Nunnally wrote to everyone she could think of — their congressional representative and senators, a local television station, the "Action Line" column in the newspaper. Soon she had accumulated a hefty file of letters and responses. People tried to be helpful, but no one had answers. Pensions seemed to be a vast unknown territory to which there were no maps, no guides.

Nobody told the Nunnallys at any time during their eight-year struggle with their pension problem that in the bowels of the federal Labor Department a pension assistance office does exist. The Labor Department doesn't publicize this office, known as the Division of Technical Assistance and Inquiries, because it's too small to respond to all the calls for help. The entire staff in the Washington office consists of 15 advisers. The department receives more than 185,000 pension inquiries a year.

Given the office's overwhelming workload, it is probable that no adviser would have spoken to the Nunnallys had they actually called. Since 1991, as a result of complaints about unanswered letters and unreturned phone calls, the office has relied heavily on an automated telephone answering service. A recording informs callers that the Labor Department cannot interpret the provisions of individual pension plans and invites them to listen to summaries of ERISA's key provisions. Should this pension "menu" not answer the question, the caller can stay on the line to talk to a live pension adviser whose role is to pin down the problem and, if necessary, ask the caller to send additional information. Advisers often encourage people to take action on their own behalf by obtaining certain documents from their plan, for example, or filing a claim for benefits.

According to a 1992 Labor Department policy statement, if people

have taken steps to help themselves and their efforts are not successful, the department may informally intercede. This means that an adviser may telephone a plan's administrator, requesting that the administrator respond to a claimant's application for benefits or send a document or make a payment that has been delayed. For simple glitches, this technique often works. The Labor Department's 1992 Annual Report to Congress states that the Division of Technical Assistance and Inquiries recovered $3,591,183 in benefits for individuals through this kind of voluntary compliance.

Most people's problems, however, require more time, more expertise, and greater resources than those that the overburdened Labor Department pension advisers can provide. In Andrew Nunnally's case, for example, everything depended on his proving that he had worked that additional month.

Before an adviser would have even agreed to inquire into the matter, Nunnally himself would have had to obtain all the pertinent documents. He also would have had to go through his social security earnings records and figure out exactly how many years he had worked for employers paying into the pension fund. This is a painstaking task that Labor Department pension advisers are not authorized to undertake.

Then Nunnally's particular problem required knowing government regulations that are beyond the expertise of Labor Department pension advisers — and of the entire Labor Department. Thanks to a 1978 government reorganization, all rules relating to pension participants' legal rights to benefits are administered not by the Labor Department but by the Internal Revenue Service (IRS). Although Labor Department pension advisers can telephone IRS staff to ask for technical assistance on specific issues, they can do this *only* if they know what questions to ask.

In Andrew Nunnally's case, the key ingredient was an obscure regulation dealing with "contiguous noncovered service." This little-known rule, uncovered by volunteer lawyer Elliott Moore, meant that Nunnally's nonunion work *could* be counted for vesting because he did it immediately after being laid off from union work and for a company paying into his multiemployer plan. It gave him the additional credit he needed. Within days after being informed of the contiguous service rule, the plan trustees found the necessary credit. On September 30, 1991, the Nunnallys received his first pension check — retroactive for nine years.

How do people get help with their pension problems? A tiny percentage luck out, as Andrew Nunnally did. Unfortunately, those who find help are the rare exceptions. For 16 years, James Hall knocked himself out working as sales manager at the offices of Lutz Appellate Printers, a small legal printing company. During his last five years, he worked in the company's Washington, D.C., office under a pension plan. In 1984, at age 58, he became disabled and retired. When he asked his former employer for a benefit statement and other plan documents, he couldn't "even get the courtesy of a reply." Finally, in 1991, a Labor Department pension adviser agreed to call the plan administrator, who was also the owner of the company. The owner denied that the company had even had a pension plan when James Hall worked there.

Ordinarily, the Labor Department would have ended its efforts at that point, but Hall had documentary proof that a pension plan had been in effect when he worked at the company (a plan summary and financial statement were on file at the Labor Department) and that he was entitled to a benefit. The owner had lied to the Labor Department adviser.

The department's Enforcement Division was called in. The employer continued to stall, refusing to produce the documents for over a year. When a court order was issued, along with the threat of a visit from a U.S. marshal, the documents were produced. In August 1993, the Labor Department told Hall that the plan's actuary was calculating his benefit and his checks would soon be in the mail. A year later, having received no checks, he got another call from the Enforcement Division. The company owner "would not cooperate," he was told. There was nothing more the Labor Department could do. It was closing the case.

Now age 68, James Hall suffers from a chronic lung problem related to a World War II injury. From his home in Mineral, Virginia, he reflects sadly that he has been trying to get his pension for "ten miserable years with zero results." What is he supposed to do now? he asks. As he sees it, "there's nowhere to turn."

One reason it is so hard for people to get help with a pension problem is that none of the three government agencies responsible for overseeing private pension plans sees individual problem-solving as its job. The Pension Benefit Guaranty Corporation (PBGC) provides information about the government's pension insurance program, but its province is limited to insured defined benefit plans that have terminated. The IRS considers itself a tax abuse watchdog, on guard against employers trying to get tax breaks for their pension plans without following the rules. Helping individual plan participants is not included in the service's view of its mission. Martin Slate, former director of the IRS's Employee Plans Division and now head of the PBGC, told the *New York Times*, "When we get a call from participants we generally refer them to the Department of Labor."[1]

The Labor Department's fields of expertise are fund mismanagement and disclosure rules. Should somebody raise questions about the investment of plan money, or should a plan administrator refuse to produce documents, as required by law, a pension adviser may ask the department's Division of Enforcement to investigate. But when the case involves a dispute over an individual's right to benefits, even when there is a clear-cut violation of the law, there is usually nothing the adviser can do. As James Hall found, administrators can simply refuse to comply, and that's the end of it. The department's deputy assistant secretary told the *Philadelphia Inquirer* in 1992, "We have no legal obligation to help people, to put it crudely."[2]

That is why there is nowhere for people to go even with relatively straightforward problems, such as how to find the right proof for a claim or decipher a document. As a result, these problems frequently remain unresolved. This inattention to citizens' problems is unique in a country where in virtually every other area of workers' or consumers' rights a government agency stands ready to assist individuals. As Frances Nunnally comments, "The government can put out the money to test ketchup, but nothing to help people with pension problems."

TRACKING DOWN A LOST PENSION

When Alice Mayo got ready to retire, she couldn't find her pension. Her old employer, Franklin Stores in Houston, where she'd worked for 20 years, no longer existed, having been bought out by another company after she left. The new owner had gone bankrupt and ended the pension plan. Alice Mayo called or wrote everybody she thought might help, but no one responded.

Finally, lawyer Cindy Hounsell volunteered to try to track down the pension. It turned out that the last owner had purchased annuities for the vested employees from an insurance company. Hounsell located the insurance company, and Alice Mayo received a statement indicating that her benefit would total $10.65 a month. Mayo knew this had to be wrong. A letter she had received years earlier from the plan's actuary said that her pension was worth ten times that amount. When the error was pointed out, the insurance company adjusted the decimal point. Alice Mayo is now getting a pension of $106.50 a month.

Lack of government resources forces people to look for help from the country's legal system, where they run into more formidable obstacles. Take James Carsten's case. He actually managed to persuade the Labor Department to investigate his small profit sharing plan because the problem involved fund mismanagement. The department's field office in Seattle, Washington, uncovered three clear violations of law by the plan administrator, who was also the owner of the small jewelry repair shop where Carsten worked. The administrator had invested the money belonging to the plan's five participants in highly speculative investments, including a large loan to himself, a risky second mortgage, and palm trees. The employees were missing $40,000 out of their $100,000 retirement fund. But the Labor Department considered the plan "too small" for it to pursue further, even *after* it had uncovered evidence of wrongdoing. A department spokesman said that they didn't have the resources to take the case to court to recover the money. The employees were told that they had the right to sue the trustee.

"You can sue!" was the only answer James Carsten got from the Labor Department, the IRS, his senators, and representative. Take the case to court, they all said.

So Carsten talked to six attorneys. "They all told me I could sue and I could even win. But then the administrator could claim bankruptcy, or he could appeal, or he could just ignore the verdict. In any case, I probably wouldn't get any of my money."

That was why the lawyers wanted $5,000 to $10,000 up front before they would take on the case. From the lawyers' perspective, this wasn't greed, it was realism. A lawsuit can be complex and costly, and if lawyers lose, they are stuck with out-of-pocket expenses and nothing to show for months or years of work. Even if a case is won and attorneys' fees are awarded, as the lawyers advised Carsten, that didn't mean that their fees would be paid. The jewelry store owner had gone out of business. Who knew whether he could pay the fees out of his own pocket? Even if he were insured, which is not required, the insurance might not have been enough to cover both the employees' missing retirement money and the attorneys' fees.

James Carsten and his fellow employees gave up. He is still bitter. "Why do *I* have to sue?" he asks. "Why, if there are laws, aren't they enforced? What good are paper laws with no enforcement powers? Small plans simply aren't protected. The government tells us the plans are covered [by the law], but as it is, the plan administrator has *absolute* discretionary authority. ERISA protection is a joke!"

Could his situation have been worse? Arguably, yes. The odds of his finding a lawyer would have been even less if, instead of suing the *trustee* for fund mismanagement, he had been suing the *plan administrator* for wrongfully denying his benefits. In some parts of the country, courts do not award attorneys' fees in benefits cases unless it can be shown that the plan administrator acted in bad faith, which is difficult to do.[3] Lawyers have to recover their fees out of the small benefits they win for their clients. How many lawyers would go to court for a share of Andrew Nunnally's $250-a-month pension?

The issue of attorneys' fees may be moot, however, since few benefits cases are ever won by claimants, even when they do manage to get their cases into court. More often than not, courts simply rubber-stamp the decisions of plan managers. As a result of the Supreme Court's decision in *Firestone Tire & Rubber Co. v. Bruch*, the plan always wins if the reasoning of plan officials is at all logical. The claimant must show that the officials' decision is not merely less sensible but an outright "abuse of discretion" (or that the officials were acting under a conflict of interest).[4] Since this standard is almost impossible to prove, most lawyers are reluctant to bring pension benefit cases to court.

Firestone Tire & Rubber Co. v. Bruch has bewildered legal experts who specialize in pension issues. According to University of Alabama law professor Norman Stein, it has raised almost insurmountable barriers to claimants' getting a fair shake in court. Professor Stein points out that in other kinds of legal issues, such as compensation or discrimination claims, courts will take a fresh (de novo) look at all the facts involved in a dispute unless an individual has already received a hearing before an impartial decision maker, such as a government agency or a neutral arbitrator. In a pension benefit situation, the only review that takes place is through the plan's own claims procedure, which is usually nothing more than an exchange of letters between the retiree and the plan administrator. Lawyer Ronald Dean points out, "In no other field of law can one side to a dispute give itself nearly unchallengeable power to decide the issues in its own favor, leaving the other side with no effective remedy."

The typical pension claims procedure goes something like this. A retiree applies for a pension. A plan administrator writes back, saying that the retiree is not entitled to a benefit because certain requirements have not been met, but the retiree has the right to appeal. The retiree then writes again, explaining that, in fact, he or she has met the requirements. (This is the appeal.) No new evidence is offered; no hearing takes place; the retiree is not represented by anyone with expertise in these matters; no impartial outsider reviews the evidence. The plan administrator writes back, saying that the requirements have not been met, and there will be no pension. (This is the denial of the appeal.) Most farcical of all is that in most cases, both the initial request and the appeal are decided on by the same person — in a small company, the owner; in a large company, an officer — despite the fact that this individual may have a personal or institutional interest in the denial: to save money for the firm or leave more money in the plan for others.

Although the claims process serves a useful purpose by correcting simple mistakes or misunderstandings, it does not provide retirees with the kind of objective, impartial review that justifies denying retirees their day in court. And in the rare instance when a pension claimant gets a court review and wins, the victory may not be worth much. The most retirees can expect is the benefit they should have gotten in the first place (sometimes with interest, sometimes not), even when a wrongful denial has cost them their jobs or their homes in the interim. The courts have generally ruled that consequential or "compensatory" damages are not available in pension claims cases.

What, then, is the incentive for plan officials to treat participants fairly? They have nothing to lose by denying people benefits and forcing them to go to court, since the worst that litigation can do is compel them to pay the benefits they were liable for at the outset. The same holds true in pension mismanagement cases, when trustees have deliberately plundered the money for their personal gain, as a result of another U.S. Supreme Court ruling, *Massachusetts Mutual Life Ins. Co. v. Russell*.[5] Thus, if the trustee of James Carsten's plan had actually stolen the money rather than investing it recklessly, a court could have ordered him to pay back the money, but the matter would have ended there. This is very different from cases in other areas of the law, in which someone harmed by another person's wrongful act is awarded additional money, "compensatory" or "punitive" damages, in part to deter others from similar actions.

"Why *not* steal the money, if that's all that will happen?" asks James Carsten.

To make the situation even more absurd, a third Supreme Court decision, *Mertens v. Hewitt Associates*, says that "third parties," such as lawyers, actuaries, and investment consultants, cannot be required to reimburse retirees for benefit losses caused by their actions.[6] If a trustee does not have enough money to repay what was lost, the retirees are out the money.

What about situations in which people believe that their benefit amounts are wrong? Those whose pensions have been paid out as lump sums instead of as monthly benefits cannot sue their plan trustees for miscalculating their benefits because they are no longer considered plan members. They don't have the "standing" to get through the courthouse door.[7]

Also out in the cold are people whose employers use pension promises as inducements to stay on the job, then renege on the promises. This happened to employees of the Price River Coal Company in Utah, whose president persuaded them to accept jobs with a new owner, Amax, by promising them that pension credit for past service would be applied toward early retirement benefits. That credit was later denied by the new owner.

Federal law allows workers to sue trustees for illegal acts, but nothing in the law allows them to sue employers for misrepresentation. Employees are prevented from suing in state courts because those courts view pensions as governed completely by federal law. "Talk about a stacked deck," says the Price River Coal workers' lawyer Zane Gill, who adds that it will be a long time before he takes another pension case. As Ron Dean notes, "With no action under state law and no remedy under federal law, participants are fair game for even the most fraudulent and malicious lies, as long as the lies are told by company officials and are about pensions."[8]

The only time workers can sue their employers under the pension law is if the company fires them or takes some other action to prevent them from getting all or part of their pensions. This is most likely to happen when employees are very close to vesting or to qualifying for special early retirement benefits.

Marjorie Reichman had worked as a bookkeeper for a small architectural firm in New York City for ten years. In 1984, just ten months before she reached age 65, she was suddenly fired. Under the pension plan's benefit formula, she was entitled to just $43,500. With the additional ten months, she would have earned almost $60,000 more. When she asked whether she had been let go because of her pension, one of the architects replied that he "wouldn't be at all surprised" if that were the case. She went to court and won.[9]

By far the most celebrated case brought under this provision of the law involved the Continental Can Company, which had set up a nationwide computerized program to identify those workers who were just short of vesting and those who were close to qualifying for the plan's special early retirement benefits. Lawyers for the United Steel Workers of America discovered that red flags had been put next to the names of those laid-off workers who were closest to qualifying for these benefits to ensure that they would not be recalled to work. The case resulted in a settlement of more than $400 million.[10]

" In recognition of your pension coming due
we are giving you your dismissal notice now..."

Reprinted courtesy of Fred Wright and UE
News Service.

Other countries are far more progressive than the United States in helping their citizens with pension problems. For example, in Great Britain, volunteer pension consultants are the principal source of information and assistance for British pension plan participants. More than 350 consultants operate out of 20 regional offices as part of the Occupational Pensions Advisory Service (OPAS). They respond to some 30,000 inquiries a year.

In 1990, Britain's Parliament passed legislation providing funding for OPAS and establishing the office of pension ombudsman. Cases that cannot be resolved by the consultants are referred to the ombudsman for a final decision. Both OPAS and Ombudsman assistance is free.

In this country, Congress took its first small step toward acknowledging the need for individual pension assistance in 1992, when lawmakers authorized the Administration on Aging to establish seven regional pension information and counseling demonstration projects as part of the reauthorization of the Older Americans Act. These projects and a national technical assistance program opened their doors in October 1993. More recently, Assistant Secretary of Labor Olena Berg directed the Labor Department's field offices to begin responding to individual inquiries. She has also initiated a pilot project to encourage pension lawyers to represent workers and retirees on a no-fee basis.

Former Senator Howard Metzenbaum's Pension Bill of Rights Act of 1994 proposed the creation of an Ombuds Office to coordinate government pension assistance and encourage more private sector involvement. Senator Metzenbaum also suggested an "alternative dispute resolution program" for cases in which going to court would be inappropriate. The program would take the form of a nonbinding "evaluation" process in which the positions of the worker and the plan's representative would be assessed by a neutral expert. This alternative would be useful for small claims, particularly in cases in which the claimants are elderly or in poor health, and for cases involving the interpretation of extremely complex statutory provisions or regulations.

For people who must go to court for their pensions, the senator's legislation would provide a more level playing field. The bill would:

- Create a presumption that attorneys' fees will be awarded to participants who win their cases;
- Provide for full court review of plan decisions denying pension benefits;
- Permit courts to award compensatory damages to reimburse individuals fully for their losses, and allow penalties to deter egregious misconduct by plan trustees.

Until reforms such as these are adopted, people will continue to be forced to play a cruel game of musical chairs when they seek help with their pensions. The Internal Revenue Service refers them to the Labor Department; the Labor Department tells them to find a private lawyer; the lawyer turns them down because there is no provision for attorneys' fees or because the case is too complex. Then the music stops and the pensioner is out of the game.

What to Do

WHERE TO LOOK FOR HELP WITH A PENSION PROBLEM

First, check with the plan administrator. It's possible that a mistake has been made. Ask for an explanation of why you were denied a pension or how your benefit was calculated. You can also request plan documents and other information. Be sure to find out how much time you have to appeal the plan's decision. This information should also be in your plan booklet.

Second, if your plan administrator is unhelpful, contact the nearest field office of the Department of Labor's Pension and Welfare Benefits Administration, or telephone its Division of Technical Assistance. You will get a recorded message, but eventually you should reach a pension adviser. If you are in one of the seven areas of the country served by an Administration on Aging pension information and counseling demonstration project, the Labor Department may refer you to that project. If you have a technical question about the pension or tax laws, call the Internal Revenue Service's Employee Plans Technical and Actuarial Division. You can also write and ask the IRS to respond with a general information letter. If you have questions about a terminated defined benefit plan, telephone the Pension Benefit Guaranty Corporation.

Third, contact a state or area agency on aging or a private group that is knowledgeable about pensions, such as a union or retiree organization.

Fourth, if you think that you may need a lawyer, consider contacting the lawyer referral service for your city, county, or state bar association. It will be listed under "Lawyers" in the yellow pages of your telephone book. In some areas, free legal services are available to people over the age of 60 or with limited incomes. You can also contact the lawyer referral service of the National Pension Assistance Project of the Pension Rights Center. Ordinarily, you must file a lawsuit within a specified number of years after the plan's final decision. It is important not to delay.

Finally, if all else fails, consider contacting your senators or representative in Congress. They may be able to help you directly or find someone to assist you. They are also very effective in encouraging government agencies to respond to their constituents' inquiries.

CHAPTER 10

The Pension Safety Net

Adjusted for your age at plan termination, the maximum guaranteeable amount of your benefit is [$1,220 a month less than you have been receiving].

—Letter from Pension Benefit Guaranty Corporation

Frank Dysart had piloted airplanes for 23 years when a heart attack grounded him. Only 45 years old, he retired on disability from his job with Eastern Airlines and moved with his wife to Pine Log, Georgia. Despite his heart condition, he was determined to make the most of retirement and thought that he had the means to do so. Eastern's disability retirement benefits were generous: $2,200 a month disability pension, plus full medical and life insurance and travel privileges.

But trouble was brewing. In 1989, the year Frank Dysart stopped flying, the airline was giving clear signs of financial strain. By October 1990, just as the Dysarts were settling into the new house in Pine Log, Eastern went bankrupt. The repercussions were immediate. Dysart's travel privileges were cut off, his life insurance was canceled, and he was informed that his medical insurance would end as of January 1, 1993. That left his pension. He knew that Eastern's pension plans were underfunded, but the government pension insurance program was in place to guarantee his benefits. Then his pension was cut by more than half, from $2,200 a month down to $980 — a yearly loss of $14,640.

Approximately 4,000 retired Eastern pilots, 200 of whom were on disability, were affected by the termination of their underfunded pension plan. Those who had earned particularly high benefits or who, like Frank Dysart, were disabled at a young age saw their benefits significantly reduced.

Studebaker all over again? Not quite. The federal private pension insurance program created by ERISA prevents the sort of devastating losses that occurred in South Bend 30 years ago. Today, few people with vested benefits from a defined benefit plan wind up with nothing. When a plan ends and there are insufficient funds to pay promised benefits, the Pension Benefit Guaranty Corporation steps in, takes over the plan, and begins paying benefits. Currently, the agency is paying benefits to more than 158,000 retirees, widows, and widowers in nearly 1,900 terminated plans for which it acts as trustee. An additional 188,000 workers from these plans will receive PBGC checks when they reach retirement age. In 1993, PBGC benefit payments totaled $722 million.[1]

The pension insurance program provides an irreplaceable safety net. Former PBGC executive director Robert Nagle describes it as "an extraordinary program, providing workers with the assurance that payment of their pensions is no longer entirely dependent on their employers' continued financial health." Pension lawyer and author Thomas Geoghegan is convinced that when the steel mills started closing in the 1980s with vastly underfunded pension plans, "there could have been riots . . . if the pensions had not been paid. . . . The PBGC took over the shuttered pension funds, paid most of the benefits, and kept everyone quiet."[2]

But the PBGC doesn't guarantee *all* benefits, and not everyone is paid what he or she would have received from the plan. Understandably, people who have to take cuts aren't happy about it; they feel that they've been cheated out of their due and they don't think it's fair. As Frank Dysart describes the pilots' situation, "Because of very stringent physical standards, many (if not most) pilots never make it to the mandatory retirement age of 60. With this in mind, Eastern pilots gave up much in negotiated pay and working conditions in exchange for [what they thought was] a fully funded disability retirement plan."

The PBGC currently insures 67,000 single employer and multi-employer defined benefit pension plans. The 41 million workers enrolled in those plans have the assurance that if their companies get into financial trouble and terminate their plans, the PBGC will pay "basic" benefits. These include the vested pensions of people age 65 and over that have been in effect for five years or longer — up to a certain limit, which increases each year.[3] In 1995, the annual cap is $30,886.32. Other guaranteed benefits include lifetime monthly survivor's benefits and most early retirement and disability benefits.

It was the combination of the cap plus his age that hurt Frank Dysart. In 1990, when Eastern stopped his plan, the ceiling on guaranteed benefits for people who were 65 or over was $25,977.24. Since he was 20 years short of age 65 — and his pension would have to be paid for that many additional years — his pension was set at less than half that amount. PBGC officials point out that although the cap can dramatically reduce the benefits of high-paid employees like pilots and executives, the amount is far more than what most people expect from their pension plans.

Other benefits are not guaranteed at all. Bill Mertens, who headed an employee benefits group at Kaiser Steel Corporation, took a special early-out package in 1985 at age 56, having worked at Kaiser for 26 years. His monthly pension amounted to $2,000. Two years later, the company filed for bankruptcy, and Mertens found his pension reduced to $512. The PBGC ruled that Kaiser's promised early retirement package was a "supplemental" benefit, not a "basic" one. Therefore, the agency didn't have to cover it. The PBGC reduced Mertens's benefit even further because he hadn't reached age 65. The former benefits manager told a congressional subcommittee, "I really thought that with the passage of ERISA, the horrors caused by bankruptcy were a part of the past. I thought these were really sacred benefits."

Higher-paid employees aren't the only ones hurt by limits on PBGC insurance. When LTV Steel stopped funding its Jones & Laughlin pension plan, the PBGC took over and immediately stopped paying the $400-a-month social security supplements to nearly 2,000 LTV steelworkers who had retired before the age of 65. These supplements, meant to bridge the gap until social security kicked in, are not insured.

Carole and Jim McMahon's benefits plummeted from $1,020 a month to $600. Jim McMahon had taken early retirement after working in the mills for 30 years. As Carole McMahon expl..ned, they saw their "bridge" benefit not as just a perk that enabled worn-out steelworkers to get out early and go fishing but as "a contract between LTV Steel management and the retiree. We gave up our jobs of $20,000 to $30,000 a year in the mill to let the active workers keep theirs."

Many workers and retirees are confused about the extent of the protection provided by the government's safety net. Many are unaware that the PBGC cannot insure *any* benefits unless those benefits are specifically provided for by a plan. Not knowing the fine print of a plan's provisions can have distressing consequences.

The PBGC was set up to be a self-supporting government corporation within the Labor Department. When the agency takes over a plan and begins paying benefits, the money comes, first, from the funds

A TRAGIC MISTAKE

Edmund Piaggi had worked for the Adams Print Works for 34 years when the plant shut down in 1984. About to turn 55 and in poor health, he didn't mind retiring early, as long as he had his small company pension. The pension plan had been set up in 1977 and hadn't had time to accumulate enough money to cover all the employees' benefits, but Edmund Piaggi and the others weren't worried. They were confident that the government insurance program would pay them their benefits.

And that was exactly what happened. In 1985, the PBGC became the trustee of their pension fund. For five years, retirees received their benefits in the mail every month, delivered like clockwork to the small houses in and around North Adams, Massachusetts. Then in 1990, the checks stopped coming, and pensioners received another letter from the PBGC asking for all the money back!

Unbelieving, Piaggi read the words telling him that the PBGC had found that he was "not entitled to benefits under your plan's provisions." Although many pension plans allow vesting credit for years worked before the pension plan started, the Adams Print Works plan did not; it said that only people over 65 or age 55 with ten years of service after the plan had started were eligible for pensions. Since the plan was not yet ten years old, nobody qualified for a benefit except the handful of people already at retirement age.

Piaggi's only income had been the PBGC checks, as was true for most of the other retirees. How were they to make the repayments? A PBGC official met with them in North Adams to discuss their options. "Quite a few of the people left in tears when they were asked how much money they thought they could make by selling their possessions and furniture by tag sale. Also those who owned their homes [were asked] how much money they could bring in." In the end, six of the retirees were found to be so poor that the agency wrote off its claims against them. Fourteen others were required to repay their "erroneously" awarded benefits. Edmund Piaggi started making repayments when he became eligible for social security. For five years he will be sending the PBGC $56 a month, exactly the amount he had been getting.

remaining in the pension plan and, second, from any money the agency can recover from the bankrupt company. The law permits the PBGC to sue a company, or its parent or other related company, for the full amount by which the plan is underfunded. In the case of Eastern, the PBGC negotiated with Continental and recovered between $115 million and $220 million, or about 20 percent of its claims. Another highly publicized intervention by the PBGC took place when the agency announced its intention to take over the pension plans of bankrupt TransWorld Airlines. Although the airline itself was broke, its owner, Carl Icahn, one of the richest people in the country, owned a large enough stake in the company to make him legally responsible for the plans' underfunding, which reportedly came to $1 billion. After lengthy negotiations, the PBGC convinced Icahn to put $400 million into the plans to keep them afloat.[4]

The TWA case is an exception. In the majority of plan terminations, when too little money remains to pay benefits, the PBGC uses its own funds to make up the difference. The agency's resources consist of premiums collected from insured plans, plus the dividends and interest earned from investing the assets of plans the agency has taken over. A plan's premiums are determined according to the number of workers and retirees it covers. For most single employer plans, the premium is $19 per person a year. For significantly underfunded plans, the premium can go higher; for people in multiemployer plans, it can be as little as $2.60. In 1993, the PBGC received a total of $913 million in premium payments, almost $200 million more than it paid out in benefits.[5]

From the perspective of pensioners, the PBGC premium is an extraordinary bargain. Even the maximum premium is small when compared to the value of the benefits the insurance program protects. To a pensioner, these benefits can be worth thousands of dollars over the course of retirement — in some cases, hundreds of thousands. Companies, of course, take a different view. Those with well-funded plans resent having to shore up shakier plans. Others go so far as to claim that premium costs could drive them out of the defined benefit plan business.

How pension plans are funded is one of the most misunderstood aspects of this generally bewildering subject. Before ERISA, almost all pension plans were underfunded. Employers simply paid benefits as they arose, so if a company went broke and closed the pension plan, there was almost never enough money to cover promised benefits. ERISA tried to stop this hit-or-miss approach by setting funding

standards aimed at forcing employers to put enough money into the
plan over a period of years to cover all benefits.

To determine how much a company should contribute each year to
defined benefit plans, plan consultants estimate how many workers will
vest, reach retirement age, die before retirement, leave the plan early,
and other possibilities. They also predict the rate of return the plan will
make on its investments and how long retirees and their beneficiaries
will live. Putting all these "actuarial assumptions" together, consultants
come up with an amount the employer must contribute each year to
cover the plan costs.

Reprinted with special permission of King Features Syndicate.

When plans start up, they usually have large chunks of unfunded
liabilities, since most employers, though not all, give pension credits to
employees for the years they worked before the plan was started. The
law generally gives a plan a 30-year period over which to accumulate
enough money to pay for all its obligations.[6]

New benefits that pension plans add from time to time, such as
raising the level of payments or offering new early retirement packages,
also cause the plan to be underfunded until those benefits are covered.
Collectively bargained plans such as those in the auto and steel industries, which provide fixed dollar amounts for each year worked (rather
than a percentage of pay multiplied by years worked), have to negotiate
increases in benefits every few years in order to keep up with inflation.
This automatically causes their plans to be underfunded. The PBGC
reports that these "flat-benefit plans," on average, are only 75 percent
funded.

For healthy ongoing plans, underfunding is normal and no cause
for concern. By the PBGC's own estimates, employees in most under-

funded plans have no reason to worry. Underfunding is relevant only if a company is in financial trouble and likely to close its plan. Had Eastern stayed in business, for example, its underfunded pension plans could have gone on paying benefits when they came due. The trouble was that the company went bankrupt and had to fold the plan in midstream.

The vast majority of the plans taken over by the PBGC were terminated because the company went into, or was about to go into, bankruptcy. These plans became underfunded in various ways. For example, in certain cases, the Internal Revenue Service permits a financially troubled company to stop funding its plan. Before Pan American World Airways went bankrupt in 1991, it had been receiving waivers for six years from the IRS, allowing it to skip pension contributions in an effort to keep the company afloat.[7] When the plans were terminated, they were underfunded by over $800 million.

Richard Brooks, who worked for Pan Am in New York City for 25 years and now runs an association of former Pan Am employees set up to counsel and find jobs for its members, is highly critical of this practice. "If the IRS had not granted Pan American six years of waivers on their obligation to their employees' pension funds," he asserts, "most Pan Am employees would be working for another airline in a financial position to have bought Pan American." In other words, Brooks believes that potential buyers of the failed airline were discouraged because of its huge pension debt, which established Pan Am's reputation as "a totally unaffordable and an impossible acquisition."

The bankruptcy left 34,000 Pan Am employees jobless and with their pension benefits frozen. At the same time, 12,000 Pan Am retirees found out that government pension protection doesn't protect everything. Anyone under 55, regardless of how many years of service they had given to Pan Am, had their pension benefits severely reduced. Overall, Brooks says, "we have paid a terrible price for our government's neglect in their duty to protect us. Since the plans' termination there have been eight suicides and 157 heart attacks, 47 of which have proved fatal."

Instead of asking for waivers, a financially strapped company may simply stop making contributions to the pension plan when disaster looms. The PBGC has found that in the five years before a pension plan is terminated, an average plan's funding of promised benefits drops from 80 percent to 40 percent.[8] For this reason, the PBGC requires a company to meet stringent financial distress standards before it agrees to take over a plan, making it unlikely that a company that is sound enough to continue contributing to its plan can cleverly contrive to dump it on the insurance program without justification.

There are a number of other reasons that plans become under-funded:

- Employers sometimes use interest rate assumptions that are more optimistic than is warranted. When employers overestimate their plans' earnings, they can then lower their contributions. The PBGC has found that when it applies its own actuarial assumptions to a terminated plan, the plan's liabilities increase by as much as 50 percent.
- Companies sometimes try to hold down current operating costs by offering workers better pension benefits, which they don't have to pay right away, in place of wage increases, which they do. Adding new liabilities to the plan, of course, increases the amount by which it is underfunded. The PBGC has pointed to TWA as an example of this practice, charging that the troubled airline made pension promises that increased its plans' liabilities by $100 million while the company was in bankruptcy.
- Sometimes, the closing down of a company itself increases the amount of underfunding. For example, many companies, particularly those in the steel, automobile, and tire and rubber industries, have special plant shutdown benefits, allowing workers to take full pensions at younger ages than they could have if the company had stayed in business. Since there is usually no way of anticipating a shutdown, these benefits can be very costly and tend not to be fully funded.
- A pension plan, even one that is originally healthy, can get into trouble because of a run on lump sum cash-outs. After Republic Steel Company was acquired by LTV, large numbers of older management employees were aware that the company was in financial trouble and exercised their right to take their early retirement pensions all at once as lump sum payments. Like a run on bank deposits, this wholesale cash-out emptied the Republic fund, which was then taken over by the PBGC.
- In a declining industry, an imbalance in the ratio of retirees to active workers can cause a plan to become insolvent. The Allis Chalmers plan, for example, had too many retirees receiving benefits in relation to the number of workers for whom contributions were being made.
- Finally, an unknown number of small plans terminate because their assets have been plundered. A 1991 study by the General Accounting Office (GAO) found that of a sample of 40 plans

trusteed by the PBGC, most having fewer than 100 participants, *one-fourth* had terminated because of fund mismanagement. Total liabilities amounted to $9.2 million. None of the violations had been reported to the Labor Department as required by law. The PBGC was not able to recover the funds in any of the terminations.[9]

The PBGC has tried to discourage the practice of underfunding in a number of different ways. One tactic is to publicize a list of the 50 largest underfunded plans. The 1993 Top 50 List, issued in November 1994, included the plans of such companies as General Motors, Bethlehem Steel, Uniroyal Goodrich, United Parcel Service, and Honeywell, Inc.[10] The 50 companies accounted for 56 percent of all the underfunding in single employer plans that year. Nearly half the underfunding came from General Motors' plans alone.[11]

Critics of the PBGC's "iffy fifty" list have pointed out that few companies on the list are likely to fold their plans, and less than a third of the underfunding was in financially troubled companies. This amount, some $12 billion, represented less than one-quarter of private pension plans' total unfunded liabilities.

Although helpful in highlighting plans with potential problems, the Top 50 List, together with statements by members of Congress and former government officials about the PBGC's own financial status, has generated widespread and needless public anxiety that a great many plans are on the verge of folding or that the PBGC itself could go under.

"S&L-STYLE TAXPAYER BAILOUT!"
"PRIVATE PENSION FUNDS IN PERIL
AS FEDERAL BACKING RUNS IN RED."
"HIDDEN TIME BOMB!"

So ran headlines during the fall of 1992, when fears of a pension insurance failure similar to that in the savings and loan industry were fanned by recessionary winds. It began in the mid-1980s with the collapse of two so-called megaliths in the steel industry — LTV Steel and Wheeling-Pittsburgh Steel — which posed the first real challenge to the insurance program. The obligations of the steel giants' pension plans were "a burden the agency cannot bear," warned *Business Week*. It added, "Despite the recent hike in insurance rates paid for by all the nation's plans, the PBGC won't be able to support those it covers when they retire." The magazine quoted Walter Olson, a senior fellow at the

Manhattan Institute for Public Policy Research, to the effect that if many more plans followed the steelmakers, it would be "like the savings-and-loan crisis, with the federal government left holding the bag."[12]

More plans did fold as hundreds of businesses failed in the late 1980s and early 1990s, and the PBGC incurred large new expenses. To insure underfunded closed-down plans was, of course, exactly the reason the agency had been created in the first place. By the summer of 1992, Pan American and Eastern had handed the PBGC $1.2 billion in new obligations. Almost 400,000 people were now dependent on the PBGC for pensions. The agency's total assets of some $6 billion were reportedly $2.7 billion below its liabilities. A $2.7 billion deficit! The press loved it.

The people running the PBGC at the time encouraged the media hype. The growing panic about the deficit was an effective way of pushing their legislative agenda. It also provided them with grounds for taking a tough stance against employers in negotiations and against retirees in the courts and in Congress.

With the change in administration in 1993, the "sky is falling" rhetoric disappeared. Secretary of Labor Robert Reich appointed a task force to examine the PBGC's finances, which concluded that the PBGC has the resources to pay all its obligations now and for years to come.

While technically the agency does have a paper "deficit," that deficit is meaningful only if *all* ailing companies were to give up the ghost tomorrow and terminate *all* their plans, and the PBGC had to pay for *all* their pension promises immediately, both current benefits and those not due for many years. None of the above is likely to happen, much less all. The PBGC is a government agency. It is not like a private insurance company or a bank that can be called upon by depositors to pay all its liabilities at once.[13] It has a positive cash flow and more than $6 billion in assets.

Although current PBGC executive director Martin Slate has repeatedly emphasized that the PBGC has enough money to pay benefits "for as far as the eye can see," he remains concerned that pension underfunding nearly doubled in recent years and that chronic underfunding of certain plans in the auto, steel, rubber, and airline industries could cause long-term problems for them and for the agency. He has noted that "today's problems are red flags for tomorrow."[14]

The Clinton administration proposed a number of specific reform measures, and in December 1994, Congress passed the Retirement Protection Act.[15] The new law establishes stricter standards to increase the contributions of underfunded plans. In addition, companies with underfunded plans now have to pay higher annual premiums to the PBGC. New disclosure rules require plan managers to alert employees and retirees to the potential problems created by underfunding. The PBGC is authorized to help participants who are unable to track down their former defined benefit plans. Finally, the law protects totally disabled retirees like Frank Dysart from devastating losses. This provision applies only to people who receive disability pensions in the future, however. "That's great for them," comments Dysart. "But what are the rest of us supposed to do?"

The greatest threat to the private pension insurance program may lie not with underfunding but with the growing number of terminations of *healthy* pension plans. The PBGC, like every insurer, relies on a stable pool of ongoing pension plans, but its premium base has been seriously weakened as a result of the elimination of premium-paying pension plans during the past decade, caused by the rush to implement less costly savings arrangements and by the practice of "pension raiding."

UNFINISHED BUSINESS

It was November 12, 1991. Bill Piatkowski and the other Studebaker "pension losers" waited uneasily in South Bend, Indiana, for the call from Washington that would tell them whether Congress had finally responded to their plea for pension justice by passing the Pension Restoration Act Amendment. Introduced in February 1991, the bill would have provided them and 38,000 other retirees who had lost vested benefits before the establishment of the PBGC with a pension of $75 for each year they had worked under a terminated plan. Someone who had worked for 20 years would have gotten $1,500 a year. The whole package would have cost the PBGC an annual payment of about $48 million initially, decreasing through attrition over the years. The sum was "large by personal standards," says actuary Paul Jackson, "but not of earthshaking importance to the PBGC."

Support for the bill was strong. Among those championing the losers were Senators Howard Metzenbaum, Brock Adams, and Edward Kennedy; the AFL-CIO and unions for the auto, steel, electrical, and oil industries; and the American Association of

Retired Persons, Gray Panthers, National Council of Senior Citizens, and Institute of Electrical and Electronics Engineers. In the weeks before the bill came to a vote, a high-level counterattack was launched by PBGC officials, bringing then Secretary of Labor Lynn Martin and Vice President Dan Quayle to the halls of Congress to join PBGC executive director James B. Lockhart III in lobbying against the bill. Their claim of a dangerous PBGC "deficit" caused some supporters of the bill to fear another S&L disaster and back off from the measure to help the losers.

When Piatkowski and the others got the call at the end of the day, they learned that the bill had lost by three votes. According to Newhouse News Service, only "an unprecedented lobbying effort by the Bush Administration" prevented its passage. The retirees were disappointed but not defeated. To this day, they are continuing their efforts to attain justice. "They're not looking for a handout," says Phyllis Spielman of St. Paul, Minnesota, a former member of the PBGC's Advisory Committee. "They're only asking for some of the pension money they were promised for years of hard work. . . . It is ironic that the very people whose plight led to the enactment of ERISA back in 1974 have never received any help from the program."

Not yet they haven't. But the fight isn't over.

What to Do

HOW TO FIND OUT IF YOUR PENSION
IS PROTECTED BY THE PBGC

Check your *summary plan description* to see whether your plan is insured. Most defined benefit pension plans are protected by the PBGC, but not all. For example, plans in which contributions are made by union members are not guaranteed. Other types of uninsured plans are those set up by religious organizations that have chosen not to come under the private pension law; plans set up by doctors, lawyers, architects, engineers, and other professionals that cover 25 or fewer employees; and plans covering only top executives.

No defined contribution plans are protected by the PBGC, since these plans are always technically "fully funded." When a defined contribution plan ends, all the money in each person's account is ordinarily paid out to that person, either in a lump sum or through the purchase of a life insurance annuity payable at retirement age.

To check on your plan's financial health, write to the plan administrator and ask for the plan's detailed financial statement, Form 5500 (for small plans, Form 5500 C/R). The forms ordinarily have an attached Schedule B, which will tell you at the top of page 2 whether the plan's consultants think it has enough money to pay all benefits that would be owed if the plan were to stop. If the plan's liabilities are greater than its assets, this could be a problem *if* the company is in financial trouble and *if* it is likely to terminate the plan. You can also contact the Labor Department's Public Disclosure Office for Form 5500s.

If you are concerned that your plan may stop, or if it is in the process of terminating and you have questions about what benefits are guaranteed, contact the PBGC's Case Operations and Compliance Department.

For information about your benefit status under a terminated plan, call the PBGC's Participant Services Division. To get the documents of a terminated plan, you can make a Freedom of Information Act request to the PBGC.

If you have trouble getting information or believe that you are being treated unfairly by the PBGC, contact the agency's problem resolution officer.

CHAPTER 11

Raiding the Cookie Jar

The pension plan is being terminated and arrangements are being made to have your pension benefits paid by a life insurance company.

Bill Hunsaker had been the manager of the Pacific Lumber Company pension plan for 20 years. He thought he knew all about his plan. It was sound and very well funded. The company owners had put in enough money to cover everyone's present and future benefits, and there was extra cash, allowing periodic cost-of-living adjustments for retirees.

Pacific Lumber was a good employer. The hundred-year-old logging operation located in northern California's redwood country was family owned. Many of its workers were third-generation employees. Bill Hunsaker himself had worked there for 47 years, moving up from mailboy to vice president for administration. The owners were concerned about the welfare of their employees and their retired workers, together numbering around 2,500, and fully supported the practice of granting "plus-ups," as their cost-of-living adjustments were called. There was plenty of money in the plan to provide them, and everyone felt confident that there always would be.

The plus-ups were a big part of Bill Hunsaker's decision to retire in 1984, the year he turned 65. His wife was an invalid, permanently confined to a convalescent home at a cost of $2,400 a month. He knew that without any boost in his pension over the coming years, inflation would dramatically reduce his ability to keep up with their expenses.

But two years into retirement, the former pension manager

discovered something he didn't know about his pension plan. He did not know that it could be legally "raided." First, he found out that Pacific Lumber had been bought by the Maxxam Group, Inc. Then the new owners informed retirees that they intended to stop the plan and purchase annuities from a life insurance company to pay benefits. It took Bill Hunsaker only a few seconds to grasp the consequences: life insurance annuities carried no cost-of-living increases. The plus-ups were gone.

The venerable old logging company had been caught up in the leveraged buyout frenzy that was just beginning to sweep the country in 1985. Pacific Lumber's new owner was Charles Hurwitz, a financier from Houston, Texas. He and his Maxxam Group had financed the takeover in part with $900 million in junk bonds brokered by the Drexel Burnham Lambert investment company. Once in charge, Hurwitz terminated the pension plan and scooped out its $55 million "surplus" to help pay down his debt.

The year Bill Hunsaker retired, it was almost unheard of for a healthy company to stop a well-funded pension plan. There was, however, a famous precedent. Just two years earlier, the German buyers of the Great Atlantic and Pacific Tea Company had announced that they were closing down the company's defined benefit pension plan, substituting a new defined contribution plan, and using the more than $200 million "surplus" in pension money for corporate purposes. The announcement made headlines, since the surplus was more than the new owners had paid for the company, but its relevance to firms like Pacific Lumber was not immediately apparent. A&P was in serious financial trouble, and plowing the pension money back into the company was seen as a last-ditch effort to save it. In contrast, Pacific Lumber was free of debt and rich in resources, including fabulous redwoods.

Nonetheless, the A&P "termination-reversion" had an enormous effect on Pacific Lumber and other companies with well-stocked pension plans. It called attention to the untapped treasure lying right under the noses of corporate managers and led to a series of government rulings that legitimized the stripping of not only the Pacific Lumber plan but also 2,000 other large plans and nearly 10,000 small ones.

As early as 1938, federal tax law allowed a company to stop a defined benefit pension plan at any time, so long as all benefits promised by the plan up to the point of plan termination were paid. The law also required that any money left over after paying the benefits go to the plan's participants, *unless* there was an express provision in the plan allowing excess assets that were created by "erroneous actuarial computation" to be paid to the employer.

When the Tengelmann Group took over A&P in 1982, the company's plan did not contain a provision authorizing it to pay excess money to the owner. The American pension consulting firm advising the new owners, however, saw nothing in the law to prevent the company from adding such a provision. The question then was whether the left-over money could be considered the result of an "erroneous actuarial computation." Yes, under a 1983 Internal Revenue Service ruling, it apparently could. After all, the plan's actuaries had mistakenly failed to anticipate that the plan would terminate!

A&P's successful maneuver did not go unnoticed. At first, however, few companies followed the termination-reversion route. Most would-be raiders were deterred by the IRS's position that it would not consider a plan terminated unless a company subsequently offered no pension plan at all to its employees or, like A&P, set up a new and different type of plan. This choice posed difficulties for management, since employees would inevitably protest the abolition of their defined benefit plans.

A number of large companies, led by the Celanese Corporation, cast about for ways to gain access to the pension money without incurring bothersome labor relations problems. Leon Irish, a lawyer then representing Celanese, told John Palmer of NBC News that the companies wanted a way of getting the surplus out of overfunded pension plans "without killing the plans."[1]

Although key government pension officials opposed the idea of allowing easier access to the pension money, Irish and other lawyers representing companies found an ally in William Niskanen, who then headed the Reagan administration's Council of Economic Advisers. At his urging, the administration issued guidelines that allowed companies to terminate their plans and buy life insurance annuities for pension benefits earned to date. Under the new rules, companies then had the option of (1) starting an identical new defined benefit plan or (2) continuing the preexisting plan for active workers but spinning off and terminating a separate plan for retirees.

These rulings coincided with, and in many cases fueled, the takeover and leveraged buyout mania of the 1980s. As Robert Kirby, chairman of Capital Guardian Trust, explained, "All of a sudden the pension funds became not just of interest to the company itself but to external potential purchasers, or raiders, or dissectors of companies. And, you know, all of a sudden it's cannibal time . . . the company is just a sitting duck."[2]

A study by the Investor Responsibility Research Center revealed that in two-thirds of the largest merger and leveraged buyout transactions, pension plans were raided.[3] By the time Congress finally tried to curb this practice in 1990, more than $20 billion had been siphoned out, affecting more than 2 million workers and retirees.

Looking back in 1991, *Time* magazine chronicled the raiding phenomenon in vivid terms:

> *Corporations scrambling for cash shut down their pension plans and pocketed the so-called excess funds.*
>
> *Some clearly acted irresponsibly, imperiling the future security of aging members of the corporate family for quick financial gain.*
>
> *Others terminated the plans as a defensive measure against hostile takeovers, knowing that the buyout buzzards circling overhead saw their well-stocked pensioners' funds as a tempting target and were eager to pick them clean.*[4]

For Bill Hunsaker, the raid on his pension fund not only shattered the assumptions of a lifetime but also made no sense in the scheme of retirement financing as he understood it. He knew that the so-called surplus money in the Pacific Lumber plan was not really "surplus" at all. Some of it was a cushion deliberately built into the plan to protect against downturns in the stock market. It was also there to provide leeway for benefit increases and cost-of-living adjustments. Finally, although some of the "extra" money was the result of a booming stock market, most of the $55 million that Maxxam scooped out was nothing more than what the original owners had been legally obligated to contribute for participants.

Like most defined benefit plans, the Pacific Lumber plan guaranteed benefits based on workers' average pay at the time they left the plan. Most workers were expected to work for many more years and retire at much higher levels of pay than they were currently earning, and the company had contributed enough money to the plan to anticipate those future increases. There was always more money in the plan than would be needed to pay benefits earned up to that time. When the plan was terminated, this money created an artificial surplus, since it exceeded the amount the plan was legally obligated to pay *at that point*.

Bill Hunsaker and the other Pacific Lumber retirees vigorously protested the stripping of their plan. They made their case to Congress, to the Reagan administration, in court, and on television. As the practice of pension raiding gained momentum, tens of thousands of other retirees, equally outraged, also tried to prevent or recoup their pension losses.

From his home in Prospect, Kentucky, Percy Penley organized 1,700 Celanese Corporation retirees to challenge their company's pension raid. He told a government task force that $380 million had been removed from his plan in order to manipulate the company's stock in preparation for a takeover. The result of all the corporate maneuvering was that plants were shut down and active workers laid off. What was at stake was not only pensions but jobs. "A few officers got rich from their stock options and golden parachutes," said Penley, "but the rank and file suffered."[5]

Like Pacific Lumber, Celanese had periodically adjusted retirees' pensions for inflation. Penley, who had been general manager of a subsidiary company and worked for Celanese for 35 years, accepted an early retirement offer on the assumption that past practices would continue. He commented bitterly, "Companies discovered a gold mine in overfunded pension funds, and have dug literally billions of dollars worth of gold out of the funds. All the retired employees got was the shaft."

Zack Carter, president of a Mobile, Alabama, shipbuilding workers local union, led his members and 800 retirees in an effort to prevent the Alabama Dry Dock and Shipbuilding Company from plundering their plan of over $4 million in surplus pension money. Unlike the Pacific Lumber and Celanese retirees, pensioners of the Alabama Dry Dock and Shipbuilding Corporation had never gotten a cost-of-living adjustment. One day the company told them that about $1 million that could have gone to boost their pensions would be used to pay fines it owed to the government for exposing them to asbestos and other health hazards. Infuriated, the retirees held rallies, conducted press conferences, picketed the company, boycotted a bank, and even held a demonstration at the Senior Bowl football game, where they handed out 10,000 posters reading, "Just say no to Pension Raiding."

American Red Cross retirees were so enraged by a proposed $400 million raid on their $740 million plan that they confronted the chairman of the board at their annual meeting in St. Petersburg, Florida. Thanks to two Red Cross retirees, Philip Gaddis, former media relations associate, and Hildegarde Herfurth, retired assistant public affairs director, the confrontation was captured in a dramatic segment on the "MacNeil/Lehrer NewsHour." American Red Cross retirees' successful public relations campaign won them significant cost-of-living adjustments in their pensions and new protections for their health insurance, but the plan was raided anyway.

As the raids continued, workers, fearful of losing their jobs, were less outspoken than retirees but felt equally betrayed — for good reason. Close to 15 percent of all workers caught up in raids were left with stripped, bare-bones plans with no cushion in case of economic bad times and no means to upgrade benefits.[6] Washington University School of Law professor Merton Bernstein comments, "If plans cash out due to high earnings, there will not be the proverbial seven fat years to balance the seven lean years." What was worse, after more than 60 percent of the raids, workers were left with no pension plan at all. Their employers told them to save for themselves through company 401(k) savings plans or individual retirement accounts.

Twenty-five percent of the workers, although given new plans identical to their old raided ones, found that their combined benefits — a small frozen benefit from the old plan and a small benefit from the new one — were much less than the benefits they would have gotten had the old plan continued. A 1986 Department of Labor study found that replacing a terminated plan with a second follow-on plan could cost the average worker as much as 45 percent of the benefits he or she would have gotten by working under the original plan.[7]

The Labor Department study looked only at larger plans. In smaller plans, because the new formulas gave very small benefits for years worked early in a career, the losses were far greater. George Blessitt, a diesel mechanic at Dixie Engine Company in Forest Park, Georgia, returned to work after Christmas vacation to find that his company had been sold and his pension plan terminated. Because his plan used a "fractional rule" formula and because, at 47, he was relatively young, his 14 years of service were worth only $1,200, payable in a single lump sum. Although the new owner offered a pension plan, it required that Blessitt begin at square one for benefits purposes. Meanwhile, his former employer had taken a tidy $225,000 in surplus pension money for himself.

THE RAID THAT FAILED

In most cases, workers and retirees were unable to prevent the raiding of their plans, but in a few instances, they wrested a share of the surplus. One notable case involved the Reeves Brothers company in Cornelius, North Carolina. In 1987, the Amalgamated Clothing and Textile Workers of America learned that the Schick Company had entered into an arrangement to buy Reeves, using loans from nine banks. The loan agreement negotiated by Drexel Burnham Lambert provided that Schick would terminate the Reeves hourly workers' pension plan and use the "surplus" money to repay the loans.

The union, which was in the process of organizing the Reeves employees, held a series of demonstrations in front of each of the banks, as well as at Drexel Burnham's offices in Washington, D.C. Embarrassed, the company called off the raid.

The roster of companies that have raided their plans reads like a Who's Who of Corporate America. Here are the top ten (in terms of reversion amounts):

COMPANY	PARTICIPANTS	DATE OF TERMINATION	REVERSION (in millions)
Exxon	1,500	8–12–86	$1,600.00
FMC Corp.	11,556	11–30–85	720.00
Union Carbide	1,920	9–30–85	504.00
Phillips Petro	11,160	9–1–86	400.00
Goodyear Tire	13,100	6–30–88	400.00
Getty Oil Co.	9,293	1–23–84	360.90
Firestone Tire & Rubber Co.	25,837	9–1–84	284.70
Great Atlantic & Pacific Tea	27,639	5–31–84	272.60
United Airlines	6,782	5–5–85	254.00
Merrill Lynch	37,859	12–13–88	242.50

Not surprisingly, some of the companies taking the largest reversions in the 1980s turned up on the lists of underfunded plans in the 1990s: Uniroyal-Goodrich Tire Corporation raided its plan in 1987 and joined the PBGC's Top 50 underfunded list in 1988, 1989, and 1990. Continental Airlines took a reversion in 1982 and was on the Top 50 list in 1989. Other companies include Tenneco, Budd, Allegheny International, Western Union–New Valley Corporation, and Goodyear Tire and Rubber Company. In fact, it seemed that the only large companies that did not scoop surplus monies out of their plans (such as GE, AT&T, IBM, Du Pont, and Kodak) were barred from doing so either by their union contracts or by defense contract rules.[8]

Although the protests of Bill Hunsaker, Percy Penley, Zack Carter, and others did not improve their own situations, their activism did help focus the attention of labor groups, retiree organizations, and the media on the issue of pension raiding. In time, the public outcry drew the attention of Congress.

The congressional debate on pension raiding was led by Senator Howard Metzenbaum and Representative William Clay. It lasted six years and in the end was never fully resolved. Discussion bogged down over the question, Whose money is it? Workers and retirees argued that the money put into the plan was their deferred wages and that under the law, it belonged to them while the plan was ongoing. They contended that a plan's character should not change solely because it is stopped. As Wilfred Godrey, a retired employee of A&P, said, "I have never thought that the funds that were in the plan belonged to anyone else except the employees."[9]

Arthur Wilson, president of Local 898 of the Oil, Chemical and Atomic Workers International Union in Delaware City, Delaware, similarly viewed the money in pension plans as "funds that were set aside and promised to secure [workers'] future. . . . My members give up important wages in exchange for an adequate pension that keeps pace with day-to-day living."[10] Workers were "livid," Wilson recalled, when in 1985 Texaco Inc. stripped $250 million from the $700 million Getty Oil Company pension fund to help pay for the takeover of Getty. A Texaco spokesman told the *Wall Street Journal* at the time that the money "can be put to better use within the company."[11]

The spokesman was reflecting the employers' side of the argument that developed during the reversion frenzy. Since pension plans are voluntary, owners argued, and the company assumes all the financial risk when it promises a defined benefit, why shouldn't it reap any unexpected gain? Circumstances change, and an employer must retain the

ability to change employee benefits. As long as the plan's legal obligations are met when a plan is terminated, the company has a right to the surplus, as a reward for managing its pension plans so well. Besides, employers pointed out, if they couldn't get at their surplus directly, they would get at it another way: by stopping their contributions to the plan. Denying them access to this money, they warned, would encourage them to underfund their plans.

In the end, Congress gave up trying to resolve the knotty question of the ownership of pension assets and instead looked to tax law to put a brake on the raiding of plans. Treasury Department officials pointed out that the money in the plans had come from contributions and investment earnings that had never been taxed. Since this money was being "recaptured" by companies and, therefore, would not be paid out to retirees in the form of taxable benefits, the government stood to lose billions of dollars in tax revenue. The fair thing, they said, was for raiding companies to pay the same amount of income taxes that retirees would have paid had they received benefits.

Congress responded by imposing a 10 percent surtax on reversions in 1986, then increased it to 15 percent in 1988. However, a 1989 General Accounting Office (GAO) study found that the Treasury was still losing a significant amount of revenue.[12] Exxon, for example, helped itself to $1.6 billion from its $5.6 billion fund in 1986, a year when it had "loss carryovers" from earlier years, allowing it to escape all income taxes and pay only the 10 percent penalty tax. Exxon told *Business Week*, "our shareholders would be better served."[13]

In 1990, Congress increased to 50 percent the penalty for companies that do not replace a terminated plan with another plan for the same workers. The tax is reduced to 20 percent if the company puts 25 percent of the surplus into a replacement plan or uses 20 percent of the surplus to boost benefits. The replacement plan can be another pension plan, but it doesn't have to be. It can also be a 401(k) savings plan.

Companies can avoid taxes altogether if they use the pension surplus to pay health insurance premiums they have promised to retirees. This huge loophole has allowed large unionized companies and defense contractors, which otherwise would have been prevented from taking money directly out of the plan, to save billions of dollars. Du Pont, for example, announced that it was transferring millions in surplus pension money to pay health benefits, thus freeing up this amount of corporate cash for other purposes.

The 1990 tax legislation, together with the ebb of the 1980s' takeover mania, has slowed but not stopped pension pirating. Companies continue to terminate their plans to gain access to "excess" funds. Between 1991 and 1993, large companies took more than $100 million out of their plans. In the case of small plans, termination may coincide with the retirement of a company owner. With larger plans, termination is often part of a corporate decision to get out of the pension business and to shift the responsibility for retirement savings to employees.

Drawing by Melody Sarecky.

For Bill Hunsaker, the raid on his plan was just the beginning of his pension nightmare. When the Pacific Lumber plan terminated in 1986, the plan trustees bought annuities for all current and future pensioners based on what they had earned up to that point, as required by law. The life insurance company the trustees chose to provide the annuities was Executive Life Insurance Company of California, soon to be a household name. Executive Life was a subsidiary of a finance company called First Executive Company, which had bought one-third of the $900 million in Drexel Burnham Lambert junk bonds used by Charles Hurwitz to finance his takeover of Pacific Lumber.

The selection of Executive Life worried Bill Hunsaker and other Pacific Lumber retirees. There had been news reports that the huge insurance company might be in serious financial trouble because of its heavy investment in junk bonds, and they were concerned that their pensions, already robbed of inflation adjustments, might be at risk. They convinced California pension lawyers Alfred Sigman and Jeffrey Lewis to take a look at their situation.

"We didn't like what we found," says Lewis. Not only was Executive Life's solvency in question, there was also evidence that the insurance company's selection stemmed mainly from its parent company's role in financing Maxxam's takeover of Pacific Lumber. If so, this situation was not only imprudent, but also a conflict of interest and a clear violation of the pension law. Lewis told a congressional committee that the pension plan managers "violated their duty to act for the sole benefit of plan participants; they wanted to reward Executive Life for its role in financing the takeover and/or to maximize recapture of plan assets, given the fact that Executive Life was the lowest bidder."[14]

On September 25, 1989, Sigman and Lewis filed suit in court on behalf of the Pacific Lumber participants, seeking to have the annuities transferred to another insurer. The lawsuit was still pending when Executive Life went bust. On April 11, 1991, the California Insurance Commission moved to take over the insolvent insurance company. Soon after, Bill Hunsaker and the other Pacific Lumber Company retirees received notices that their benefits would be reduced by 30 percent.

Some 86,000 annuitants in 46 states were affected by the failure of Executive Life. The fallout from the largest insurance company failure in history was tremendous. Accountant James W. Seddon, 76, of Mount Vernon, New York, was dismayed and angered but not entirely surprised when he heard the news. Retired for 12 years from Revlon Corporation, he had been concerned ever since he learned that the company was replacing his pension with an annuity — from Executive Life. Like Pacific Lumber, Revlon had been a family-owned, paternalistic-type company until 1985, when it was taken over by Mac-Andrews and Forbes Holdings Inc., owned by Ronald Perelman, another corporate raider. First Executive Company helped finance the $2.7 billion takeover by buying $370 million worth of Drexel Burnham junk bonds. Perelman then raided Revlon's $214 million pension plan, buying $85 million worth of annuities from Executive Life to pay promised pensions and raking off more than $100 million in "surplus" pension money for the corporation.

Executive Life payouts were reduced by 30 percent. What had happened, Seddon wondered, to the federal pension insurance program that was supposed to protect their benefits? And what would happen to people whose companies didn't offer to make up the difference when Executive Life failed?

What Seddon didn't know was that in 1990 the Pension Benefit Guaranty Corporation reversed an earlier position and announced that it would not backstop annuities. In companies that were not inclined to be generous — and most were not — the annuity pensioners would have to rely on protections at the state level. The risk, in other words, belonged to the pensioners, not the company!

The protections to which the PBGC referred were provided by state guaranty funds, which, under state law, require healthy life insurance companies to cover the claims of insurers that become insolvent. These protections turned out to be sadly inadequate. Three states and the District of Columbia didn't even have guaranty funds or any other provisions to pay the annuities. California had passed a law effective January 1, 1991, setting up a state guaranty fund, but its protections did not apply to companies that were insolvent on or before that date, such as Executive Life. In each of the 46 states that had some sort of guaranty fund at the time, there were limitations on who was protected (some did not protect nonresidents, for example), as well as ceilings on the amounts guaranteed. These amounts varied widely among states and left large gaps in most, according to an April 1991 report by the GAO. "This patchwork of coverage," said Joseph F. Delfico, director of income security issues for the GAO, "allows some retiree annuitants to slip through the cracks of state protections."[15] As many as 3 to 4 million retirees with annuities totaling $50 billion were at risk nationwide.

James Seddon testified before two congressional committees and appeared on CNN, and Pacific Lumber retirees were featured on an "NBC News White Paper," "20/20," and local television. The result was that more states set up guaranty funds, and existing guaranty funds were strengthened. Charles Hurwitz and Ronald Perelman agreed to pay the missing 30 percent of the Pacific Lumber and Revlon retirees' benefits.

Thousands of other retirees with Executive Life annuities continued to receive truncated pensions until April 1992, when the various state guaranty associations agreed to a so-called quick-pay plan covering 90 percent of all annuitants. This plan left out annuitants in Colorado, Louisana, and the District of Columbia, and it provided no back payments.

David Certner, lawyer and pension expert who heads the economic team at the American Association of Retired Persons, says, "It's essential that Congress act to make sure that we never have a repeat of these disastrous experiences." At present, the only requirements are that plan trustees act prudently in choosing an insurance carrier and that plan participants be told which company has been selected. These measures would have been insufficient to protect Executive Life annuitants, since the company was rated AAA by Standard & Poors at the time the annuities were bought by the Pacific Lumber and Revlon plans, and it didn't fail for another five years.

A recent study by Southern Finance Project director Tom Schlesinger shows that although state guaranty funds have been strengthened, they continue to offer a hodgepodge of inconsistent and inadequate protections.[16] One response would be to allow companies to substitute annuities for PBGC-protected pensions only if those annuities are sold by life insurance companies licensed in states with funds providing the same level of protection as the PBGC. In 1994, Montana representative Pat Williams introduced legislation into Congress that would require the PBGC to serve as insurer of last resort.

What to Do

How to Protect Yourself
if Your Plan Is Overfunded

If yours is a single employer defined benefit pension plan, check to see whether your plan is overfunded. Write to your plan administrator or the Department of Labor's Public Disclosure Room to get your plan's most recent financial statement, Form 5500 or Form 5500 C/R. Specify that you want the complete form and *all* attached schedules.

Look at Schedule B to see whether your plan is overfunded. If the amount of assets is greater than the amount of liabilities, the difference would be "surplus" should your company decide to terminate your plan. *Note:* Multiemployer plans are not allowed to take reversions of surplus assets.

Find out whether your pension plan's document permits the company to "recapture" the surplus. The plan document is available from the plan administrator or the Internal Revenue Service Employee Plans Division in the District Office closest to the plan's main office. If the plan permits the company to take the surplus, this will be stated in the document. (Such a provision must have been in the plan at least five years before the money is taken by the company. If not, the plan can still be terminated, but the excess money must be distributed to the workers and retirees.)

Should your company decide to terminate the plan for the purpose of extracting pension surplus, it must notify you and other participants in advance, to give you the right to comment on the legality of the termination and on the insurance carrier that has been selected for the payment of annuities. This can give you time to protest, if appropriate, and to check the security of your future annuities.

Call the state insurance commission in the state where your insurance company is located to find out about protections provided by its guaranty fund. Ask whether you would be protected if the insurance company providing your annuity failed. This is especially important if the insurance company is located in another state. Also, check on the maximum dollar amount that is guaranteed by the state fund.

PART III

THE PENSION STAKES

The Largest Lump of Money in the World

Throughout the United States, from Flatbush to Peoria to Hollywood, the word "pension" conveys security in old age — the monthly check that stands between people and poverty. There is one exception: Wall Street. In the world of corporate finance, "pension" conjures up images of high-stakes financial deals — takeovers, leveraged buyouts, mergers, and acquisitions. Forget the monthly check: "pension" means simply "the largest lump of money in the world."[1]

Three and a half trillion dollars![2] It boggles the mind. Pension funds are this country's largest single source of private capital. Over two-fifths of the money in these funds is invested in the stock of companies, making them the owners of nearly one-fifth of corporate America.[3]

Pensions are also the biggest part of our savings. They are so important that, according to Stanford economics professor John Shoven, they accounted for all of our national savings during the 1980s, and by 1990 they represented more than 17 percent of the nation's wealth.[4]

These funds have been growing at astronomical rates, tripling during the past decade. This is principally because they earn such huge investment returns.[5]

Private plans are already the largest of all institutional investors.

They are so large, in fact, that the investment decisions made by the managers of these funds can affect the lives of people throughout the country, determining whether companies decline or prosper, which communities survive and which do not.

Pensions are unique because of their size and because of their potential for being long-term investors. Money put into a pension fund for workers today may not have to be paid out for 30 or 40 years, when those workers retire. In the meantime, their money can help finance corporate retooling and expansion that will create jobs for their children and pay for research into new technologies or products that can improve their quality of life. In other words, sound pension investment strategies can reflect the long-term interests of present and future pensioners — and everybody else — in new jobs, an expanded national economy, reduced living expenses, and revitalized communities. Or they can do the opposite. Pension investments can support corporate decisions that close plants, slice jobs, choke off expansion, and stagnate long-term research.

Many people have a stake in keeping this great pool of money available for investment just the way it is now. They include not only the wizards of Wall Street, but also the caretakers and servicers of pension plans: the officers of corporations that offer plans; the heads of banks, insurance companies, and financial institutions that invest the money; the professional consultants and investment managers who offer advice and other services. Together, these groups form what has been called a "veritable pension/industrial complex."[6] Organized into influential trade associations, they meet regularly in Washington, testify at congressional hearings, disseminate reports, and maintain ties with those in Congress and the administration who make pension rules. Pension plan participants, community members, and others who seek a voice in pension policy need to know who the players are and just what effects these giant funds are having on America.

CHAPTER 12

The Pension Fund
Was Just Sitting There

The stakes are very high, the temptations are great and the potential for conflicts-of-interest are heightened in these transactions.

—David M. Walker, former Assistant Secretary of Labor

Kannapolis — "city of Cannon" — was the quintessential company town. Just down the road from Charlotte, North Carolina, Kannapolis was owned virtually lock, stock, and barrel by Cannon Mills, maker of towels and sheets. The workers' houses, the main store, and most of the land inside the town limits belonged to the mill. Some thought that the mill "owned" the workers too. Kannapolis was an anachronism, they said, a throwback to nineteenth-century paternalism, and then some.

In the early 1980s, the "city of Cannon" came crashing into the twentieth century. The elderly owner, Charles Cannon, known locally as "Mr. Charlie," died, and his heirs sold the mill with all its property to a California financier named David Murdock. No "Mr. Charlie," Murdock immediately began selling off the small clapboard houses in which textile workers had lived for generations, paying nominal rent. The store went, and so did everything else that wasn't turning a dollar for the mill.

The dismantling of the last of the company towns made headlines all over the country. Even former critics of Cannon-style paternalism professed shock at the crassness with which the new owner cast off responsibility for his employees. Selling off the houses and the company store was only the beginning. Nobody knew about the games David Murdock was playing with the workers' most valuable security of all — their well-stocked pension plan.

As later revealed in court papers, the new company officers put in place by Murdock, who were also pension trustees, quietly took millions of dollars of the pension plan's assets and invested them in the stock of companies that Murdock wanted to take over, among them Occidental Petroleum, Kaiser Cement, and Dole Pineapple. Murdock's plan was to use the pension fund stock, together with his other holdings, to gain control of these companies.[1] The plan didn't succeed. The target companies fought off Murdock's takeover attempts by using a tactic called "greenmail": they bought their own stock from the pension fund at a price higher than its value, which gave the fund a windfall of $30 million.

The weavers and dyers of Kannapolis went about their business completely unaware of the high-stakes game being played with their pension money on Wall Street. They were not consulted. Indeed, had Murdock's takeover attempts succeeded, the textile workers themselves would have won nothing. The stock transactions had no purpose other than allowing Murdock to take over the other companies.

The fact that the pension fund ended up with a profit did not help the workers either, since their employer had no intention of letting the $30 million go to raise their pension benefits. As owner of Cannon Mills, Murdock had the right to terminate the pension plan and take out the $30 million as a "reversion," which is exactly what he did. He then bought annuities from a life insurance company for the 13,000 workers and retirees, sold Cannon to Fieldcrest, and went home. The party was over.

Well, not quite over, thanks to the Amalgamated Clothing and Textile Workers' Union. At the same time that Murdock was playing with the pension plan, ACTWU had been trying to organize the Cannon workers. Led by Bill Patterson, the union's corporate affairs director, workers unearthed details of the pension manipulation and filed a lawsuit under ERISA, charging that plan trustees had violated their duty to invest plan assets solely in the interests of participants and challenging Murdock's right to keep his ill-gotten gains.

Ultimately, the case was settled and David Murdock put $1 million back into a fund for pension beneficiaries. Bill Patterson says, "The vigilance of workers and retirees was critical to disclosing the unlawful action of the trustees and recovering some of the assets for pensioners."[2] But the damage had been done. Their company was sold, many workers had lost their jobs, and the community of Kannapolis was altered forever. Why? Mostly because, in the words of an often-quoted Doonesbury cartoon, "The pension fund was just sitting there."

DOONESBURY copyright G. B. Trudeau. Reprinted
with permission of UNIVERSAL PRESS SYNDICATE.

Takeovers, leveraged buyouts, and other high-stakes transactions
have redrawn the economic map of America over the past decade.
Thousands of Americans have been thrown out of work, and community after community has been irrevocably changed. Although pension
funds did not cause merger mania, the "footloose capital" they provided
played a critical and sometimes decisive role in the restructuring of a
great many companies.[3]

Pension money is "footloose" because the plan trustees can invest it
wherever there is the promise of a good return to the pension fund and
without regard to the desires of the owners of the money, that is, the
workers and retirees. Beyond their charge to get a reasonable dollar-
and-cents return, pension fund managers are free agents.[4] As in the
Cannon Mills situation, they can and do use pension money in takeover
attempts and other power-play transactions without getting workers'
approval or even informing them of their intentions.

The freewheeling economic power wielded by fund trustees has
given rise to a number of troubling problems. One of them, as former

Labor Department administrator Robert Monks told a group of pension lawyers in 1991, is that "[c]onflict of interest permeates . . . the private pension system."[5]

In the Cannon Mills case, the trustees, who were also company officers, used the pension plan to enrich their boss, the company owner. In other situations, trustee-officers have used the pension money to try to protect their jobs. A classic *conflict of interest* involved a 1981 attempt by the Grumman Corporation's pension fund trustees to thwart a takeover of their company by the LTV Corporation. When LTV announced its plans to buy a controlling interest in Grumman by paying more for its stock than its value, the corporate officers running Grumman's pension plan, who stood to be ousted if LTV took over, refused to sell the fund's shares. Not only that, they arranged for the pension plan to buy another million and a half shares in company stock to block the takeover.

Ordinarily, the matter would have ended there. It didn't only because the Labor Department's top pension official at that time, Ian Lanoff, happened to read about the transaction in the *Wall Street Journal* and ordered an investigation. In the lawsuit that followed, a federal appeals court ruled that the company officers had not shown that they had acted "with an eye single to the interest of participants and beneficiaries." The court noted that the trustees, faced with obvious self-interest, should have hired an outside independent trustee to determine whether blocking the takeover was also in the interests of the workers and retirees.[6]

In addition to buying and selling stock to block or fuel takeover attempts, pension fund managers can achieve the same results by the way they vote on corporate decisions requiring stockholder approval. The same kinds of conflicts of interest are present in these proxy voting situations as in the direct investment of pension money. For example, the beleaguered officers of a company that is a takeover target, fearing for their jobs, are likely to vote or direct their fund managers to vote pension stock in favor of "poison pills" or "shark repellents," anti-takeover amendments to their corporate charters or bylaws. If these strategies aren't enough to discourage a raid, managers may vote for proposals giving themselves "golden parachutes," large severance packages to protect them in the event they are forced out.[7]

In most cases, the company's pension fund does not hold enough shares of its own stock to carry the vote alone, as Grumman did, so company officers call on friends at other companies to help them out. In their book *Power and Accountability*, Robert Monks and Nell Minow report that in the midst of the takeover-leveraged buyout binge of the 1980s, chief executive officers of some of the nation's leading companies wrote and called one another asking for support of initiatives aimed at protecting their companies against takeovers. The implied promise was, "You support me on this one, pal, and I'll support you when it gets to be your turn."[8]

Pension plan trustees and managers generally support takeovers even when they aren't trying to enrich company owners or save the jobs of company officers, because they have an interest in seeking short-term investment profits. Making a "quick buck" in order to reap a short-term gain is almost irresistible to pension plan managers. It looks great on that year's bottom line. In the case of defined benefit plans, a higher return on investments can also lower a company's required contribution for that year. Smaller pension expenditures can then show up as a tidy profit to the company on its year-end balance sheet. The problem is, as management expert Peter Drucker has put it, "Long-term results cannot be achieved by piling short-term results on short-term results."[9]

The desire for quick profits can influence plan managers to sell stock in a company that is a takeover target to a corporate raider offering a high price for the stock, or to vote the plan's shares in favor of the takeover, since that will boost the value of the stock. As investment manager Robert Kirby told *Fortune* magazine, "Every money manager's lucky day is when a raider launches an offer for his big holding. . . . Most money managers will vote for anything that makes the stock go up tomorrow."[10]

In pursuit of high short-term returns, pension fund trustees and managers have invested billions of pension dollars in leveraged buyout (LBO) arrangements in which investors pool their money to buy companies — and often close them down. Bob Lutz, a retired engineer from Grand Rapids, Michigan, and other retirees of Lear Siegler are still bitter about the devastation of their company as the result of a takeover financed by an LBO fund. After the workers lost their jobs and the retirees saw their hopes for cost-of-living adjustments evaporate, they learned that millions of dollars in the LBO fund came from another large defense contractor's pension plan.[11] Bob Lutz is "sure as heck" that the engineers retired from that company wouldn't have wanted their money to be used to destroy his old firm.

The question in all this is, Would the takeover frenzy have raged unchecked for a decade had the trustees who controlled the pension funds looked beyond their own personal and corporate interests to determine how workers and retirees wanted their money to be invested?

And what about current high-stakes transactions? *Pensions & Investments* reports that in 1993 the top ten corporate funds had $2.75 billion invested in buyouts and acquisitions.[12]

The Ten Largest Corporate Pension Funds in 1993[13]

COMPANY	FUND (in billions)
AT&T	$54.0
General Motors	50.8
General Electric	37.7
IBM	33.9
Ford	27.0
Du Pont	22.8
NYNEX	18.4
Bell South	17.4
Bell Atlantic	17.2
GTE	16.9

Employers' enthusiasm for high short-term investment yields contributes to a second problem, unnecessary buying and selling of stock by pension funds. The extreme form of this practice is called churning. According to a 1987 Labor Department study, 30 percent of larger defined benefit plans had common stock turnover rates in excess of 100 percent.[14] This means that those plans bought and sold securities worth more than the total amount of money in their pension funds that year. A 1991 Institutional Investor Project pilot study of turnover in large pension funds by economist Carolyn Kay Brancato found that the large, actively managed private plan she analyzed held only 12 percent of the same stocks at the beginning and end of a five-year period.[15]

A pension fund manager can easily buy and sell hundreds of thousands of shares of many different companies several times in one day. Most pension managers trade stock through the New York Stock Exchange. In 1993, more than half of all NYSE transactions were in the form of "block trades" consisting of the buying or selling of 10,000 or more shares of stock. More than one-fourth of these trades did not take place on the floor of the stock exchange but through computerized buy-and-sell agreements arranged "upstairs" from the exchange. There was an average of 5,841 block trades a day in 1993 involving more than 35 billion shares of stock.[16]

Money managers argue that their business is to maximize return for the fund and that they can do this by trading frequently. Moreover, they stand to lose their corporate clients if they do not show significant gains in the short term.[17] There is no evidence, however, that high turnover produces a better investment return. In fact, a Labor Department study found that the rate of return for plans with low stock turnover was slightly higher than the rate of return for plans with high turnover.[18]

Not only does all this buying and selling fail to benefit the pension funds, it also encourages a short-term mind-set within the companies whose stock is being traded. It compels company executives to focus solely on this year's profits rather than on long-term research, retooling, and investment in future production. Nicholas Brady, secretary of the treasury in the Bush administration, told a 1990 meeting of business executives that the obsession with quick gains was preventing American companies from investing in research and modernization and putting them at a competitive disadvantage with Japanese firms that invest for the long term. "As pension funds have grown to the size they are today," Brady warned, "they must realize that short-term trading techniques can't possibly contribute in an important way to their performance, much less to national goals."[19]

Another harmful consequence of unnecessary buying and selling of stocks, critics say, is that it prevents pension funds from serving as watchdogs of corporate management. As short-term investors, pension funds have no incentive to try to hold corporate officers accountable for their management decisions. Monks and Minow point out that a lack of oversight on "corporate governance" can contribute to the entrenchment of inefficient company managers, which in the long term can lower the value of a company's stock and may eventually cost workers their jobs.[20]

Concerned that pension money is not being invested solely with the interests of plan participants in mind and for their long-term benefit, government officials and others have taken steps to reduce conflicts and to nudge pension fund managers toward taking the longer view in investing. For example, during the height of the takeovers and LBOs, when pension fund managers felt pressured to maximize investment returns by accepting all tender offers, the Labor and Treasury Departments published a letter saying that plan managers were not required to take the quick buck if they believed that the pension plan would ultimately achieve a higher return by holding on to an investment.[21]

To deal with conflicts of interest in the voting of stock, the Labor Department issued a ruling in 1988 establishing that pension funds were subject to the same obligation to act solely in the interests of workers and retirees in proxy voting as they were in investing plan money.[22] This ruling gave rise to firms offering to assume the job of voting stock solely in the interests of participants. However, many companies are reluctant to use these proxy voting services because they do not want to give up control of the voting power. In the event of a takeover attempt, the company officers and plan trustees want to be able to vote the pension stock to protect themselves. Some experts are convinced that the Labor Department's ruling will have little effect unless federal law is changed to require that all nonroutine voting decisions be made by independent third parties.[23] At a minimum, plan trustees should be required to tell workers and retirees how they voted their stock. A proposal that this be federal law was made in 1990 by then Secretary of Labor Elizabeth Dole, but it was later withdrawn.[24]

Convinced that plan managers will not voluntarily cut down on excessive buying and selling of stock, Senators Nancy Kassebaum and Robert Dole proposed legislation in 1990 that would have imposed a 5 percent penalty tax when pension fund managers buy and sell the same stock within a six-month period and a 10 percent tax if the stock is turned over within less than 30 days. Former Senator Terry Sanford introduced legislation in 1992 that would have applied to pension funds the same "short-short" rule that prohibits mutual funds from making more than 30 percent of their income from shares held for less than three months.[25]

Labor adviser Randy Barber and economics professor Teresa Ghilarducci propose a stick-and-carrot approach to encourage plan managers to take a longer view. They suggest that pension fund transactions be taxed when stock is held for less than one year, with a refundable tax credit when stock is held for more than five years.[26]

In part to address concern about high turnover, an increasing number of plan managers have begun investing in index funds. These funds buy stocks according to their relative weights in a major market sampling, or "index," such as the Standard and Poor's 500 or the Wilshire 5,000.[27] Indexing solves the problem of unnecessary turnover and allow plans to invest in companies for longer periods of time.

Another method of achieving a longer-term investment horizon is "relationship investing." Instead of adhering to the so-called Wall Street rule of selling off a company's stock because of dissatisfaction with management, some corporate pension plan managers are saying that they intend to become long-term holders of securities and take an active role in ensuring the efficiency of the management of the companies in which they invest. This approach addresses both the conflicts and the churning problems and achieves the primary goal of its proponents: encouraging corporate executives to be more responsive to the interests of their shareholders.

Until recently, the use of relationship investing to achieve corporate governance goals has been limited to government pension funds, notably the large California state pension funds. Now, however, several large private plans have announced their intentions to exercise their power as shareholders and act as watchdogs. A spokesman for the Campbell Soup Company pension plan told the *Wall Street Journal* that as part of its relationship investing strategy, the plan's money managers have been instructed to vote Campbell's stocks against companies that elect more than three inside directors. The plan may also become involved in issues related to the salary levels of corporate officers.[28]

General Motors has announced plans to put $325 million of its pension money into a relationship investing fund run by Dillon Read & Co. Other funds have begun experimenting with corporate governance issues in overseas companies in which they hold stock.[29] One less controversial position being put forward requires that a majority of the members of corporate boards of directors be outsiders (not company officials) and that boards evaluate their own performance periodically.[30]

Indexing and relationship investing can help reduce conflicts of interest and churning but they also contribute to another problem: the high degree of concentration of pension fund money in the stocks of large blue-chip companies.

Pension fund investments, for all their activity, remain concentrated in a narrowly circumscribed investment world. At the end of the third quarter of 1993, private noninsured pension plans held 44 percent of their assets in corporate stock.[31] Large defined benefit plans surveyed by Greenwich Associates in 1993 reported having 57.9 percent of their assets in stock.[32]

Much of this stock is in America's largest corporations. In 1990, then Assistant Secretary of Labor David Walker noted that private and public pension plans "now own over 25% of all corporate equities and over 50% of many Fortune 500 companies."[33] The 20 largest pension funds owned an average of 7.7 percent of the top ten U.S. companies in 1989, including 10.6 percent of General Motors, 9.1 percent of IBM, 9 percent of Phillip Morris, 8.5 percent of GE, 7.4 percent of Exxon, and 6.1 percent of AT&T.[34]

As more funds choose indexing and relationship investing, the degree of their concentration in these companies could increase even further, since these companies are the most heavily represented in index funds and most likely to be the targets of corporate governance efforts.

The problem is that heavy concentration of fund investments in blue-chip stock, rather than in new shares being sold by new or expanding companies, does little to contribute to the country's economic growth. Buying "old" stock does not, for example, provide new jobs in small businesses or result in new products or services. Nor does it address the needs of communities for investments in housing, roads, and schools.

Partly in response to the concentration problem, policymakers have been exploring ways to encourage pension funds to invest more creatively, outside their present narrow universe of capital markets. Currently, few private funds seek such investments.

The Labor Department has long taken the view that among investments providing comparable returns and levels of risk, plan trustees can choose those that create jobs for workers, reduce day-to-day expenses of pensioners, or enhance their communities.[35] Only recently, however, have *economically targeted investments* (ETIs) attracted public interest as a viable means of moving pension capital into long-term investments that reflect the broader economic concerns of the people whose money is being invested.

Olena Berg, assistant secretary of labor for pension and welfare benefits, a champion of ETIs, defines targeted investing as "investments that produce competitive or even superior risk-adjusted rates of return, while at the same time boosting the health and productivity of the U.S. economy."[36] She is convinced that pension assets can and should be invested productively to provide capital to affordable housing projects, start-ups, and small businesses.

Until now, the practice of investing pension assets with the goal of helping plan participants and improving their communities has been largely limited in the private sector to certain multiemployer plans in the construction industry. These plans have developed innovative ways of using pension money to increase the availability of jobs for union members while also increasing the supply of housing in members' communities.[37] The AFL-CIO's pioneering Housing Investment Trust (HIT), begun 30 years ago, has created 31,000 housing units and provided 21,000 jobs in construction and other industries. Its return on investment has averaged 9.28 percent over the past five years. Legislation passed by Congress in 1993 is giving a significant boost to HIT's efforts. In 1994, under the Community Investment Demonstration Program, the U.S. Department of Housing and Urban Development (HUD) provided $100 million in rental assistance to low-income individuals living in housing units built or renovated with pension fund financing.[38]

The Clinton administration is searching for additional ways to encourage pension fund investments in projects that will spur economic growth.[39] In its 1993 report, the Commission to Promote Investment in America's Infrastructure recommended the creation of a National Infrastructure Corporation, which would encourage pension fund investment in roads, bridges, schools, airports, water treatment systems, and other public facilities. The commission noted that pension funds, with their enormous capital pools and unparalleled ability to provide long-term investments, are essential participants in any effort to cover the estimated $40 billion to $80 billion annual shortfall in needed infrastructure spending in the country today.[40]

Critics of ETIs argue that the introduction of nonfinancial factors into the investment decision compromises the primary objective of pension funds, which is the income security of pensioners. Yet the strong track record of HIT and other ETIs shows that it is possible for fund managers to put the interests of pensioners first and also "do good" with their money.[41]

One unexplored target that would directly promote the financial well-being of plan participants is "elder investments," aimed at reducing the day-to-day expenses of people living on fixed pensions. These might include high-yield, low-risk investments in housing, transportation, and technology for the elderly, as well as in pharmaceutical companies specializing in drugs for older people, nursing homes, hospices, for-profit hospitals, and home health care providers.[42]

The success of efforts to promote ETIs will depend on establishing mechanisms that will both enable pension funds to invest in ETI projects and attract them with a good rate of return. For example, pension funds have not traditionally invested in infrastructure projects because the usual financing tool, tax-free municipal bonds issued by cities and states, carries a lower yield to compensate for tax breaks, which tax-exempt pension funds don't need.

Another impediment is simply a lack of information. It is extremely costly for pension funds to search out new types of investments. The Labor Department is now developing a clearinghouse to identify sound ETIs and provide information to pension fund managers.

Just as economic issues are the focus of ETIs, social and moral issues are the concern of other attempts to influence pension fund investment practices. The goal of these efforts has been to promote good corporate conduct, such as affirmative action or environmentally sound policies. With *socially responsible investments* (SRIs), as with ETIs, the emphasis has been on prudent investments and sound voting policies that first ensure workers' and retirees' secure and enhanced pension benefits and only then take other considerations into account. To date, SRI advocates have directed most of their efforts at convincing pension funds to commit to a policy of excluding from their portfolios securities issued by companies that fail to adopt and comply with certain principles. The following are examples of nonfinancial criteria on which companies have been excluded from fund portfolios:

- **Sullivan principles:** Companies were excluded if they had operations in South Africa and did not adopt certain fair employment practices aimed at preventing discrimination against blacks.
- **MacBride principles:** Companies are excluded if they have operations in Northern Ireland and do not adopt certain fair employment practices aimed at preventing discrimination against Catholics in Northern Ireland.
- **Valdez principles:** Companies are excluded if they are considered to be environmentally destructive.

The Social Choice Account offered by the College Retirement Equities Fund of TIAA-CREF, as part of its supplemental retirement annuity, has in the past screened out from its portfolio any company that:

- Has economic ties to South Africa;
- Has operations in Northern Ireland *and* has not adopted the MacBride principles or operated consistently with such principles;
- Produces nuclear energy;

- Has a significant portion of its business in weapons manufacturing;
- Produces and markets alcoholic beverages or tobacco products; or
- Engages in activities that result or are likely to result in significant damage to the natural environment.[43]

ETIs represent a significant response to the pension concentration problem. As they grow, they will be extremely important in promoting the economic security of participants and the revitalization of the U.S. economy. Most ETI advocates, however, like those urging pension funds' involvement in corporate governance, overlook a key element in the equation: a means of determining the interests of the individuals whose money is being invested. So far, most ETI (and SRI) proponents have been content to leave investment decisions to the judgment of plan trustees and have not tried to develop ways to solicit input from participants.

A proposal that would have ensured participant involvement in plan decision making was offered in 1989 by Indiana Representative Peter Visclosky, who introduced legislation to require that all plans be managed jointly by employee and employer representatives.[44] The Visclosky bill sparked a firestorm of opposition from business leaders, who objected on a variety of grounds, but principally on the ground of risk. Since the corporation "takes all the risk in defined benefit plans, it should be the one to decide how much risk and how to take it," was the way *Pensions & Investments* editor Michael Clowes recalls the argument.

Labor unions, which strongly supported the Visclosky proposal, responded that the money belongs to the workers as deferred wages, and they are the ones with the ultimate risk, since the company would be sure to reduce benefits if investments went sour. Joint trusteeship, argues Michael Calabrese, former pension counsel for the AFL-CIO, would have the positive effect of "aligning the pension plan's interests as perceived by money managers, who simply see plans as pots of money, with the true, multiple interests of workers." Those interests include "the security of their jobs, the prosperity of the plan sponsor, economic growth, and the environment of their communities." Some employers object that participants lack the financial sophistication necessary to help in plan investment and stock voting decisions, and that it would be difficult to devise a mechanism for joint trusteeship for very small plans.[45] However, in Great Britain, joint trusteeship has been in effect informally in plans for many years. The British Parliament is slated to pass legislation requiring an equal number of worker and management trustees in plans with 100 or more participants.

A compromise approach, which would also address the difficulties of devising a mechanism for joint trusteeship for very small plans, has been suggested by Georgetown law professor Roy Schotland. He proposes including employee representatives on pension plan boards but leaving ultimate control with the employer. This arrangement, he told a congressional committee, would assure that plan managers would be "more aware of participant views, and participants more aware of their plans' operations and strengths or weaknesses."[46]

Former Senator Howard Metzenbaum's Pension Bill of Rights would establish voluntary participant advisory committees that could send worker and retiree representatives to trustee meetings, review investment and proxy voting decisions, and make nonbinding recommendations. In the case of plans too small for a formal committee to be necessary, the plan trustee could solicit the views of participants through yearly proxy voting and investment preference questionnaires. The trustees could also respond to written requests from workers and retirees for information about specific votes or investment decisions.

The Visclosky proposal was dropped, but the questions it raised remain unanswered: how can workers and retirees ensure that their money is being used to advance their interests and that their funds' investment practices are promoting the economic growth of the nation?

What to Do

How to Have a Say in
the Way Your Pension Money Is Invested

Many plan trustees assume that participants have no interest in knowing where their money is invested or how stock held by the plan is voted. If you are concerned, speak up.

For information about your plan's investment practices, ask your plan administrator for *Form 5500 or Form 5500 C/R*. You can also call the U.S. Department of Labor's Public Disclosure Room to request a copy. Form 5500 will tell you who is managing your money; how much the plan manager is being paid; how much of the plan's money is in stocks, bonds, real estate, and other assets; and how much money the plan earned on investments. If there are 100 or more people in the plan, a list of all the plan's investments as of the end of the plan year will be attached to the form.

Ask the trustees how the plan's stock was voted on key issues. They are not legally obligated to tell you, but you can point out that it's your stock that was voted. Discuss one or more of the following with the plan's trustees:

- Investments you believe the plan should (or should not) be making.
- Social concerns you would like to see reflected in your plan's portfolio.
- The willingness of the trustees to allow employee and retiree representatives to participate in an advisory capacity in your plan's investment and proxy voting decisions.

If you are a member of a multiemployer plan, ask your union trustees to explain the plan's investment policies and find out whether those policies truly represent members' long-term interests.

If you discover investment practices by plan trustees that you believe do not further your economic interests, contact the nearest field office of the U.S. Department of Labor's Pension and Welfare Benefits Administration.

CHAPTER 13

The Pension Players

There is no political capital in working on the pension system in this country.

—Former Representative Rod Chandler[1]

It happens every spring. The cherry blossoms appear in the nation's capital and members of the pension industry's largest lobbying group gather in one of the city's vast hotel ballrooms. The annual legislative conference of the Association of Private Pension and Welfare Plans (APPWP) brings together many of the major players in the pension game: representatives of corporations, the banks, insurance companies, and pension consulting firms who make up APPWP's membership and have a financial stake in operating or servicing plans, and members of Congress and the administration, who appear on APPWP's podium to discuss their current legislative or regulatory initiatives.

Most conference speakers express views sympathetic to their business-oriented audience, calling for less government interference and more relaxed regulation of private pension plans. But conference organizers are also careful to invite speakers who mention reform proposals that the audience is sure to oppose. Thus alerted, APPWP members can prepare to head off any threats to the status quo.

Talk of radical change, such as worker participation in plan investment decisions, immediately puts members on red alert. In record time, chief executive officers of major corporations will be on the phone to key members of Congress. Contributions from political action committees will begin to flow toward legislators likely to stand against the proposal. Other reform proposals unleash grassroots strategies. For example, in the campaign against efforts to curb pension raiding, APPWP members canvassed the districts of key congressional committee members to find business owners willing to tell their representatives that they would shut down if denied access to "surplus" pension money. The specter of unemployed constituents and lost campaign support helped defeat the more stringent proposals to stop raiding.

On most legislative campaigns, APPWP works closely with the ERISA Industry Committee (ERIC), an organization of 128 Fortune -200 companies, 40 of which are also APPWP members. Both APPWP and ERIC have budgets of over $1 million and staff to lobby full-time on pension issues. For additional help in supporting or opposing legislation, they regularly call on the Financial Executives Institute and actuarial and other pension groups. They are often joined as well by larger multi-issue trade associations such as the U.S. Chamber of Commerce, the American Council of Life Insurance, and the National Association of Manufacturers.

Pension industry lobbying resources stand ready to be mobilized on very short notice. Not long after the APPWP's 1993 conference, a Senate floor vote was unexpectedly scheduled on a bill that would have permitted retirees to sue pension plan consultants for losses resulting from the consultants' bad advice. APPWP, ERIC, and the American Council of Life Insurance were able to orchestrate what the trade paper *Pensions & Investments* called a "massive lobbying campaign" to defeat the measure. *P & I* reported that a letter was "hand-delivered to every senator on the eve of the debate ... signed by 87 employers and organizations including IBM Corp., International Paper Co., Ameritech Corp., Chevron Corp., Rockwell International Corp., NYNEX Corp., and Weyerhaeuser Co."[2] The Senate vote was canceled.

For statistical ammunition, plan-side lobbying groups turn to the Employee Benefit Research Institute (EBRI). Documents filed with the IRS show that EBRI was founded in 1978 by the country's 13 largest actuarial firms. Each agreed to contribute $25,000 a year and serve as a trustee of the new research group, which would "promote, improve, and further the common business interests of persons involved in the employee benefit field."

Fifteen years later, as of the end of 1993, EBRI and its EBRI Education and Research Fund affiliate reported assets of $4.7 million and a 47-member board of trustees. In addition to officials of 13 consulting firms, EBRI trustees included representatives of 14 of the nation's largest corporations, 12 insurance companies, and four banks. Twelve of the companies listed on the EBRI board also belong to APPWP and ERIC. Among those with overlapping memberships are corporate giants such as Du Pont, Amoco, AT&T, and Boeing, and the life insurance companies Aetna, Equitable, and CIGNA.

EBRI publishes numbers collected by government agencies in its own format with its own emphasis. Unlike the bleak image of private plans portrayed by the government studies, the figures in EBRI reports consistently paint a rosy picture. They convey the message that the private system is in fine shape and getting better. For example, when government studies show a substantial decline in private pension participation, EBRI counters with reports that appear to show an increase.[3] The difference is that EBRI's numbers are based on a "civilian" workforce that includes government employees, almost all of whom are plan members, and also on figures that include savings plans, to which many employees have contributed only small amounts.[4] Economist Thomas Woodruff, who served as executive director of the President's Commission on Pension Policy, points out that figures such as these give a "distorted and much overstated view when discussing federal policy regarding private pensions."[5]

Given the formidable phalanx of pension industry groups and the millions of dollars they spend each year to block changes in the system, one might conclude that participants seeking reform don't have a chance. Yet Congress has passed four major pension equity laws since ERISA, as well as a number of other important pension reforms opposed by APPWP and its industry allies. Several factors account for these victories by participants, but one of the most important has been the willingness of wronged individuals to speak out against pension injustice. Despite the lopsided odds, courageous citizens have often carried the day.

The fight for widows' benefits was such a time. In 1983, Congress was asked to pass legislation requiring plans to provide survivor's benefits to widows and widowers of employees who died before they had reached early retirement age. APPWP, ERIC, and EBRI, along with other industry groups, vigorously opposed the bill, contending that life insurance provided adequate protection for widows and threatening that employers would close their plans rather than pay the additional cost of these widow's benefits.

Then Geraldine Compton made the trip from her tiny mining community of Phelps, Kentucky, to tell Congress her story. It was a simple but powerful tale. Her husband had worked for 27 years as a repairman for a coal mining company. He had always assured her that whatever happened to him the pension would be there for her. Then he died four hours before his fifty-fifth birthday. That was "too early," ruled the plan administrator. The widow wouldn't get a dime. "Nothing," she told a congressional committee, "has ever seemed so unfair to me in my whole life."[6] Within the year, Congress changed the law to provide survivor's protection for widows and widowers regardless of the age at which their spouses died.[7]

The power of people like Geraldine Compton and the other widows who testified on this issue cannot be overestimated. They toppled the plan-side Goliaths because they were able to focus attention in a dramatic way on a plight shared by tens of thousands. The executive director of a pension industry group once offered to drop his opposition to a piece of reform legislation if participant groups would promise never again to arrange for individuals to appear as witnesses at congressional hearings. The offer was not accepted, as he had known it would not be.

Drawing by Margaret Scott.

Other factors come into play as well, of course. The widows would never have won without the backing of an array of groups representing participants. This informal coalition ranged from large national organizations such as the American Association of Retired Persons, the Older Women's League, and the AFL-CIO, to smaller advocacy groups such as the National Senior Citizens Law Center and the Pension Rights Center. The larger groups alerted their constituents to the issue, testified at congressional hearings, and lobbied individual members of Congress; the smaller ones provided technical assistance to congressional staff, testified, and arranged for the widows to appear before Congress and on national television.

Former Senate Labor Subcommittee chief counsel Michele Varnhagen notes that when participant-side groups make pensions a priority and devote resources to it, as they did in the 1980s, they can be extremely effective, particularly when, as in the case of the widows' legislation, the issues are easy to explain to their members and to the media. This, she says, "is because, given a choice, lawmakers want to protect women and retirees."

Ultimately, however, the widows' victory may have depended less on lobbying strategies than on the way members of Congress viewed the issue's impact on another player — the ultimate stakeholder in the pension game: the American taxpayer. What finally convinced lawmakers to reject the business groups' arguments and approve widow's benefits was the principle of "tax equity." Simply put, this principle says that because taxpayers are underwriting the pension system, they have the right to expect it to meet certain standards of fundamental fairness for all Americans. Denying benefits to a coal mine repairman's widow because he died "four hours too soon" did not meet those standards.

The extent to which pension policy is determined by tax considerations often surprises people. Yet all Americans pay more in taxes (or receive less in government services) than they would if there were no private pension system. In 1995, the tax breaks on pension contributions and investment earnings will cost taxpayers nearly $30 billion.[8]

Some industry advocates argue that the revenue loss should not be a factor in policy decisions, since much of the untaxed money will be taxed in future years when it is paid out to retirees as pension benefits. However, as Georgetown law professor and former Treasury official Daniel Halperin notes, "The way the calculations work, the Treasury never recovers all that it has lost. This is true even when people do not retire to lower tax brackets." The taxes that would have been paid on investment earnings over the years are never recouped. Most importantly,

Professor Halperin adds, "the lost taxes are not available to the Treasury to meet today's needs, including the need to reduce the federal deficit."

If the revenue loss for state, city, county, federal government, and military pensions is added to that of private pensions, the tax subsidy grows to an astronomical $69 billion, the largest of all federal tax expenditures. The Treasury loses more revenue from the tax-favored treatment of pension plans than from the tax deduction granted to home owners for interest on their mortgages, or from the tax exemption for employees' health insurance payments.[9]

Because pensions so directly affect the amount of revenue the government receives each year, the two tax-writing committees of Congress — the Senate Committee on Finance and the House Committee on Ways and Means — often play a decisive role in developing pension policy. It was tax considerations that determined the way Congress finally curbed pension raiding. Without deciding whether the practice was right or wrong, lawmakers found that companies owed tax revenue on the "surplus" funds and upped the penalty tax on that basis. Another example of the duality underlying most pension legislation was the 1992 law requiring income taxes to be withheld when employees withdraw their pension or savings money before they reach retirement age. This law raised revenue and discouraged preretirement cash-outs of pension funds.[10]

Viewing pensions from a tax policy perspective can lead to stronger protections for individuals, but it has its disadvantages as well. For one thing, significant public issues can be overlooked when they occur in plans that involve minimal tax loss and, as a result, are of little interest to the tax committees. An example is the trend toward "top hat" and "supplemental" pension plans. A growing number of companies are setting up these executive-only plans, typically in addition to a company-wide plan. These plans remove a key incentive for employers to set up or improve plans for rank-and-file employees — providing for their own retirement — and thus raise important policy concerns. But because they do not have the tax advantages of conventional plans, they have not been subjected to congressional scrutiny.

Another disadvantage of linking public policy concerns to tax policy is that when the two objectives conflict, pension security for individuals nearly always loses. This happened in 1990 when AT&T, IBM, Du Pont, and other large companies with overfunded pension plans used the tax revenue argument to convince Congress to let them take "surplus" pension money for a five-year period to pay their retirees' health insurance bills. Retirees protested that this shift of monies would give

the companies an excuse to end their practice of granting cost-of-living adjustments. Their protest fell on deaf ears because members of Congress saw the measure as a way of raising revenue: the companies would not be taking tax deductions for their health insurance payments. In 1994, lawmakers quietly extended this legislation to help finance the General Agreement on Tariffs and Trade (GATT).

The tax committees share authority over certain pension issues with the Senate Committee on Labor and Human Resources and the House Committee on Economic Opportunity (formerly the Committee on Education and Labor). These labor committees look at the issues from the perspective of worker protection and have traditionally been supportive of participants' rights. Turf battles regularly occur between the tax and labor committees. The resulting compromises, although advancing participants' interests in some cases, make pension legislation extremely complex.

There are pension issues for which the labor committees have full responsibility, notably those involving enforcement of participants' rights, disclosure, and mismanagement of funds. Even here, conflict-of-interest problems arise. These committees are structured to balance the concerns of companies and unions. When business and labor are on the same side, as sometimes happens, it is politically difficult for committee members to champion the rights of workers and retirees. For example, proposals by retirees to allow courts to award them punitive damages when trustees deliberately mismanage their pension money find little support on the labor committees. Both union and company officials serve as trustees of multiemployer plans, and they are flatly opposed to any measures that would increase the liability of trustees.

Ironically, the complexity of pension issues and their generally low profile in the press may serve to facilitate reform and blunt the lobbying efforts of the industry. A political action committee contribution may influence a lawmaker's vote in the short term, but the perception on Capitol Hill is that there is no political capital in pensions: a reelection campaign will not be won or lost on the basis of a pension vote. For that reason, members generally delegate work on these issues to committee staff, knowledgeable professionals with an understanding of the technical aspects of pensions and of the competing interests at stake, who work hard to come up with reasonable compromises. With rare exceptions, their bosses act on their recommendations.

The basic problem with pension legislation is that division of authority among several committees with radically different objectives slows and fragments the process of reform. The survivor's benefit legislation, which was a response to a highly visible, easily grasped problem, took ten years.

Highly technical, less dramatic issues take even longer. The reforms that emerge from this process tend to be piecemeal, partial measures at best.

For a brief period, one congressional committee did focus on the overall retirement income concerns of individuals. Beginning in 1990, a House Select Committee on Aging subcommittee, headed by New Jersey Representative William Hughes and New York Representative Sherwood Boehlert, held a series of hearings and a congressional symposium aimed at developing realistic long-range pension policies. In 1993, Congress abolished the committee in a budget cut. A similar committee in the Senate, the Special Committee on Aging, has not addressed pension issues since 1989, when it was chaired by the late Senator John Heinz.

In theory, the roster of major pension players ought to include the government agencies with pension regulatory authority: the Department of the Treasury (which includes the Internal Revenue Service), the Department of Labor, and the Pension Benefit Guaranty Corporation. But each of these agencies keeps strictly to its own program objectives in proposing legislation; none has assumed the challenging task of formulating comprehensive, long-range retirement income policies.

Interest in such a broad examination of pension policy was revived in 1994 in bills introduced by Representative William Hughes and Senator Joseph Lieberman that would have created an 18-month Commission on Retirement Income Policy.[11] A similar bill had been introduced earlier by then Senator (later Secretary of the Treasury) Lloyd Bentsen. These bills left the appointment of a commission to Congress and the president, leading some critics to express concern that it would be too politicized to develop realistic recommendations.

Alternatives to a congressional commission would be a new presidential commission, an administration task force, or a permanent independent government agency similar to the Securities and Exchange Commission, the National Labor Relations Board, or the Environmental Protection Agency. In addition to developing long-range policy recommendations, the agency could be given authority to protect participants and coordinate the activities of the many agencies now involved in the day-to-day regulation of plans. Significantly, countries that have recently taken the lead in formulating private pension reforms, such as Great Britain, Canada, and Australia, have pension policy commissions, boards, or committees that were established by their legislatures.

What to Do

How to Become a Pension Player

Becoming a pension player is as easy as writing a letter to your senators or representative in Congress to tell them that you think pensions are important. Pinpoint a specific concern. Ask why there's no government agency to develop pension policy and help individuals. Protest against rules you consider are unfair, investment practices you think are wrong, or the lack of inflation adjustments in private pensions.

Your letter will be read not by the senator or representative but usually by a staff member. When the office receives a number of letters on the same subject, a memorandum is written to someone higher up, and the issue may eventually reach the top of the ladder. Make a follow-up phone call; it helps focus staff attention on the issue. Raise the issue at a town meeting where the member of Congress is speaking, or at a candidates' forum. Try to arrange a personal meeting with your senators or representative.

Also, contact staff members of one of the tax or labor committees specializing in pensions. They are the ones who decide which reform proposals will move through Congress. Drop a line to the president and to the secretaries of the Treasury and Labor. Letters and phone calls give policymakers a sense of which issues matter to people.

It is helpful to alert radio and television talk show hosts to your concerns. If a local program has "open phones," call in and suggest a show on pensions. And write to financial columnists, many of whom base their articles on queries from readers, and to newspaper editors. Even if your letter isn't printed, it will have an effect on whoever reads it; the next one on the subject, yours or someone else's, may well be featured.

If you belong to a retiree group, a women's or religious organization, or a union or professional association, ask the officers to put pensions on the policy agenda. If they have already done so, find out what the group's positions are on the issues and make sure that the group knows yours. Join with friends or coworkers to form your own grassroots group to campaign for pension justice.

PART IV

PEOPLE WITHOUT PENSIONS

Do It Yourself!

Nearly everyone knows the fable of the grasshopper and the ant. All summer, the story goes, the carefree grasshopper sings and dances while the industrious ant busily stores up food for the winter. When cold weather comes, snug in her home with plenty to eat, the ant turns her back on the starving grasshopper and tells him to go dance.

What does Aesop's fable have to do with American retirement policy? Oddly enough, this fable was invoked in connection with two events that occurred almost simultaneously in the first year of the Reagan administration. The first, widely reported, was the enactment by Congress in November 1981 of a law that made it possible for people covered by pension plans to get tax deductions for their contributions to individual retirement accounts.[1] Undersecretary of the Treasury Norman Ture explained that his administration's strong support for this legislation stemmed from the view that people can and should make their own provisions for retirement. He told the *Washington Post*, "The evidence of the past suggests that people do not behave like grasshoppers. They are much more like ants."[2]

Two days after the *Post*'s article appeared, a second, almost unnoticed, event occurred, reflecting the philosophy of the ant. The Reagan administration published what seemed at first to be obscure, narrowly focused regulations related to a handful of bonus plans set up by a few banks. The regulations said that employees who authorized their employers to put part of their earnings into these plans would not be taxed on what they contributed.

They turned out to be a veritable gold mine for people with money to shelter from taxes. For the first time, employees were given tax breaks for their contributions to company savings plans. This change was part of a deliberate strategy on the part of the administration "to encourage private savings and minimize regulatory burdens on businesses that wish to use deductible employee contributions to promote retirement savings by employees."[3]

The changes stunned the pension world. One actuary told *Pensions & Investments*, "We were shocked, and then pleasantly surprised that the government would allow pre-tax contributions. And our clients were pleasantly surprised."[4]

The 401(k) stampede was on. As word of the new regulations spread, companies raced to set up tax advantages that seemed too good to be true. Between 1981 and 1985, the number of 401(k)s and the assets invested in them more than doubled. By 1986, over 37,000 of these plans were on the books, with investments totaling $182.8 billion. The anthills were fast becoming mountains.

By mid-decade, a counterreaction had set in. Treasury officials, aghast at the unforeseen drainage of tax revenue, proposed the elimination of both 401(k)s and deductible IRAs for people with pension plans.[5] But it was too late to halt the juggernaut. Brokerage houses, insurance companies, and mutual funds, which were having a field day managing the new plans, bombarded Congress with protests. When the dust settled, certain compromises had been reached. The Tax Reform Act of 1986 placed limitations on contributions by higher-paid employees, but both 401(k)s and deductible IRAs for people with pension plans survived.[6]

The new law significantly slowed the amount of money going into IRAs, but it hardly caused a blip in the growth of the 401(k) behemoth, since the limit it placed on deductible contributions was far above what most people were putting in anyway. Between 1987 and 1991, the number of 401(k)s again more than doubled. By 1991, there were nearly 115,000 of these plans covering 19.5 million workers. They had almost $448 billion in assets.[7] The revenue loss to the Treasury is unknown.

The mirror image of the advancing tide of 401(k)s has been the quiet ebbing of pension plans paid for by employers. Between 1983 and 1993, the number of full-time private sector workers in traditional pension and profit sharing plans declined by 30 percent.[8] This retreat from pensions reflects an astounding reversal in national retirement policy.

Today, for two-thirds of Americans working full-time in the private sector, do-it-yourself retirement is the only option.[9] How are the 48 million Americans outside the pension system preparing for winter?

CHAPTER 14

Pots of Gold?

A 401(k) is the richest deal you'll ever find.

—Jane Bryant Quinn, *Making the Most of Your Money*[1]

Vicky Bernard will tell you straight off that she loves 401(k) savings plans. Why? "Because ours sent my husband to law school!"

In 1987, at age 36, Lucian Bernard decided to quit his sales job with BioScience Labs and go back to school. The Bernards would probably not have been able to swing the expense without the cash from his 401(k) at BioScience. He had begun contributing to the plan three years earlier, putting in the maximum the company would match, on a two-to-one basis, and had $11,000 in the kitty. Even with a 10 percent penalty and income tax payable when he took it out, the 401(k) covered a giant chunk of his law school tuition.

Now running a solo law practice in Cincinnati, Ohio, he is not covered by any pension plan. His only retirement income at this point will be social security and, at age 65, a pension of $35 a month from BioScience's defined benefit plan. But with two children aged 10 and 7, who has the time to think about retirement? Though both the Bernards work, he admits wryly that they "live pretty much hand to mouth. We may be able to put something aside in the next couple of years for the kids' college funds." Savings for retirement? Maybe later. Welcome to the 401(k) fan club.

U.S. News & World Report has called them "the most powerful savings tool available."[2] And in theory, they may be. These 401(k) plans and their nonprofit counterparts, 403(b)s, allow people to set aside significant sums in savings and, in many cases, receive matching funds from their employers. The main incentive to use them is that employees get tax breaks for their contributions, that is, their taxable income is reduced by the amounts they put into their 401(k) accounts. If someone earning $40,000 a year could afford to make the maximum contribution allowed by law — $9,240 in 1995 — that person would pay income taxes on only $30,760. Because of this feature, 401(k)s are often called salary reduction plans.[3]

How do 401(k) plans work? Most commonly, companies allow employees to contribute up to a specified percentage of pay. On average, employees contribute 5.5 percent of earnings, with higher-income employees putting in about 2 percent more than the lower-paid.[4] In addition to the tax deferral on contributions, taxes on investment earnings do not have to be paid until the money is taken out of the account.

As with pension plans, companies take a tax deduction for their contributions. Unlike with pension plans, they aren't obligated to put any money in if they don't want to — and many employers don't. If they do put something in, they can match an employee's contribution up to a total of $30,000 a year or 25 percent of pay, whichever is less. Those companies that do contribute generally put in 50 cents for every dollar employees put in, up to 6 percent of salary.[5] Very few provide as generous a contribution as BioScience's two-to-one match.

Employer matches usually do not vest immediately, although employee contributions do. Typically, employees must work for five years before they earn a right to the employer contribution. Often the employer's contribution takes the form of company stock rather than cash.

Employers ordinarily choose which 401(k) investments to offer their employees. Under recent regulations, if employers act prudently in selecting the investments and offer three or more different types of funds, they will not be held responsible if the investments go sour. Many large companies offer a variety of choices. A menu of five or six is common. Honeywell reportedly gives employees participating in its 401(k) plan 14 investment options; the World Wildlife Fund offers 45 choices in its 403(b) plan.

Another attraction of 401(k)s is their portability — a better word might be accessibility. All vested accumulations in these accounts can be transferred into another employer's plan if workers change jobs. Or they can be cashed out. However, unless employees have reached age 59½ or are totally disabled, they must roll the money over into an IRA within 60 days or they will be required to pay a 10 percent penalty plus income tax on the full amount.

Many plans allow people to withdraw all or part of their contributions to a 401(k) while they are still working under the plan to pay certain types of expenses. These may include a mortgage on a first home, a child's college tuition, or emergency medical costs. Again, a penalty is assessed and taxes must be paid on the withdrawals. Some plans also permit employees to borrow against their accounts, something financial planners are increasingly recommending to clients.

All in all, the nuts and bolts of 401(k)s are fairly straightforward and easy to understand, which is one reason employees like them. People also like the clarity of the regular account statements they receive showing how their money is growing. Access to the money before retirement is a major drawing card, and so is the power to direct investments.

For millions of American workers, 401(k)s are replacing traditional pension and profit sharing plans. Although the overall percentage of private sector employees participating in some kind of private retirement plan has remained fairly constant for the past 20 years, the percentage in defined benefit plans declined by 13 percent and the number in non-401(k) defined contribution plans fell by 28 percent between 1984 and 1991.[6] According to Internal Revenue Service statistics, companies dropped more than 34,000 pension and profit sharing plans, covering more than 2 million people, over a two-year period starting in October 1991.[7]

Small businesses in particular have substituted 401(k)s for pension and profit sharing plans.[8] In large companies, the substitution of 401(k)s for pensions has been less evident, since in many cases the old-style pension plans continue to exist alongside the new savings plans. However, companies make no improvements in the old pension plans; they channel all new company retirement contributions into the 401(k) plans as company "matches."

This shift has gone largely unnoticed by employees. Many welcome the simplicity and portability of 401(k)s, in contrast to the abstruse rules and obscure formulas of pension plans in which employees have no say about how their money is invested and, in the case of defined benefit plans, frequently no idea how their benefits are calculated. As Michael Clowes, editor of *Pensions & Investments*, has noted, the defined benefit plan is largely "an invisible benefit" for which employers get little or no credit, since their contributions go largely unremarked by employees. In contrast, employer matches for employees' 401(k) contributions are frequently perceived by workers as magnanimous "free gifts."

Few employees stop to realize that, especially in cases in which the 401(k) has supplanted the defined benefit plan, the "gift" goes to the employer. Employers consider 401(k)s a "cheap treat," far less costly than pension plans.[9] After all, a company has to contribute (if it contributes at all) only for those employees who can afford to pay in first. The employer is also relieved of most of the money management costs and investment risk, and increasingly the day-to-day administrative costs. As Wyatt Asset Management's Lou Valentino told *Pensions & Investments*, "Participants aren't sophisticated enough to really understand the cost shift and are unlikely ever to reach that point."[10]

A 401(k) plan typically costs a company that chooses to match employee contributions about 1 to 2 percent of its total payroll costs, compared with the average 7 percent it costs to fund a defined benefit pension plan.[11] Even when employers contribute nothing to a 401(k), they gain goodwill, since these plans are usually presented to employees as the greatest money-making "opportunity" since the gold rush. In business circles, as *Fortune* magazine has noted, 401(k)s have become the butt of a questionable joke: "What begins with F and ends in K and means screw your employees?"[12]

Drawing by Tom Chalkley.

If 401(k)s are liked by employees and are cheaper for employers, what's the problem? One is that a lot of the money in 401(k)s won't be used for retirement. "As much as 50 percent of the money in retirement plans is not staying there for that purpose," says Theodore Benna, president of the 401(k) Association and the consultant who persuaded the Reagan administration to open the door to tax-deductible 401(k) contributions.[13] When an employee leaves a job, he or she is entitled to receive a lump sum distribution of whatever money has accumulated in the 401(k) account. The employee can ask the plan administrator to roll the money over into an individual retirement account or another retirement plan, or the employee can cash the money out and spend it, paying the penalty and income taxes. The majority follow the cash-out course. As Vicky and Lucian Bernard discovered, the temptation to dip into 401(k) funds and spend them long before retirement is just too great.

Business Week reported that in 1988, a mere 30 percent of 401(k) participants who changed jobs put their money into another retirement plan. The rest used it to buy a house, pay off a mortgage or other loans or debts, or consumed it in some other way. More recent Labor Department statistics suggest that as many as four-fifths of workers under age 55 who take lump sum distributions when they change jobs are cashing out their nest eggs.[14]

To help stem the flow out of these plans, Congress passed a law effective in 1993 requiring companies that give 401(k) money directly to departing employees to withhold 20 percent of it for taxes. There's no withholding if the transfer is made directly to an IRA or to another plan. But penalty or not, "it is the knowledge that you could get the money out if you need it that encourages people to put the money in in the first place," says James Klein, executive director of the Association of Private Pension and Welfare Plans.[15]

The second major flaw of 401(k) plans is that employee-managed investments tend to be too conservative, so that earnings, a critical element of the 401(k) equation, tend to be too conservative to provide retirees with significant income. According to a Hewitt Associates survey of medium and large employers, one-third of all employee 401(k) contributions are invested in guaranteed investment contracts (GICs), which are sold by insurance companies and promise to pay a certain level of interest for a given period of time, much like a certificate of deposit.[16]

Investors tend to like GICs because they are "safe" as compared with more volatile stock investments, but they are by no means "guaranteed" in the sense that many people believe they are. GICs carry no government insurance, and their safety depends entirely on the solvency of the insurance company that sells them. A few years ago, GIC holders lost millions of dollars when Mutual Benefit Life and Executive Life

Insurance Companies collapsed on their junk bond holdings and the state guaranty funds that might have backed them decided that they were not required to insure 401(k) money. The workers took the hit.

All too aware of the risks of Wall Street, and unfamiliar with that world, "most people tend to be too conservative and go into investments that could be outrun by inflation," Merrill Lynch vice president Donald Underwood told *Newsday*.[17] One result is that 401(k)s have rates of return 2 or 3 percentage points below that of defined benefit plans.[18]

After GICs, 401(k) plan assets are most heavily invested in the stock of the companies sponsoring them.[19] Overall, these investment trends can mean an annual return of 2 percent for low-risk investors.[20]

Low returns on 401(k) investments and preretirement cash-outs present serious problems, but by far the most troubling aspect of 401(k)s is that most moderate- and lower-income employees either cannot afford to contribute to these plans at all or put in too little money too late in life to amass significant savings for retirement. The median income of employees given a chance to contribute to 401(k)s is $12,000 a year higher than the income of those not offered participation.[21] Just over one-fourth of private sector workers who earn between $20,000 and $25,000 a year put money into 401(k)s, in contrast with more than three-fifths of those earning over $75,000.[22]

The main reason people don't participate in 401(k) plans, of course, is that they can't afford to. Half of all year-round, full-time workers earn less than $26,701 a year.[23] Even people who sell these plans see this as a big problem. As the director of marketing for Massachusetts Mutual Life Insurance Company told *Pensions & Investments*, "When there is so little money left for a lot of the non-highly compensated employees after paying bills, making savings deferrals to the 401(k) plan can be a hard sell."[24]

Joseph Perkins, an executive at Polaroid, observes, "It doesn't matter how much you educate people about the need to contribute — how guilty you make them feel about not saving — or even how generous the company match is, most folks have to keep up with their payments on their mortgage and car. If they have enough left over after paying for their food, clothes, electricity, and so forth, they'll save for their kids' college education. Once the kids are grown and the mortgage paid off, okay, then they may put money into the 401(k), but by then it's almost too late."

The numbers are tricky when it comes to pinning down how many people actually contribute to 401(k)s. The insurance companies, mutual funds, and consulting firms that sell and service these plans publish surveys showing high participation rates. Many workers in companies offering 401(k)s, however, are not given the opportunity to participate. The tax law's "coverage exclusion" rules give employers a great deal of leeway in designing their plans. As a result, "eligible" workers are often only those whom the employer considers likely to put in some money.

Union workers and those in low-wage jobs may simply be carved out of a plan, significantly narrowing the number of "eligible" employees. Hewitt Associates reports that four-fifths of the 485 companies it surveyed excluded union workers from their 401(k) plans, and nearly a third did not offer these plans to their nonunion hourly employees.[25]

Many surveys, like the Hewitt survey, count as 401(k) participants all employees who have ever contributed, even if they are not currently putting money into the plan.[26] Also, surveys tend to be highly selective. Those by consulting firms may, for example, be limited to their clients.

Although starting early is universally acknowledged as the key to making a 401(k) savings plan work, younger employees have other financial commitments. Those who wait until they're older to contribute aren't going to be able to set aside enough over a sufficient period to make much of a dent in their looming retirement costs.[27] More than half of all participants between the ages of 51 and 60 have account balances of $10,000 or less. *The median account balance for all 401(k) contributors is $5,000.*[28]

Recognizing that higher earners — who don't need tax incentives to encourage them to save — were taking disproportionate advantage of 401(k)s at immense cost to the Treasury,[29] Congress limited the extent to which 401(k)s can skew their benefits. The Tax Reform Act of 1986 more closely tied the amounts company officers and owners can put into these plans to the amounts contributed by other employees. Now the basic requirement is that the average share of income contributed by a plan's highest-paid employees cannot exceed the average share contributed by the other eligible workers by a specified amount, generally by no more than 2 percentage points.

Let's say that a company owner wants to contribute the maximum $9,240 to the company's 401(k) plan on his own behalf, then match that amount on a two-to-one basis in order to reap the full $30,000 of employee plus employer contributions allowed. If the owner is getting a salary of $150,000 a year, that would require him to make a basic contribution of 6 percent of pay. The law says essentially that he and the other company officers can contribute an average of only 2 percentage points above the average percentage of pay put in by all the eligible employees. This means that their average contribution must be at least 4 percent. (This average includes zeros for any eligible employees who do not contribute.)

"The idea was that you wanted a system that assured that the low-income got meaningful retirement benefits," says Harry Conaway, a former Treasury official who helped draft the reform proposals. The linkage of tax benefits for the affluent to those for the less affluent, Conaway explains, "puts a premium on employers' encouraging and selling the plan to the low-paid."[30]

The linkage tests have encouraged employers to implement a variety of creative approaches to educate their employees about the magic of compound interest and tax deferral; it has also prompted most larger employers to add the lure of matching contributions. It has not, however, been notably successful in attracting moderate- and lower-income people into 401(k)s. They are still less concerned about tax breaks than about paying this month's bills. In 1992, as a result of low participation rates, two-thirds of the companies surveyed by Hewitt Associates had to limit contributions from higher-paid employees.[31]

Even those who roundly condemn the "paternalistic and protective policies" of traditional plans and paint glowing pictures of the opportunities for "self-reliance" and "employee self-management" presented by 401(k)s reluctantly concede that the potential of a win-win opportunity afforded by these plans has yet to be widely endorsed by employees.[32]

Were 401(k)s purely extras for the wealthy — icing on the retirement income cake — they wouldn't raise such serious policy questions. But the bottom line of the 401(k) phenomenon is that people are now told to save for themselves what they would have gotten under old-fashioned company-paid plans, and that lower- and moderate-income people simply aren't doing it. In the meantime, billions of dollars of tax revenue are lost to the federal treasury *without* raising the national savings rate.[33]

Advocates of 401(k) plans believe that over time the new savings plans can do the job. A John Hancock Insurance Company report argues that more people would put money into 401(k)s if it were easier to take it out for nonretirement purposes.[34] The Association of Private Pension and Welfare Plans contends that the linkage tests are a problem, discouraging companies from offering 401(k)s. The APPWP is lobbying for legislation that would eliminate those requirements for employers that offered eligible employees a dollar-for-dollar match on contributions up to 3 percent of income and a 50 percent match on additional contributions up to 5 percent of income. It claims that this would encourage more companies to set up 401(k)s and make it possible for more people to contribute.

These approaches "go in exactly the wrong direction," responds Phyllis Borzi, former employee benefits counsel for the House Subcommittee on Labor-Management Relations. "All they would do is provide more tax shelters for those who don't need them — and less money for retirement for rank-and-file workers." She points out that under the APPWP proposal, employers would have no incentive to encourage lower-paid employees to join the plans. In fact, the fewer employees contributing, the less employers would have to match! Even if *no* employees contributed, employers could put in the full amount allowable for themselves. Borzi believes that a more realistic measure would be the one proposed by former Senator John Heinz and Missouri Representative William Clay in their Retirement Income Policy Act of 1985. That proposal would have allowed employers to continue to offer 401(k) plans, but only if they were supplemental to an adequate company-paid retirement plan. Consultant Robert Paul has proposed that rather than allowing employees to contribute to 401(k)s, they be permitted to make tax-deductible payments to defined benefit pension plans.

An efficient way of ensuring that all workers at all income levels profit from 401(k)s would be to permit employees to match the contributions of their employers — in other words, to reverse the current arrangement, which depends on the employee contributing first. Management-level employees with extra money to save would have a strong incentive to convince the employer to make contributions (so that they could get tax breaks on their savings), and this would ensure that all employees would get something from the plan. Vermont Senator (then Representative) James Jeffords initially put forward this "reverse match" concept in 1987. It has been incorporated in proposals by the Profit Sharing Council of America.[35]

To address the problem of cash-outs, the 1993 Congressional Symposium on Women and Retirement recommended locking in all employer contributions to 401(k)s and other plans until the worker is age 59½. This would ensure that the money is there for retirement.

A more draconian approach to all 401(k) problems would be simply to end the deductibility of employee contributions. This concept was twice suggested by the Reagan administration. It is an alternative that could appeal to members of Congress who are troubled by the nation's mounting tax expenditures and escalating retirement income inequality.

Although only 15 percent of the private workforce now has a 401(k) as a sole retirement plan (and another 8 percent has one to supplement a pension plan), the numbers are growing fast.[36] The proliferation of these plans that shift both the cost and the risk of retirement savings from employer to employee is arguably the most important single phenomenon affecting people's retirement since ERISA. It's self-reliance versus paternalism, and the early signs indicate that it's going to be a long, hard winter, even for ants.

What to Do

How to Make the Most of a 401(k)

If you have the chance to participate in a 401(k) and can afford to do so, you should begin contributing as early as possible in your career and try to put something into the plan every year. While estimates vary, experts generally say that people earning $25,000 will need to save almost $250,000 in their 401(k)s to maintain their standard of living in retirement. If your income is $50,000, the amount shoots up to $1 million. What does this mean you should save? A rule of thumb is that if you are 35 years old now, you can probably finance a comfortable retirement if you put away at least 10 percent of your income each year for the rest of your working life. At age 45, you should save 20 percent. If you don't start saving until you're 55, you need to save half of your income.

If your company offers matching contributions and you are financially able, you'll want to get the maximum employer contribution. *Newsday* columnist Jerry Morgan calls matching money "probably the largest return on your investment you will get."

Contributing to your 401(k) is only the first step. You then have to monitor your investments. "Diversify among the choices given," Morgan advises, "taking a little more risk than you normally would, because it can pay huge rewards over time. Check your investments regularly, comparing them with similar ones outside the program. If they are doing well, stick with them. Inertia can work for you as well as against you."

If you think that the investment options selected by your plan trustee aren't as good as they should be, speak up. The trustee may be relying on the advice of a consultant and be unfamiliar with other investments. If you are concerned about possible mismanagement, contact the Labor Department field office nearest you.[37]

Make sure that any projections about likely earnings reflect the returns your investments will actually get *after* investment management and other costs have been subtracted. Projections should be translated into today's dollars, taking into account future inflation rates, then divided by the number of years you expect to live after you stop working. Finally, figure out how much would be left after you pay taxes. Will that amount plus social security, other savings, and any pension be enough to live on?

CHAPTER 15

A Four-Letter Word

Millions of Americans working in small companies without a retirement plan are jeopardizing their future quality of life.

—Patricia Saiki, former administrator, Small Business Administration[1]

Serge Belanger has owned and operated a language school in Washington, D.C., for 27 years. An elegantly dressed man in his mid-fifties, he has never been covered by a pension plan, nor have his employees.

"For me, 'plan' is a four-letter word," he jokes. "Seriously, I've put a little money aside from time to time. I'll have social security and Medicare. I think I'll get by, but of course, if I had to draw on my savings for very long, I suppose they'd run out."

He has considered setting up a pension plan for his school, which employs up to 100 people. All but about six employees are "less than full-time." The school offers a health plan, but "the nature of our business [teachers work sporadically as demand dictates] makes it hard to offer a pension plan. You can't set up a plan for just a few people, and if everybody were covered, it would break the bank."

For Serge Belanger, the traditional incentives for setting up a retirement plan don't work. He is not looking for a "management tool" that will tie employees to his school or ease them out when they become too old. He's not making enough of a profit to be looking for tax breaks for either his business or himself, and although he'd certainly like to be sure that he'll have enough to live on if he ever has to close the school, he's far more concerned about keeping his business going for the next 10 or 15 years than about what might happen after that.

He also doesn't have to provide a pension plan to keep up with his competitors. None of his employees has asked for one. Why should he take on an extra cost when he already has to pay for his employees' social security, workers' compensation, and unemployment compensation and, in addition, has voluntarily undertaken to provide them with a health insurance plan?

Serge Belanger is far from being the only employer without a retirement plan. *More than four-fifths of private employers do not have plans.*[2] Most of these planless firms are very small.[3] The smaller the company, the less likely it is that it will have a plan. For example, only about 15 percent of businesses with 25 or fewer employees have plans, contrasted with 88 percent of companies with 500 or more employees.[4]

In addition to the size of a firm, other predictors of whether a business will have a plan are whether its employees are unionized, how much they are paid, and the type of work they perform. Plans are most common in unionized, high-wage manufacturing companies. Lower-wage, nonunionized firms that provide services rather than produce goods are the least likely to have plans.[5] Also, plans are rare among new businesses with young employees. *Overall, one-third of private sector workers are employed by businesses that have no retirement plan for any of their employees.*[6]

A refrain one hears from business groups is that employers are not setting up pension plans because of the cost and complexity of adapting to new pension rules. Although it is true that the law changes of the 1980s (requiring plans to provide benefits for more people and imposing new funding requirements and restrictions) have spawned extremely complicated new regulations, the burden of complying with these rules ranks near the bottom of the list of reasons businesses give for not establishing plans. Most employers point to economic concerns. In response to a Small Business Administration survey, more than 60 percent of employers cited their own economic concerns as their principal reason for not having plans; only 6 percent cited costly or burdensome regulations.[7]

This makes sense, since there is no need for an employer to deal with complex rules in order to have a retirement plan. Any employer can set up a simple plan called a Simplified Employee Pension (SEP). It involves only a few easy-to-understand rules and no federal filing or reporting requirements. A firm that opts to establish a SEP contributes a uniform percentage of pay to individual retirement accounts for all employees who have worked three or more years.[8] The employer makes the contributions, fills out five blanks on a government form, and gives copies to the employees, along with a statement of how much has been contributed for them.[9] That's all that is required.

ASK THE EXPERTS

Lorraine and Ken Decker are financial planners in Houston, Texas. They spend their lives helping other people plan for retirement. When *Fortune* magazine decided to do a cover story on how much people needed to live on in retirement, the editors went to the Deckers, who profiled eight of their clients. They calculated that 30-year-old Nancy Sims, who earns $30,000 a year at her job as a government relations specialist, would need $1.8 million in retirement savings by age 65, and that Lionel and Katherine Sosa, ages 50 and 35, who earn $165,000 running an ad agency and a public relations firm, would need $7.1 million. These amounts include the lump sum value of their future social security benefits as well as pensions and all savings.[10]

When it came to setting up a retirement plan for themselves and their employees, the Deckers say, that the choice was simple: a SEP. Lorraine Decker reports, "we looked at all the options, and this is what made sense for us. No hassle, just a straightforward arrangement. We and our employees would have pensions at retirement, and our company would get a tax break. It was an ideal starter plan for a small company like ours," she says.

Despite their simplicity, SEPs account for only slightly more than one-fifth of the plans that very small employers now have.[11] In large part, this is because more complicated plans can be tailored to employers' personal and corporate concerns. Complex plans allow employers the flexibility of leaving a significant percentage of their workforce out of their pension and profit sharing plans and to pay much larger benefits to higher-paid and older employees at the expense of others. The rules that draw the lines between what is and is not permitted are convoluted, but they afford substantial dollars-and-cents benefits to company owners and their top officers.

SEP rules do not provide employers with the same leeway in structuring their plans, and they deny employers control over fund money. That is why they are so clear. There is no need for the protections afforded by the complicated rules of other plans.[12]

The Small Business Administration survey went beyond asking employers why they did not have plans and asked what it would take to persuade them to set them up. Not surprisingly, a significant percentage (36.2

percent) said that they would be interested in establishing plans if they had increased profits or greater income stability, or if the economy improved. What was puzzling was that an almost equal number (36.4 percent) said that nothing would induce them to start plans. They simply had "no interest" in them.[13] The survey did not ask why employers had no interest in starting plans. The response might well have been, "Why should I?"

The likelihood is that most employers without plans are unaware of the importance of pensions to their employees or to themselves. Like Serge Belanger, they are so caught up in keeping their businesses going that they don't have time to stop and think about what will happen when they or their employees become too old to work.

A great many employers without plans have no idea that most retirees without pensions live almost entirely on social security payments. They also do not know that those payments average less than the minimum wage.[14] Those who have thought about retirement may rationalize that their employees don't need pension plans because they are free to set up individual retirement accounts.

IRAs were created 20 years ago as part of ERISA, specifically for people working for companies without pension plans. Current law allows employees without plans to deduct contributions of up to $2,000 a year from their income taxes and to delay paying taxes on these amounts—and on investment earnings—until the money is paid out, usually at retirement age. In addition, employees participating in their employers' pension or 401(k) plans can fully deduct their IRA contributions if their incomes are less than $25,000 a year ($40,000 if married). According to a Center on Budget and Policy Priorities estimate, 70 percent of taxpayers are eligible to contribute to deductible IRAs.[15] However, fewer than 5 percent of those eligible actually do.[16]

The law also permits employees who are members of other retirement plans and have earnings above the income limits to contribute to IRAs, and more than 3 percent of taxpayers in this group do. Although they cannot deduct their contributions, they can defer taxes on their investment earnings—an attractive tax break.

All told, 7 percent of workers put money into IRAs. *Nearly three-fifths of IRA contributors also participate in their employers' plans.*[17] They are also financially better off than those without IRAs, with a median income of between $30,000 and $40,000 a year.[18] Those employees who have IRAs in addition to other retirement plans report incomes of almost three times the incomes of people who have no plans.[19] As in the case of 401(k) participants, most IRA contributors are getting tax breaks for money they would have saved in other forms, at a cost to all taxpayers of more than $8 billion this year.[20]

Another common assumption is that workers without pension plans will have acquired substantial amounts of money by retirement age from other sources. This may be true for those people lucky enough to inherit wealth or own a house they are willing (and able) to convert to cash. However, that group generally consists of higher-earning, college-educated employees who are very likely already covered by retirement plans. Half of all households with at least one member age 65 to 74 have less than $9,700 in personal savings other than their homes and cars.[21]

One of the reasons so many employers are unaware of the importance of pensions is that the media often convey the impression that rather than being in need of additional income, older Americans are too well off. This image comes from two sources. The first are studies emphasizing the wealth of the elderly. Statistics show that half of the age 65 to 74 population have more than $81,500 in total assets.[22] But a large portion of that wealth is in the form of the houses the elderly live in and the cars they drive, not income-producing assets. Also, the studies emphasize household wealth, combining the wealth of couples, and overlook the nearly half of the 65 to 74-year-old group who are not married. The median total wealth of those retirees is only $42,000, with only $8,700 of that amount representing nonhousing worth. Half of the retirees in this group have yearly incomes of under $11,700 a year.[23]

The second statistic relied on by the media to paint glowing pictures of the golden years is the fact that over 87 percent of the elderly live above the government's official "poverty level."[24] That makes it seem as if they have enough money to pay their bills for food, gas, electricity, transportation, housing, and medical expenses not covered by Medicare. Far from it. The poverty level for an older person in 1993 was $6,930. For a couple it was $8,740.[25] The poverty level is arrived at by estimating what it costs to provide a minimally adequate diet for a healthy person over age 65 and multiplying by three. Since older people are assumed to eat less than younger people, their poverty level is lower than that for the under age 65 population. However, most experts believe that the elderly need an income equal to twice the poverty level to avoid being "economically vulnerable."[26]

Another fact that employers without plans may not know is that they and their employees are paying for the pensions of others. Everyone pays for pensions as *consumers* of goods and services. The firms that have plans pass pension costs, along with other labor costs, on to consumers. A Bureau of Labor Statistics survey shows that in 1993, 2.9 percent of the total labor costs of American businesses went to pensions and savings plans.[27]

People without pension plans also pay as *taxpayers*. When one group in the country gets a tax break, everyone pays for it. Another way that people without plans "pay" for others' pensions is as *retirees*. Everyone's social security benefits are smaller because of the existence of company and union plans. If the United States did not have a private sector system that paid off so well, especially to those in leadership positions with influence on social policy issues, this country, like others, would have a far more adequate social security program for everyone.

Those well served by the private system have strong incentives to keep the program at its current low levels. Were social security payments to be raised to provide more realistic payments to average workers, there would be little justification for continuing tax-favored treatment for plans providing very large benefits to high earners.

* * *

The two key characteristics of our private system are (1) that plans are tied to employers, and (2) that they are completely voluntary. Are there ways within this system of encouraging more employers to have plans?

Since plans are currently sold to employers by appealing to their self-interest, most proposals have sought to make plans more attractive to them. For example, several years ago Arkansas Senator David Pryor floated the concept of tax credits for small businesses that set up new plans. The notion was that although a tax deduction might not be of much interest to a small company with limited profits, an additional tax credit could be of great interest. Unfortunately, to avoid penalizing company owners who had already done the right thing by setting up plans, the tax credits would have to be available to all small businesses, making the proposal a very costly proposition at a time of great concern about the federal budget deficit.

The Pryor proposal was aimed at employers' corporate interests. Other suggestions have been geared to appeal to the personal interests of company owners and officers. One proposal, put forward by the New York State Bar Association's Employee Benefits Committee, would lift any restrictions on benefits of plan officials if the plan provided minimum benefits — 2 to 3 percent of pay — to other employees. Above the minimum, there would be no vesting, integration, or backloading rules. Within certain limits, the employer would have complete flexibility as to the design of the plan.[28]

In 1991, the Bush administration came up with a variation on this approach. Instead of applying it to pension plans, the proposal involved allowing small employers to contribute the minimum benefit to a savings plan. Called POWER (short for Pension Opportunities for Workers' Expanded Retirement), the measure would have changed the rules for salary reduction SEPs (SAR-SEPs), which are mini-401(k) plans with their own rules. A for-profit employer with fewer than 25 employees can have a SAR-SEP if half of all eligible employees contribute their own money to the plan. The amounts that company owners and officers are allowed to contribute to these plans cannot be more than 125 percent of the average percentage of pay contributed by all the other eligible employees (including those who don't contribute), and no more than the limit for tax-deferred employee contributions — $9,240. POWER would have expanded SAR-SEP eligibility to companies with 100 employees and ended both the requirement that half the employees contribute and the tie-in between the amounts put in by high-paid and low-paid employees, if the company contributed at least 2 percent of pay for all the non-highly paid.

The proposal was criticized by employer advocates, who claimed that no small businesses would use the new plans — the minimum benefit was too high — and by employee advocates, who asserted that the minimum was too low and that it would encourage even more companies to abandon existing pension plans in favor of savings plans.

A different kind of approach was developed by Senator James Jeffords in his 1987 Pension Portability Act. He proposed the creation of portable pension plans similar to SEPs but paying lifetime monthly benefits. The Jeffords proposal went nowhere, largely because mutual funds and other financial institutions, such as life insurance companies, that now market pensions and savings arrangements have little to gain in promoting such simple plans, since they compete with plans that are more complicated and, therefore, more profitable.

No voluntary approach will ensure that every employer will have a plan, but remarkably little has been done so far to see how educational efforts could expand pension coverage. One effective way to educate employers about the importance of pensions, and to alert them to the availability of simple plans, would be for Congress to authorize the sale of U.S. retirement plan bonds to small companies interested in establishing new Savings Bond SEPs. The Treasury could then promote these plans as part of its very successful savings bond marketing efforts.

The only government effort to date to educate employers about SEPs produced an astonishing response. Frank Swain, the Small Business Administration's chief counsel for advocacy during the Reagan administration, told a pension industry group that the demand for a SBA booklet about SEPs was greater than that for any publication in the history of the Small Business Administration. Would Serge Belanger set up a pension plan if there were an all-out campaign directed at encouraging him to do so? "Possibly," he says.

What to Do

HOW TO CONVINCE YOUR EMPLOYER
TO SET UP A PENSION PLAN

Many employees have found that the most effective way of persuading their employers to set up a pension plan is to give them information about SEPs. You may want to let your boss know that SEPs do not require government reporting, and allow companies the leeway to contribute only in those years when they can afford to. Also, you can point out that setting up the simplest SEP, the IRS Model SEP, only involves five easy steps:

Step 1 requires calling the Internal Revenue Service and asking for Form 5305-SEP, the form for the IRS Model SEP.

Step 2 is figuring out what percentage of pay to contribute. The same percentage must be contributed for all employees up to 15 percent of payroll, or $22,500, whichever is less.

Step 3 is selecting which employees to include. Employers are required to include only employees over age 21 who have worked three out of the preceding five years and earn more than a specified amount ($400 in 1995), but many include employees who have worked shorter periods.

Step 4 is filling out the five blank spaces on Form 5305-SEP and giving copies of the form (which includes questions and answers about SEPs) to each employee, together with a statement of the amounts contributed for that employee.

Step 5 is deciding where to invest the SEP contributions and then mailing the check or checks. SEP money can be invested in any financial institution that offers individual retirement accounts. The employer can choose the institution or ask each employee where he or she would like the money to be invested.

That is all that is required. The employer gets a tax deduction for the amounts contributed, and the employees do not pay taxes on the money until it is withdrawn, usually at age 59½ (earlier withdrawals result in a 10 percent penalty tax plus income tax) or in the case of disability or death. The financial institution reports to the employee and the government, and the employee can change where the money is invested.

Profit and nonprofit employers of any size and self-employed persons can set up an IRS Model SEP.

PART V

WHAT IS TO BE DONE?

No More Fiddling

"We've been fiddling with the system and fiddling with it for years," says Paul Edwards. "We need people to say it's a mess, there's no way this system is going to work, and it should not be supported." The burly former factory worker from Springfield, Massachusetts, now in his mid-fifties, is a passionate advocate of overhauling the private pension system. He is also an example of the way that an outraged sense of justice can change lives.

Paul Edwards had given little thought to pensions before he ran into Ed Johnston at a meeting of the Gray Panthers in late 1975. He heard Johnston describe how he and other workers at the Perkins Machine and Gear Company in West Springfield had seen their pensions go down the drain when their company and its underfunded plan closed in 1972. They lost again in 1974 when Congress failed to make any provision in ERISA for those whose pensions had been lost before the new law was enacted.

Edwards was shocked. At the time, he was a skilled machine tool operator making diesel engine parts for American Bosch. His own pension was secure, he thought, but he joined Ed Johnston and other retirees from around the country to fight for legislation to restore their pensions. The two of them formed the grassroots Pension Losers' Committee.

Edwards grew to admire his new friend tremendously. Johnston had served as an army artillery sergeant in World War II and as president of his union local at Perkins. He was smart, proud, and witty. Seeing such a man, then in his late sixties, working as a janitor outraged Edwards. Still, he had no idea what his friend's pension loss had really cost until he dropped by Johnston's house one day and found him hunting through a shoe box for loose change. He was trying to see whether he'd saved enough quarters to buy the eyeglasses he urgently needed. It was a scene Paul Edwards was never to forget.

Then in 1986, Edwards became a pension loser too. American Bosch had been sold to United Technologies, which decided to close the 75-year-old Springfield plant. "They shipped most of our work overseas, with the balance placed in a brand new plant in a low-wage environment," says Edwards. "I was among 1,200 workers and supervisors who hit the street." Paul thought he could handle this plant closing, his third. He and a hundred others were not prepared for what happened next. They were informed that in the event of a plant closing, a provision in the plan promised pension benefits to all workers who were age 50 with 25 years of service. He was 48 and had 24½ years — two years short of getting the pension he'd worked for.

Unlike Ed Johnston, Paul Edwards didn't lose his entire pension, and his loss didn't plunge him into poverty. He will get a monthly check of $400 if he waits until the year 2003 to collect his benefit. Between his social security and the state pension earned by his wife, Maria, a social worker, they will get by. But the loss hurt badly. He estimates that he's lost $80,000 in benefits and that by the time he finally collects his pension, it will have been reduced by inflation to about a third of its original value. "It's a giant ripoff for the American worker. The companies lead you on for their own purposes — letting you think you'll win big if you stay with them. Then it's 'Oh sorry, you lose, better luck next time.' That's wrong. Besides, for most there is no next time."

Millions of workers "aren't even in the running" for a pension, Edwards emphasizes, "since there is no pension structure on site for them to plug into." They will get nothing from the "trickle-down" voluntary system, which allows employers to skew pension benefits for their own profit as a way of inducing them to offer plans that might benefit others as well. "It doesn't work," Edwards says. Since his plant closed, he has held a number of jobs in small companies, none of which offered him a pension. Why? It's simple. They didn't have to and, in fact, might have been at a competitive disadvantage had they done so.

"The problem with the current pension system," Edwards says, "is that the employer is the gatekeeper. That just doesn't make sense. These plans are this country's substitute for decent social security benefits. Most employers are not offering pensions, and the ones who do often cancel or retract or tear them into pieces. And everyone is paying for all those tax breaks, including the poor suckers who can't even get a piece of the action!"

Now chair of the Citizens' Commission on Pension Policy, a grassroots activist group formed in 1978, Paul Edwards is convinced that the country needs a completely new private pension system — a universal system in which all workers have part of their paychecks put aside for the day when they are too old to work. A lot of people agree with him. Others believe that the voluntary private pension system can be changed and made to work. Still others want to throw out pensions altogether and pay for old age through an expanded social security system.

Voluntary or mandatory? Public or private? What are the alternatives? What do we do now?

Drawing by Bill Greaney. Reprinted courtesy of the Citizens' Commission on Pension Policy.

CHAPTER 16

Making the Old
Way Work

*For too long policymakers have been content to just try to
plaster over the cracks in the walls in the private pension
system. That no longer makes sense.*

—Citizens' Commission on Pension Policy[1]

Senator Howard Metzenbaum came to Congress in 1974, the same year
that ERISA was passed. The new pension law had taken seven years to
hammer out. "At the time, we thought we had reformed the private
pension system."

In fact, the reform process had just begun. Over the next two
decades, Senator Metzenbaum, who became chairman of the Senate
Labor Subcommittee, played a pivotal role in getting reforms that filled
loopholes in ERISA through Congress. But even that didn't do it.
Today, 20 years later, complaints are still pouring in from both individuals disappointed by their plans and business owners disgruntled by the
frequent changes in the laws and the complexity of pension rules. "The
system," he has concluded, "is still failing too many people."

Senator Metzenbaum retired from Congress in 1994, but not
before leaving a final legacy to American workers: a blueprint for
comprehensive reform of the private pension system. The Pension Bill
of Rights of 1994 aims at improving pensions within the existing
employer-based voluntary private system. Although some of its provisions
are contained in other legislation pending in Congress, Senator
Metzenbaum's is the only bill to propose total reform of all aspects
of private plans — except their voluntary nature. Employers would
continue to determine the type of plans they offer and the amount of

benefits they pay. They would retain control over plan investments. The difference would be that almost everyone who worked under a plan would be a winner.

At the heart of this proposed legislation are simple concepts of fair play: that people should be able to understand pension rules, earn benefits fairly, have a say in how their money is invested, receive the help they need to enforce their rights, and be compensated for any wrongs they suffer. The bill consists of ten basic rights:

1. Employees have the right to be included in a pension plan sponsored by their employer.
2. Employees have the right to fair treatment in earning retirement benefits.
3. Employees have the right to timely, accurate, and understandable information about their pension and welfare benefits.
4. Employees have the right to receive information about and have a voice in the investment of pension plan assets.
5. Employees have the right to an adequately funded pension plan with investments that promote their long-term economic security.
6. Employees have the right to government assistance to protect their pension rights.
7. Employees have the right to effective judicial enforcement of their pension rights.
8. Widowed and divorced spouses have the right to equitable treatment.
9. Employees have the right to pension portability.
10. Employees have the right to be protected against fraud and mismanagement of their pension money.

The bill challenges a number of the basic principles on which private pension plans have traditionally operated. For example, reforms enforcing the first two rights would make it unlawful for employers to exclude workers from their plans arbitrarily or to provide benefits or contributions favoring higher-income and older employees. These measures challenge the long-standing assumption that employers won't set up plans if they can't use them for their personal or corporate purposes.

The Pension Bill of Rights also rejects the notion that it is permissible for company owners to make plan contributions only for those employees who can already afford to save for themselves. Instead, it stipulates that if employers contribute first, employees who are able to do so can match their companies' contributions.

The bill challenges the concept that workers should have no say in where their pension money is invested or how stock held by the plan is voted. The proposed legislation would require plans to establish pension advisory committees to involve workers and retirees in plan investment decisions and to inform them of how stocks held by their plans are voted.

Opponents of pension reform always issue the warning that "if you tinker with the system, employers will bail out." But Senator Metzenbaum does not believe that this will happen. "If you design a system that is understandable and fair to all, people will ultimately accept that system."

As minority counsel for pensions of the Senate Labor Sub-committee, Michael Gordon was present when ERISA was born. He was one of the people directly responsible for the landmark legislation. Now an attorney in private practice in Washington, Gordon looks at the changes in the nation's economy over the past 20 years and concludes that "an employment-based system may no longer be the best way to deliver the goods." Even if we maintain a voluntary system, which he favors, he has come to believe that we need a more radical restructuring than even the reforms Senator Metzenbaum has proposed.

"Traditional employment ties have become looser for greater portions of the workforce," Gordon points out. There are more part-time, intermittent, and self-employed workers than ever before. More businesses contract out for employees. Most job opportunities are now in small business, which has always had difficulty providing pensions. Automation and computer technology have made many workers' skills obsolete. Job changing is a fact of life for most workers, and changing jobs means losing pension credits.[2]

However, although fewer people stay with the same company for a lifetime, most work at the same occupation most of their lives. For that reason, Gordon has been exploring the concept of *occupation-based* pension plans. All employers in a particular field — construction, electronics, transportation, and so on — would contribute to a single pension fund. Funds could be organized as either defined contribution or defined benefit plans, with contributions from both employers and employees. Job changers, at least within the same occupation, would not be penalized.

Models already exist. One is the plan set up by Andrew Carnegie in 1905 for college professors. The Teachers Insurance Annuity Association–College Retirement Equities Fund (TIAA-CREF) is the largest of all private pension plans. Colleges and universities throughout the country make contributions to TIAA-CREF for their professors and other employees, who may also contribute to the plan. Professors retain their plan membership when they change jobs so long as they continue to work for a college or university contributing to the plan. TIAA-CREF is a defined contribution pension plan. The amounts accumulated in an individual's account are converted to an annuity paid out in lifetime monthly benefits at retirement.

The National Rural Electric Cooperative Association also has an industrywide plan for its members. Efforts have been made by engineers and nurses to set up nationwide pension funds in their professions, but so far, employers have not responded.

Multiemployer plans are also occupationally based but are usually limited to one craft or trade — bricklayers or pipefitters, for example — rather than the broad range of construction workers. They are also confined to one geographic area and to members of a particular union. Attempts at arranging reciprocity agreements between multiemployer plans in different regions of the country have not always been successful, primarily because they conflict with a local union's interest in retaining its membership.

Occupation-based pensions supplement the government's social security program in France. Employers and employees both contribute to pension plans called *caisses*. There is a *caisse* for workers in the service and trade industry, another for government employees, and a third for farmers who are not self-employed. Self-employed persons have their own *caisses*, one each for farmers, tradespeople and industrialists, craftspeople, and professionals. The French approach, however, differs from Michael Gordon's proposal and from current U.S. occupation-based plans in two key respects. First, the *caisses* are not advance funded but operate on a pay-as-you-go basis. Second, the French pension system is a compulsory scheme, which Gordon generally does not support.[3] Looking back at the early 1970s when ERISA was passed, Gordon says, "We have to create a retirement system for a world that looks entirely different. I think we have to break the 'employer nexus' for a pension and replace it with an 'occupational nexus.' "

Gordon's plan would go a long way toward solving the problem of pension portability: workers would take their pension credits with them when they changed jobs within an occupation. Extend that notion a little farther, and you reach another concept: the creation of *private competitive retirement funds* available to all employees.

Michigan Senator Philip Hart put such a proposal before Congress back in 1973. His Retirement Benefit Fund Act of 1973[4] was based on ideas outlined by consumer advocate Ralph Nader in a speech to a pension industry conference. Hart and Nader envisioned a restructured private pension system managed by competitive private financial institutions committed exclusively to the investment of pension money and the payment of pension benefits. They would be federally licensed, regulated, and insured. Employees, rather than employers, would choose where they wanted their pension contributions invested. Each worker would be limited to participation in one fund at a time; all contributions from all jobs would go to this fund, whether made by the employer or by the worker. Fund participants would have the right to vote for the directors of their funds and to express their preferences on investment policies and proxy votes. If they became dissatisfied with their funds' investment practices or performance, they would have the right to transfer to other funds.[5]

Ralph Nader notes now that "a lot of people thought the Hart bill made a lot of sense — it was just ahead of its time. Actually, the bill has aged well. It could be readily updated to reflect concepts developed in recent years."

All these proposals could significantly expand pension coverage while keeping the system voluntary. For example, both Senator Metzenbaum's Pension Bill of Rights Act and the occupational funds envisioned by Michael Gordon would greatly simplify plans, thereby reducing administrative costs and making them more attractive to employers. Plans that were fairer and more understandable would also be more attractive to employees.

The retirement funds contemplated by the Hart bill would have an institutional interest in selling pensions. They could significantly increase the popularity of plans by marketing the notions that every worker needs more than social security for retirement and that pension savings can help the economy by spurring new jobs, community revitalization, and long-term economic growth. As another "carrot," these retirement funds could be structured to permit participating employers to receive preferential treatment for loans.

Legislation setting up the retirement funds might follow the "reverse match" concept, allowing employees to contribute only if their employers contributed first, thus encouraging upper-management employees with clout to pressure their employers to contribute. Provision could also be made for employers to make pension contributions for their household workers.

But nobody contends, not even the strongest advocates of voluntarism, that a voluntary program will ever be able to ensure that *all* workers will receive pensions. There will always be employers (and employees) who believe that they cannot afford to put money aside today for what seems to be a far distant retirement. For that reason, there is a growing sense within the pension world that the United States will eventually have to follow the lead of its principal global competitors and adopt a compulsory scheme.

What would a mandatory pension system look like?

CHAPTER 17

New Directions

> *The Congress hereby finds and declares that . . . the older*
> *people of our Nation are entitled to . . . [an] adequate*
> *income in retirement in accordance with the American*
> *standard of living.*

—Older Americans Act of 1965[1]

Teresa Ghilarducci was still in high school when Congress battled over
and finally enacted ERISA. Pensions couldn't have been further from
her mind. Today, a slight, dark-haired woman of great energy, whose
own retirement is still many years away, she thinks about pensions
virtually every day. "You can't live in South Bend and not think about
pensions," she notes wryly.

Professor Ghilarducci teaches economics at the University of
Notre Dame, not far from the empty lot where the Studebaker plant used
to be. Coincidentally or not, she has become an expert on the economics
and politics of private pensions. She lectures extensively and has published a book on the subject.[2] Her conclusion after years of study?
"Changing the system we've got is not enough. If the money's going to be
there for everyone, in the long run, pensions should be mandatory."

Ghilarducci recommends gradually eliminating employer-based
pension plans and replacing them with a universal pension scheme.
Boards of trustees, including employee representatives, would invest the
funds, steering investments toward employment-generating activities.

Mandatory contributions to a universal pension system is by no
means a new proposal. Donald Grubbs and Robert Paul, two of the
nation's most prominent pension consultants, have been urging adoption of a minimum universal pension system (MUPS) since the early

1970s, several years before ERISA. They are credited with convincing the President's Commission on Pension Policy to recommend a MUPS approach in 1981.[3] The proposal by the President's Commission contains the prototype of a mandatory pension system. Every employer would contribute a minimum of 3 percent of payroll to a pension plan. Every employee over age 25 with one year of service and 1,000 hours of employment would participate. Vesting would be immediate, and benefits could not be integrated with social security.

The Commission proposed a special MUPS tax credit for small businesses equal to 46 percent of their contributions (up to 3 percent of payroll). Company plans would be managed through pension trusts, insurance companies, or other financial institutions. Employers that did not wish to administer their own plans could send their contributions to a clearinghouse under the Social Security Administration with authority to invest funds in private capital markets. Investments would be administered by an independent board of trustees appointed by the president.[4]

The Commission's report failed to engender a national pension policy debate — at least in part because of the change in administrations in 1981. Then in 1992, Senators Brock Adams and Howard Metzenbaum reintroduced the subject with their Private Pension Reform Act — Retirement 2000,[5] which called for a mandatory universal pension system to be phased in by the year 2000. Employers would be required to make 3 percent tax-deductible contributions for their employees to either "portable pension accounts" in their own company plans or accounts with financial institutions such as mutual funds, banks, life insurance companies, or credit unions. The bill incorporated recommendations made by the Institute of Electrical and Electronics Engineers and was endorsed by the Older Women's League and the Citizens' Commission on Pension Policy.

How big a pension would a 3 percent MUPS provide? Let's take someone earning $25,000 a year. Assume that the person's employer contributed 3 percent of pay over 40 years (costing the employer $750 a year). How much would that person receive in lifetime yearly payments at age 65? To figure it out, make the following assumptions: no inflation, so interest rates reflect a real rate of return on investments; a rate of return on investments of 4 percent; an increase in real wages of 2 percent a year; and a life expectancy of 20 years at age 65. Under those assumptions, that person's lifetime yearly pension would be less than 14 percent of what the worker was earning the last year before retirement.

If social security payments amounted to 40 percent of earnings, or $10,000, the worker's total retirement income based on a minimum pension *and* social security would be $13,250 a year, or 53 percent of preretirement earnings. According to experts, this person would need almost 30 percent more to live modestly in retirement. It is for this reason that critics have claimed that a 3 percent MUPS is not enough.

In 1991, Representative Sam Gibbons proposed a higher minimum contribution — 6 percent — if a voluntary pension system finally proved ineffective. The Pension Coverage and Portability Improvement Act of 1991[6] would have required employers to set up savings plans to which employees could contribute up to 25 percent of pay or $30,000, whichever was less. After five years, if fewer than 75 percent of all private sector workers were participating in this retirement savings scheme, the legislation would have begun phasing in a compulsory 6 percent contribution.

Neither the Gibbons bill nor Retirement 2000 got anywhere in Congress. Yet the idea of a mandatory universal pension system has begun to attract support, not only among workers and those who represent their interests but also in the business community. A growing number of employers recognize the advantages of leveling the playing field so that pension contributions become a way of doing business rather than an optional "extra" expense. Even some conservative economists are recognizing that the notion that everybody will save enough for retirement if offered tax inducements to do so is pie in the sky.

The immediate questions raised by proposals for mandatory universal pensions have to do with their cost. How can employers pay for them? How can the Treasury make up the revenue loss?

As an added business expense, the cost of pensions can be paid by passing it on to consumers through higher prices, or by taking it out of existing profits. A third and likelier option is for the employer to pay for pensions out of the company's existing budget, which is primarily the payroll. Should that option be taken, many fear that it will lead to layoffs.

There are several responses to the job concern. First, unlike other mandatory benefits such as workers' compensation, unemployment taxes, the minimum wage, or social security, compulsory pensions would create investment capital that in turn could create new jobs. This would be especially likely to happen if workers are given a say in how their pension money is invested.

Second, rather than simply increasing an employer's costs, new pension benefits could be paid for by reducing the amount of future wage increases. Since more than half the workforce would be affected as new recipients of pension contributions, a curb on wage increases for that many people could hold down increases in the prices of goods and services, leaving workers no worse off financially.

Finally, requiring all employers to provide pensions would correct the inequity between employers that are "doing the right thing" by providing retirement benefits and others that unfairly avoid the cost.

Ultimately, the argument comes back to the fact that everyone will need more than social security to live on in retirement. A straightforward system in which all employers automatically take part of all their employees' paychecks and put that amount aside for them may be the most efficient way of making sure that "something more" is there when they retire.

What about costs to the Treasury? Professor John Guarrera, an engineer and vice chair of the Citizens' Commission, estimates that if every company in the country were to get a tax deduction (or credit) for making a 3 percent pension contribution for all employees, the cost to the Treasury would be about $9.2 billion a year.[7] How could Congress make up the loss?

One controversial answer is to end tax breaks for pension contributions above the minimum. For example, if only the first 3 percent of pay were deductible but an employer contributed 8 percent, either the employer or the employee would be taxed on the 5 percentage point difference. Investment earnings on the additional contributions would also be taxable each year instead of when paid out in retirement. Variations of this kind of system are in effect in Australia and Sweden.

A second approach to the revenue concern is to impose a small tax on all the money in pension funds. Guarrera points out that a yearly tax of one-half of 1 percent assessed on the current $3 trillion in private pension funds would offset the revenue loss from universal coverage. In fact, the tax revenue might actually increase, since the total amount of pension savings would go up so dramatically under a mandatory system. A small tax on pension funds might mean that investment earnings were slightly less and that the benefits they paid were reduced by a small amount. But the offsetting advantage would be that every employee in the private sector was earning a pension.

Most mandatory pension proposals call for a new minimum system to be established on top of the existing social security system. A proposal put forward recently by the American Society of Pension Actuaries (ASPA) would redesign pensions *and* social security as well.[8] Under the ASPA proposal, all full-career workers would get the same dollar amount in social security benefits, as they do in Great Britain and

Canada. The amount would be equal to the poverty income level for an elderly person. This new social security system would be financed by taxpayers through general income tax revenues instead of by employer payroll taxes.

The new plan would also call for tax-sheltered 401(k) savings plans to be available to all workers age 40 and older. People over 40 would be encouraged to save 4 percent of that part of their earnings each year that exceeds the poverty level; those over 50 would be encouraged to save larger amounts. This staggered approach takes into account the fact that most people don't — or can't — do much about retirement saving before age 40. Employers would be allowed to match employee contributions up to certain limits. People who are unable or unwilling to take advantage of savings plans would be encouraged to continue to work if they are able.

The restructured social security and savings plans proposed by ASPA would play a role secondary to that of a redesigned private pension system. Employers, except for new and very small businesses, would be required to contribute to minimum mandatory pension plans for all employees who work more than half-time, and permitted to supplement those benefits with more generous *voluntary* plans.[9] Minimum contributions would be immediately vested and adjusted for inflation both after retirement and, if employees change jobs, between their leaving a defined benefit plan and retirement. Benefits, paid out over a retiree's lifetime, would not be integrated with social security. Survivor's benefits would not be automatic but could be chosen by workers.

Since all these sources together — minimum pension, social security, savings, and work — would still not give everyone a retirement income equal to what ASPA calls a "national retirement policy goal," employers would be given incentives to offer additional voluntary pension plans.

What would be the incentives? First, the government would relax certain rules, such as those limiting the amount of pay that can be taken into account in calculating benefits. Second, only those employers that structured their plans to meet the national goal would be allowed to take tax deductions for all their pension contributions. Third, small businesses that set up plans would get a one-time 14 percent tax credit.

These incentives reflect ASPA's view that it may be necessary to give a good deal to business owners and executives to get a good deal for rank-and-file Americans.[10] How good a deal? ASPA's new voluntary pension plans would include virtually every worker over age 21 who works in the same line of business. Vesting would be reduced to three years, and workers could not cash out pension money before early retirement age. All pension benefits would be adjusted for inflation both before and after retirement, and employees would have the chance to trade in their fixed benefit for an indexed benefit. "It would help employees to recognize the value of their pension for what it is," says actuary Ed Burrows. "It's often not what they think."

Less satisfactorily, the new pension plans would also be integrated with social security to a greater degree than is now permitted and could skew benefits more toward older employees.

At the heart of the ASPA proposal is the notion that any new pension system should have as its goal the replacement of a certain percentage of a retiree's earnings rather than merely meeting basic expenses equally for everyone. For example, most pension consultants estimate that lower-income people need between 85 and 90 percent of what they were earning before retirement, and higher earners need between 60 and 70 percent to live as they lived before. (A somewhat lower cost of living for everyone is anticipated after retirement because taxes are generally reduced, and less money is needed for work-related expenses such as transportation and clothing. Medical expenses, however, are likely to be higher.)

Income replacement is a concept that has long been accepted in this country — and is reflected in the private pension system. However, it is the subject of increasing scrutiny. People are asking why a tax-supported private system should assure someone earning $100,000 a year $70,000 in retirement? Why shouldn't high earners be expected to replace income above a certain level without government help?

An alternative approach would be to support a social security and pension system that provides income necessary for basic expenses. Anything above that level would be financed without direct or indirect government support. The retirement policy goal would be to ensure a specific dollar amount to all full-career workers no longer able to work because of their age.

What should that level be? In 1981, the White House Conference on Aging recommended using the intermediate budget for retired couples as a benchmark for measuring income adequacy for the elderly. Developed by the Bureau of Labor Statistics, the retired couples' budgets measured the amounts needed by older couples to buy "market baskets" of goods and services in various cities around the country. The baskets were not overflowing. The intermediate budget provided a retired couple with enough money for one and three-quarters eggs a day, two bottles of beer a week, and eight movies a year.[11] For a couple living in a city, the money amounted to $10,226 in 1981. In 1994 dollars, this would have been $15,866.[12]

A grassroots group called the Committee for a National Pension Plan, working out of Las Vegas, Nevada, has put forward a proposal for a mandatory pension system and restructured social security. This plan would merge the current private pension and social security systems into a single government program. Everyone over age 59 who is completely retired would receive an amount equal to the national average wage. This benefit would go to homemakers as well as people who worked outside the home. The new system would be financed by a national sales tax on all products and services.

The engine behind the National Pension Plan is 78-year-old Peter Montagnoli, retired painter and former GI. Montagnoli retired in 1969 after he was injured on the job and denied a pension. Since then, with his wife Blanche, he fires off newsletters to pension activists around the country, many of whom are buddies from the Blue Devils, his World War II 88th Infantry Division, who served with Montagnoli in Italy. Their stories of pension loss are ammunition for his frequent radio talk show appearances and newspaper interviews.

He recalls that when he went to Washington in 1980 to testify before the President's Commission on Pension Policy, "there was a whole lot I didn't know about pensions. But there was a lot they didn't know too." His sales tax idea seemed "radical" at the time, he says, though it is quite similar to the value-added tax in place in most European countries. Now people who once rejected the concept as "socialism" are beginning to give it a second look.

A footnote: Although Peter Montagnoli's advocacy efforts have not yet persuaded the country to adopt his National Pension Plan, they have paid off in another way. In the spring of 1994, *25 years after his pension had been denied,* he received a check for $1,800 in back pension payments. Now he is receiving $39 every month. He estimates that he is still due about $100,000 in back payments, but, he says, "at least it's a start."

The problematic state of the pension system has led a number of people to conclude that the way to go is to scrap private plans and expand the social security system. Social security is considered by many — expert and ordinary citizen alike — to be the country's most successful social program, in terms of both efficiency and customer satisfaction. In more than half a century of operation, it has never missed a payment. The program paid $302.4 billion in benefits to 42.2 million people in 1993, with an administrative cost of only 1 percent.[13]

A supporter of expanding social security is University of Michigan professor Howard Young, who was actuary for the United Auto Workers Union. These auto-industry plans became models for private plans around the country. Based on a lifetime of work with private pension plans, Young has come to the conclusion that they leave too many people out and are plagued with too many problems involving coverage, vesting, and portability. He also laments the potential for "unfair plan provisions, shoddy administrative practices, inadequate financing, and other abuses."

An expanded social security system would be essentially free of the pension system's management problems and would provide nearly universal coverage, immediate vesting, and full portability. It would pay out defined benefits indexed for wage changes and inflation both before and after retirement. The system would cost employers no more than a private sector MUPS and relieve them of the administrative and regulatory burdens imposed by private plans.

But expanding social security would have its drawbacks. One would be loss of investment capital if the pay-as-you-go structure of social security were used to cover benefits formerly provided by private pension plans. If an advance-funded second tier of social security were adopted instead, as is more likely, economists and others fear the results of too much government-directed investment in the stock and bond markets.

One way to address these problems is simply to take the money targeted for benefits over and above what the social security system now pays and invest it in the private sector. The new funds, Professor Young suggests, could go to investments that are explicitly related to economic growth: postsecondary education for all adults, infrastructure, public-private consortia, and the like.

But how sound is social security? In their 1994 report, the program's trustees warned that social security may run out of money by 2025, the year the last of the baby boomers turn 65. Would putting our eggs in that basket prove just as risky?

Robert Ball, a former social security commissioner and the country's foremost expert on the system, agrees that increased life spans and lower birth rates will necessitate adjustments. But, he says, the program was designed with these demographic changes in view. "Social security benefits are not too high," he adds, "and the program can be brought into balance without reducing benefits by relatively minor adjustments: increasing contributions from both employers and employees by 1 percentage point in the year 2020; covering state and local employees who are not currently in the program (the only exempted group of any magnitude); using the savings from the Bureau of Labor Statistics' revision of the COLA index; and imposing additional taxes on the benefits of comparatively well-off retirees."

Such changes, Ball emphasizes, "are well within the traditional principles of the 60-year-old program. The real dangers for those counting on social security benefits lie in proposals for fundamental change." As examples, he cites those proposals intended to privatize parts of the program, to turn the system into a welfare program by means-testing the benefits, or by a so-called "blanketing in," which pays benefits to people regardless of whether or not they have worked in covered employment, or made contributions, or been dependents of those who have.

"Social security has turned out to be a terrific investment for today's retirees," says professor Merton Bernstein, coauthor of a book examining the social security system.[14] "They get back more than they would have earned had they invested their contributions (and their employers' contributions) on their own."

Added to that, people have protection in the event of disability and for their surviving spouses and children throughout their work lives. They also get cost-of-living adjustments that would have been unavailable had they invested privately.

Most experts agree that, with adjustments, social security will continue to be a very good deal in the future. Although actual rates of return on the retirement portion of social security will not be as high as in the past, they will still be impressive. And if you add in the other protections, in Professor Bernstein's words, "it's a system that can't be beat."

Why not simply require all workers to save a certain percentage of income each year until they retire? In other words, approach a minimum universal pension system from the other direction: by forcing employees, instead of employers, to put the money aside.

A mandatory savings plan would circumvent the huge political problems of mandating an employer-paid system. Congress could require all private sector workers to set up separate pension accounts for a certain percentage of their earned income. Longtime pension lawyer Leon Irish has suggested a 5 percent savings rate. Under his scheme, employers would be free to match employees' contributions but would not be compelled to do so. Required contributions and employer matches up to a cap would be tax deductible. Employees could also make additional tax-deductible contributions up to specified limits. Payouts would take the form of inflation-adjusted lifetime benefits starting at social security retirement age, although lump sums of up to 20 percent could be considered.[15]

A compulsory savings system is also attractive as a way of stimulating the economy by raising the savings rate. Writing for the *Brookings Review*, William Gale and Robert Litan point to the disturbing drop in national savings over the past two decades and the potentially disastrous consequences for the American economy.[16] Most economists see deficit reduction as the way to restore economic growth, a route requiring painful tax increases and massive cuts in government spending. Gale and Litan suggest that the same objective can be achieved by increased individual savings, which would not only supplement the retirement income of taxpayers but also "foster economy-wide growth and raise future living standards."

Mandated savings systems have become popular in a number of other countries. The government of Chile put into a place a mandated savings system in 1981. All workers are required to save 13 percent of their earnings in competitive private financial institutions chosen by them and regulated and insured by the government. Mandated savings take the place of both pensions and social security and provide retired full-career workers with about 40 percent of what they were earning before retirement. They receive guaranteed lifetime benefits that are adjusted for inflation.

Systems similar to that in Chile have recently been set up in Argentina, Colombia, and Peru.[17] Approximately 20 countries in Asia, Africa, and the Pacific and Caribbean islands, such as Malaysia, Singapore, and Fiji, have mandated savings systems in which the government invests the money and sets the rate of return. The government investments, however, tend to produce low returns, with the result that some countries have abandoned their savings systems in favor of social security–type pension plans.

Significantly, says World Bank economist Estelle James, there is little opposition to a Chilean-type mandatory savings system, because workers do not consider the required contributions a tax. She says that they "see a direct linkage between their contributions and their benefits."[18] The World Bank recently issued a report recommending mandated savings systems for all countries.[19]

Support for mandatory pensions, expanded social security, or compulsory savings rests on the premise that individuals cannot be left to their own devices to save for retirement, and society must help them see to it. This kind of paternalism goes against the grain of quintessential

American notions about self-reliance and independence. Why shouldn't everyone take responsibility for his or her own retirement?

Although a philosophy of "rugged individualism" has inspired America in many areas, it may be a dangerous illusion where retirement security is concerned. To be sure, most people are aware that they probably can't work forever. Many also realize that working for companies with good pension plans and saving for retirement early in their careers can make all the difference in their golden years. The problem is that what people know is not necessarily what they are able to do.

Realistically, most people have little choice in where they work, and those who do are necessarily more concerned with take-home pay that will pay today's bills than with pensions that will pay tomorrow's. As for savings, is it really "rational" to save early in a career for something as remote as retirement? For the overwhelming majority of workers, immediate expenses — kids, schools, mortgages — can, and arguably should, consume their total budget for many years, possibly until their fifties. By then, of course, the math will be too hard; they won't be able to save enough.

The voluntary system we now have is already heavily paternalistic. The *government* mandates that all Americans underwrite the tax subsidy for pensions and savings plans. *Employers* decide whether to have plans and which employees should get benefits, and how much they should get. And *pension fund managers* choose where workers' money should be invested. Proponents of mandatory programs argue that they are merely taking this paternalism one step further in order to make the system work for everyone, not just for those who draw the lucky straws.

Is a compulsory scheme the best hope for retirement security, or can new incentives make a voluntary system do the job? There are no easy answers and precisely for that reason there is the danger that lawmakers will try to duck the issue. Congress and the administration already show signs of avoidance: either they advocate doing nothing or they say that people ought to save for themselves. All that is needed, they claim, is to teach Americans a lesson in personal responsibility. Each individual should save enough income every year to provide the hundreds of thousands of dollars they will need in retirement; they can then be instructed in the wonders of compound interest and tax deferral, initiated into the mysteries of the stock and bond markets, and persuaded not to spend their savings before retirement age.

Talk of educating people to save for retirement is, of course, based on nothing more than wishful thinking. There is no evidence whatever that "education" can do *that* job. Such talk is merely a way for politicians to buy time and does not constitute a national retirement income policy.

Americans must act now to confront the challenge of shaping a pension system that works — both to provide income stability for older Americans and to spur economic growth for the economy — by demanding sweeping reform. Meeting the challenge will require courage, creativity, and commonsense on the part of elected officials and those who elect them.

Change in a democracy is always painful and slow, but inevitable. Pension policy is at a crossroads. The old system has failed; the new directions are as yet uncharted. It is now up to us to choose which road to take.

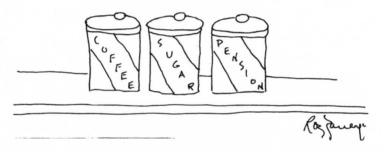

Drawing by Roz Zanengo. Copyright © 1980 by The New Yorker Magazine, Inc.

AFTERWORD

Pensions in Crisis was written to inform and spur debate, not to prescribe solutions. Nevertheless, readers may be curious about the authors' own views. Based on today's political and economic realities, the clear and present need of every citizen to have retirement security, and recommendations made thus far, these are the approaches that we think make the most sense.

First, Congress should adopt a *retirement income policy goal* to ensure an adequate level of income for all full-career workers when they retire. The benchmark for adequacy should be the dollar amount a retiree needs for basic living expenses, as determined by a new Bureau of Labor Statistics retired person's budget.

Second, a new system for achieving the policy goal should include the *current social security system* supplemented by *substantially modified employer-paid pension and savings plans*. Private pension plans should be required to conform to the provisions of the *Pension Bill of Rights Act of 1994*, ending inequities for workers and homemakers in those plans. Investment of pension monies should be handled by *regional retirement funds* that would be private, competitive, federally regulated, and insured and run by professional money managers supervised by a board of directors elected by workers and retirees. The funds could expand coverage by effectively marketing pensions to employers. Inflation adjustments could be provided by allocating a portion of fund assets to the purchase of new Treasury "index" bonds.

Third, *savings plans* should be required to shift to a "reverse match" concept, limiting employee contributions to the amounts put in by employers, as a way of increasing the likelihood that these plans will benefit people of all levels.

Fourth, Congress should create a *Pension Protection Agency* to assist individuals in enforcing their pension rights, review federal pension policies, and coordinate the activities of all federal agencies regulating retirement income programs, other than social security.

Fifth, in the event that employer-paid pension coverage of full-time private sector workers does not at least double by the year 2015, Congress should mandate a *universal pension system*, requiring all employers to withhold 5 percent of workers' pay and contribute it to regional retirement funds selected by employees. The revenue loss could be made up by imposing a tax on plan assets and ending tax breaks for contributions above the minimum.

Where do you stand? We want to know.

NOTES

PART I. THE PENSION PATCHWORK

CHAPTER 1. AN AMERICAN DREAM (PENSIONS AND RETIREES TODAY), PAGES 3–10

1. Quoted in Donald Bartlett and James Steele, "Pensions Aren't Always a Sure Thing," *Philadelphia Inquirer*, October 27, 1991 (part of the series "What Went Wrong with America").

2. The 1995 average yearly social security benefit for a retired worker is approximately $8,376. Office of the Actuary, Social Security Administration, 1994 (unpublished estimate). The average retired couple's social benefit is $14,136.

3. At the time Bill Piatkowski retired, half of all newly retired workers had savings of less than $9,819, not including their homes and cars. Susan Grad, "Income and Assets of Social Security Beneficiaries by Type of Benefit," *Social Security Bulletin* 52, no. 1 (January 1989), table 5, p. 7. A more recent study found that in 1989, half of all households between ages 65 and 74 had less than $9,700 in personal savings. Congressional Budget Office, *Baby Boomers in Retirement: An Early Perspective*, September 1993, p. 70, table C-7. See discussion in Chapter 15.

4. Approximately two-thirds of the elderly poor living alone are widows. They suffer poverty rates five times higher than that of elderly couples. The Commonwealth Commission on Elderly People Living Alone, "Overview and Recommendations," in *Old, Alone and Poor: A Plan for Reducing Poverty Among Elderly People Living Alone*, April 16, 1987, p. 5.

5. President's Commission on Pension Policy, *Coming of Age: Toward a National Retirement Income Policy*, 1981, p. 21. See also John A. Brittain, *Private Pensions and the*

Economic Status of the Aged, 1979 (prepared for Pension and Welfare Benefits Administration, U.S. Department of Labor).

6. Towers Perrin, *Retirement Income Throughout the World*, 1990, p. 30.

7. C. Eugene Steurele and Jon Bakija, *Retooling Social Security for the 21st Century: Right and Wrong Approaches to Reform* (Washington, D.C.: Urban Institute Press, 1994), p. 96.

8. Some experts consider work to be a fourth leg of the stool; others point to Supplemental Security Income. SSI provides income to people over age 65 (or those who are blind or disabled) whose income and assets fall below specified levels. In 1995, SSI payments for older individuals are $5,496 a year; for couples the amount is $8,244. They went to individuals who had $2,000 or less in assets and unearned income of less than $5,736 a year, and to couples with assets of $3,000 or less and unearned income of less than $8,484.

9. Daniel J. Beller and David D. McCarthy, "Private Pension Benefits," in *Trends in Pensions 1992*, ed. John A. Turner and Daniel J. Beller, U.S. Department of Labor, 1992, p. 235, table 10.2. If lump sum payments from pension and savings plans are included, the percentage increases from 34 percent of private sector retirees to 41 percent. Beller and McCarthy, p. 236, table 10.3. Half of all lump sums paid in 1989 were less than $5,000. Beller and McCarthy, p. 257, table 10.15. These figures on pension benefit receipt are from a 1989 Census Bureau Survey. This survey was repeated in September 1994, and the results are scheduled to be released in the spring of 1995. Throughout this book, every effort has been made to use the most recent available government pension statistics.

10. *Inland Steel Co. v. NLRB*, 170 F.2d 247, 251 (7th Cir. 1948), *cert. denied*, 336 U.S. 960 (1949). The exemption of pensions from wage-price controls during World War II and the Korean War also played a critical role in pension growth. See Alicia H. Munnell, *The Economics of Private Pensions* (Washington, D.C.: The Brookings Institute, 1982), pp. 10–12.

11. Daniel J. Beller and Helen H. Lawrence, "Trends in Private Pension Coverage," in *Trends in Pensions 1992*, p. 75, table 4.1.

12. Arnold Hoffman and John Mondejar, "Pension Assets and Financial Markets, 1950–1989," in *Trends in Pensions 1992*, p. 426, table 16.1.

13. Ralph Nader and Kate Blackwell, *You and Your Pension* (New York: Grossman Publishers, 1973).

14. Subcommittee on Labor, Senate Committee on Labor and Public Welfare, *Legislative History of the Employee Retirement Income Security Act of 1974*, vol. III, April 1976, p. 4747.

CHAPTER 2. PENSION TENSION (PENSIONS AND RETIREES TOMORROW), PAGES 11–18

1. Senate Special Committee on Aging, *A Report of Conference Proceedings, 10th Anniversary of the Employee Retirement Income Security Act of 1974*, 98th Cong., 2d Sess., 1985, p. 54 (statement of Senator John H. Chafee).

2. Pension and Welfare Benefits Administration, U.S. Department of Labor, et al., *Pension and Health Benefits of American Workers: New Findings from the April 1993 Current Population Survey*, May 1994, p. A-2 table A2. This figure includes workers participating in employee stock ownership plans, stock bonus plans, and

other employer-financed retirement plans. *It excludes workers participating only in primarily employee-financed savings plans, such as 401(k) and 403(b) plans.* The number of full-time private wage and salary workers participating in pension and profit sharing plans is 24 million. If part-time workers are included, the number is 25 million. The participation rate for all private wage and salary workers in these traditional plans is 28 percent. Adding participants in savings plans gives a total of 38 million workers, or 43 percent of all private sector workers, participating in some kind of private retirement plan (36 million, or 50 percent, of full-time private sector workers). Also see p. B2, table B-2.

3. Pension and Welfare Benefits Administration, *Pension and Health Benefits of American Workers,* p. A-2, table A2. If savings plans are included, the percentage of full-time workers participating in private retirement plans has remained fairly constant during the past two decades. In 1972, the participation rate was 48 percent; in 1993, it was 50 percent. A recent Social Security Administration study of currently employed workers between the ages of 25 and 54 notes that 50 percent of all private wage and salary workers in this "prime working years" age group report participation in a pension or savings plan, and that 52 percent report participating either in the plan of a current employer or that of a former employer. If contributions to an individual retirement account and/or a plan on a second job are counted, the overall retirement plan participation rate goes up to 56 percent (59 percent for full-time workers). John R. Woods, "Pension Coverage Among the Baby Boomers: Initial Findings from a 1993 Survey," *Social Security Bulletin,* vol. 57, no. 3, Fall 1994, p. 15, tables 1 and 2.

4. Pension and Welfare Benefits Administration, *Pension and Health Benefits of American Workers,* p. 2.

5. Timothy M. Smeeding, "Cross National Comparisons of Poverty, Inequality and Income Security Among the Elderly in Eight Modern Nations," presented at the National Academy on Aging Executive Seminar on Poverty and Income Security, June 29–30, 1992, p. 2: "In no other country [in the study] do we consistently find that the aged and near aged have greater income inequality than that found in the USA. Among the very oldest group, the U.S. clearly has the greatest degree of inequality found in all nations."

6. Tax breaks for private pensions will cost the U.S. Treasury nearly $30 billion in lost tax revenues in 1995. Joint Committee on Taxation, U.S. Congress (unpublished estimate). See discussion in Chapter 13.

7. Board of Governors of the Federal Reserve System, *Flow of Funds Accounts: Flows and Outstandings, Third Quarter 1994,* December 1994, p. 96, tables L.121 and L.123. $3.5 trillion. See discussion in Chapter 12.

8. Pension and Welfare Benefits Administration, findings from 1991 Form 5500 annual reports (unpublished), p. 62, table E.4. The 43 million participant figure cited here differs from the 38 million Current Population Survey (CPS) number in note 2 principally because the Form 5500 data is based on financial reports filed by plan administrators with the federal government; whereas the CPS uses the responses of individual workers and retirees. Because each study provides different statistical categories, it is not possible to refer to the findings of just one study. For example, the Form 5500 results provide a breakdown of the number of participants in defined benefit plans noted here, and the number of private sector workers' defined contribution primary and supplemental plans cited in note 9. The

CPS data in note 2 distinguishes between workers in traditional pension and profit sharing plans and 401(k) type plans.

9. Pension and Welfare Benefits Administration, findings from 1991 Form 5500 annual reports (unpublished).

PART II. THE RULES OF THE GAME

INTRODUCTION: WINNERS AND LOSERS, PAGES 21–24

1. American Express Company *proxy statement*, March 18, 1993, pp. 14–17.

2. Pension and Welfare Benefits Administration, U.S. Department of Labor, "Abstract of 1991 Form 5500 Annual Reports," *Private Pension Plan Bulletin* vol. 3 Summer 1994, p. 5, table A2.

3. Pension and Welfare Benefits Administration, "Abstract," p. 4, table A1.

CHAPTER 3. IT JUST ISN'T FAIR! (RULES FOR GETTING INTO A PENSION PLAN), PAGES 25–36

1. There is no precise statistic indicating how many private sector workers are excluded from pension plans. Eleven percent of *all* workers over age 25 excluded from their employers' retirement plans are excluded because of their job category. Bureau of the Census, U.S. Department of Commerce, "Preparing for Retirement: Who Had Pension Coverage in 1991?" *Statistical Brief*, April 1993, p. 2 (this figure is larger than 10 percent because it includes participants in government and military plans — where participation is almost universal — as well as employees who choose not to contribute to savings plans). Eight percent of *private sector* employees excluded from their employers' retirement plans are excluded because of their job category. Pension and Welfare Benefits Administration, U.S. Department of Labor, et al., *Pension and Health Benefits of American Workers: New Findings from the April 1993 Current Population Survey*, May 1994, p. B-5, table B4 (figure is smaller than 10 percent because it includes employees who choose not to contribute to their firms' savings plans).

2. Nancy Altman, "Rethinking Retirement Income Policies: Nondiscrimination, Integration, and the Quest for Worker Security," *Tax Law Review* 42, no. 3 1987, p. 444.

3. An even larger percentage of employees could be excluded if the Internal Revenue Service determined that the employees included in the plan represented a reasonable classification that did not discriminate in favor of highly paid company officers and owners.

4. *Hearings Before the Senate Special Committee on Aging*, 99th Cong., 1st Sess., June 14, 1985 (statement of Madeline Sapienza). See also Spencer Rich, "Gaps Abound in Pension Plans," *Washington Post*, June 15, 1985.

5. Companies can exclude 30 percent of their employees from a plan for any reason. They can exclude more, twice that number in some cases, if the group of employees covered is a reasonable business classification, such as salaried employees only, and the plan (combined with other plans for the employer) passes certain

mathematical tests. These tests generally compare the average contribution or benefit (as a percentage of pay) provided under the plans for the company's highly paid employees with the average contribution or benefit for other employees. If the average for the non–highly paid employees is at least 70 percent of the average for the highly paid, the plan will pass the tests.

6. Pension Reform Act of 1994, H.R. 4367, 103d Cong., 2d Sess.

7. Pension Bill of Rights Act of 1994, S. 2531, 103d Cong., 2d Sess.

8. *Toward a Disposable Work Force: The Increasing Use of "Contingent" Labor: Hearings Before the Subcommittee on Labor of the Senate Committee on Labor and Human Resources*, 103d Cong., 1st Sess., June 15, 1993 (statement of Jimmie Ruth Daughtrey).

9. Steven Pearlstein, "Business and the Temp Temptation: A Permanent Situation," *Washington Post*, October 20, 1993.

10. *Toward a Disposable Work Force* (statement of Richard Delaney).

11. Pearlstein, "Business and the Temp Temptation."

12. *Toward a Disposable Work Force* (statement of Sen. Howard M. Metzenbaum).

13. *Toward a Disposable Work Force* (statement of Richard Delaney).

14. Labor letter, "Lease, Don't Hire," *Wall Street Journal*, March 16, 1993.

15. As a practical matter, the leasing provisions provide little protection to most workers, since they only require that they be counted as "employees" for purposes of determining whether the plan satisfies the 30 percent (or other) coverage exclusion tests. Thus, if an employer decides to exclude all leased truck drivers from the plan and fewer than 30 percent of the workers fall into this category, they do not have to be included in either the employer's or the leasing company's plan.

16. *Pensions: Here Today, Gone Tomorrow? Hearings Before the Labor Subcommittee of the Senate Committee on Labor and Human Resources*, 102d Cong., 2d Sess., August 4, 1992 (statement of Margaret Hubbard).

17. Workers can no longer be denied plan participation because they are too old thanks to the 1986 Omnibus Reconciliation Act (OBRA), Public Law No. 99-509.

18. Certain plans that must allow employees to earn benefits right away can delay participation. For example, the pension plan for college and university professors, Teachers Insurance Annuity Association–College Retirement Equities Fund (TIAA-CREF), requires a two-year wait for participation. Similarly, simplified employee pensions (SEPs) can limit plan membership to employees who have worked three out of the preceding five years.

19. Pension and Welfare Benefits Administration, *Pension and Health Benefits of American Workers*, p. B-3, table B3.

20. Chris Tilly, "Reasons for the Continuing Growth of Part-time Employment," *Monthly Labor Review*, March 1991, p. 10.

21. Bureau of Labor Statistics, U.S. Department of Labor, *Employee Benefits in Medium and Large Private Establishments, 1991*, May 1993, p. 127, table 122.

22. Part-time and Temporary Worker Protection Act of 1993, H.R. 2188, 103d Cong., 1st. Sess.

CHAPTER 4. STRANDED IN BUCKEYE (RULES FOR GETTING SOMETHING OUT OF A PENSION PLAN), PAGES 37–48

1. Pension and Welfare Benefits Administration, U.S. Department of Labor, "Abstract of 1991 Form 5500 Annual Reports," *Private Pension Plan Bulletin* 3 (Summer 1994), p.5, table A2.

2. Calculated from Pension and Welfare Benefits Administration, "Abstract," p. 5, table A2.

3. Calculated from Pension and Welfare Benefits Administration, "Abstract," p. 5, table A2. If defined contribution plans are added, including workers' own contributions to savings plans, vesting rates rise significantly, to 76 percent of private sector workers participating in plans in 1988. They increase further when vesting on prior jobs and lump sums are counted. See John R. Woods, "Pension Vesting and Preretirement Lump Sums Among Private Sector Employees," *Social Security Bulletin*, vol 66, No. 3, Fall, 1993, p. 3, table 3 and p. 8.

4. Bureau of the Census, U.S. Department of Commerce, "Preparing for Retirement: Who Had Pension Coverage in 1991?" *Statistical Brief*, April 1993, p. 2 (statistics include government as well as private plan participants).

5. Donald S. Grubbs, Jr., "Summary of Report," *Study of the Cost of Mandatory Vesting Provisions* (1972) in Subcommittee on Labor, Senate Committee on Labor and Human Resources, *Legislative History of the Employee Retirement Income Security Act of 1974*, vol. I, 1976, p. 662.

6. Subcommittee on Labor, *Legislative History of the Employee Retirement Income Security Act of 1974*, vol. II, 1976, p. 1605 (statement of Sen. Harrison A. Williams, Jr.).

7. Tax Equity and Fiscal Responsibility Act of 1982 (TEFRA), Public Law No. 97-248.

8. Tax Reform Act of 1986 (TRA), Public Law No. 99-514. Certain plans covered by union contracts were allowed to wait as long as January 1, 1991. The law requires plans to provide 100 percent vesting after five years or, in the alternative, graded vesting. Graded vesting provides employees with 20 percent of their benefits after three years and 20 percent additional each year thereafter, with 100 percent of the benefit vested after seven years.

9. U.S. General Accounting Office, *Private Pensions: Impact of New Vesting Rules Similar for Women and Men*, August 1990.

10. Remarks in the *Congressional Record*, June 23, 1993.

11. *Pensions: Here Today, Gone Tomorrow?: Hearings Before the Subcommittee on Labor of the Senate Committee on Labor and Human Resources*, 102d Cong., 2d Sess., August 4, 1992, p. 107 (statement of Joan Kuriansky).

12. John A. Turner, *Pension Policy for a Mobile Labor Force*, W. E. Upjohn Institute, Kalamazoo, Mich., 1993, p. 20, table 3.2.

13. Sheila Zedlewski, *The Urban Institute's Dynamic Simulation of Income Model*, January 1988.

14. Pension Portability Improvement Act of 1993, H.R. 1874, 103d Cong., 1st Sess.

15. Turner, *Pension Policy*, p. 184. Vesting is immediate under France's mandatory pension system (and break-in-service penalties for time taken off for childbirth and military service have been abolished since 1910). However, Germany requires ten years of service and age 35, or 12 years of service, to vest.

16. A "year" for vesting purposes may be the calendar year, the plan year, or any other 12-month period chosen by the plan.

17. Tom Baden, "Retirement Security an Illusion For Many Workers," Newhouse News Service, 1991.

18. *Congressional Symposium on Women and Retirement: Hearings Before the Subcommittee on Retirement Income and Retirement of the House Select Committee on Aging,* 102d Cong., 2d Sess., September 24, 1992, p. 59 (statement of Vicki Gottlich).

19. The pension law says that multiemployer plans are not required to provide individual benefit statements until the Labor Department issues regulations specifying their content. Although the department has proposed regulations twice, it has never issued them in final form. The American Institute of Public Accountants has called on the Labor Department to close this troubling gap in the information available to individuals. Kathy M. Kristof, "Pensions System Reform Seen," *Los Angeles Times,* May 15, 1994.

CHAPTER 5. CHANGE FOR A CUP OF COFFEE (RULES FOR CALCULATING BENEFITS), PAGES 49–62

1. Daniel J. Beller and David D. McCarthy, "Private Pension Benefits," in *Trends in Pensions 1992,* ed. John A. Turner and Daniel J. Beller, U.S. Department of Labor, 1992, p. 247, table 10.10. More recent numbers show that in 1992, half of all people over age 65 receiving private pensions were getting less than $4,013 a year. This number is lower than the 1989 figures because it includes widows and widowers in addition to retired workers. Susan Grad, *Income of the Population 55 and Older, 1992,* Social Security Administration, May 1994, p. 81, table V.C.7.

2. Assistant Secretary of Labor Olena Berg recently noted, "the gulf between men and women in the amount of pension benefits received . . . continues to widen. In 1978, the average amount of pension benefits received by women ($1,630) equaled 47 percent of those received by men ($3,480). Eleven years later, using 1978 dollars, the median amount of pension benefits received by women ($1,350) averaged only 37 percent of those received by men ($3,690)." Olena Berg, statement at "Pensions Not Posies Campaign" press briefing, May 12, 1994.

3. Beller and McCarthy, "Private Pension Benefits," p. 247, table 10.10. Later data indicate that the *average* annual benefit for all private pension recipients age 65 and over is $6,243. Bureau of the Census, U.S. Department of Commerce, preliminary data for *Money Income of Households, Families, and Persons in the United States: 1994* (unpublished).

To give a realistic picture of how much people are getting from the private pension system, experts rely on median, rather than average, figures. The median shows the midway point — half of the people surveyed are above and half are below the figure. Averages, by contrast, are influenced by the highest and lowest extremes. As Secretary of Labor Robert Reich has observed, "Averages don't always reveal the most telling realities." His example: he, at 4 foot 10, and professional basketball player Shaquille O'Neal, at 7 foot 2, have an average height of 6 feet. Frank Swoboda, "Reich Reinvents 'Competitiveness,'" *Washington Post,* September 24, 1994.

4. Esther Champion's total retirement income after a lifetime of work outside

the home is $695.68 a month: $550 from social security, $96.17 from *Consumer Reports*, and $49.51 from a Newspaper Guild pension.

5. *Pensions: Here Today, Gone Tomorrow?: Hearings Before the Subcommittee on Labor of the Senate Committee on Labor and Human Resources*, 102d Cong., 2d Sess., August 4, 1992 (statement of Esther Champion).

6. Georgia C. Marudas, "Pulling the Rug Out: Pension Funds Only as Healthy as the Company," *Baltimore Evening Sun*, March 27, 1991.

7. Bureau of Labor Statistics, U.S. Department of Labor, *Employee Benefits in Medium and Large Private Establishments*, 1991, May 1993, p. 87, table 82.

8. Final pay formulas cover 65 percent of participants in defined benefit plans. Bureau of Labor Statistics, *Employee Benefits in Medium and Large Private Establishments*, p. 87, table 82.

9. Bureau of Labor Statistics, *Employee Benefits in Medium and Large Private Establishments*, p. 80, n. 34.

10. Bureau of Labor Statistics, *Employee Benefits in Medium and Large Private Establishments*, p. 87, table 82.

11. Bureau of Labor Statistics, *Employee Benefits in Medium and Large Private Establishments*, p. 87, table 82.

12. Bureau of Labor Statistics, *Employee Benefits in Medium and Large Private Establishments*, p. 80.

13. These figures apply to someone retiring after January 1, 1988. See United Mine Workers of America Health and Retirement Funds, *Summary Plan Description: 1974 Pension Plan and Trust*, 1989, p. 22.

14. Ruth Simon, "Look Before You Leave," *Forbes*, November 14, 1988.

15. The Clinton administration proposed the elimination of age-weighted profit sharing plans but withdrew the proposal after opposition from business groups.

16. Bureau of Labor Statistics, *Employee Benefits in Medium and Large Private Establishments*, pp. 83, 97, table 94.

17. In one case, a federal court of appeals ruled that employees in Richard Nichols's situation should receive a pro rata share of their subsidized early retirement when they satisfied the requirements for such benefits while working for the new employer. *Gillis v. Hoechst-Celanese Corp.*, 4F.3d 1137 (3rd Cir. 1993), *cert. denied*, April 18, 1994. In another case, in another part of the country, a court ruled the opposite. *Hunger v. AB*, 12 F.3d 118 (8th cir. 1993), *cert. denied* 129 L.Ed. 2d 811 (1994).

18. Internal Revenue Code Sec. 411(d)(6) says that if a plan is amended to eliminate a special early retirement benefit and a person continues working for the same company, she gets a pro rata share of the benefit at the time the original terms of the plan are satisfied. Diane Hill's situation differed from Richard Nichols's because she continued to work for the same employer, GM, after her plan rules changed, while he found himself working the same job but for a different employer.

19. *Pensions: Here Today, Gone Tomorrow?* p. 5 (statement of Mary Green). Mary Green was making $34,512 when she was forced to retire. Had she been allowed to work to full retirement age, she would have gotten a benefit of $1,414 a month from the pension plan. Because she was forced to retire at age 60, her benefit was reduced to $998 a month. Her plan's offset integration formula reduced her benefit further to $840 a month at age 65.

20. Bureau of Labor Statistics, *Employee Benefits in Medium and Large Private Establishments*, p. 91, table 88. See also Bureau of Labor Statistics, *Employee Benefits in Small Private Establishments, 1992*, May 1994, p. 78, table 77.

21. Office of the Actuary, Social Security Administration, 1994 (unpublished estimate).

22. Nancy Altman, "Rethinking Retirement Income Policies: Nondiscrimination, Integration, and the Quest for Worker Security," *Tax Law Review* 42, no. 3 1987, p. 484.

23. Public Law No. 99-514.

24. The only exception is in the case of top-heavy plans, those in which at least 60 percent of the benefits or contributions go to company owners or officers. As part of the 1982 tax law, Congress said that integrated plans must provide lower-paid employees with minimum benefits equal to 2 percent of pay for ten years or contributions of 3 percent of pay for years worked after 1986.

25. *Pensions: Here Today, Gone Tomorrow?* p. 5 (statement of Mary Green).

26. Pension Reform Act of 1994, H.R. 4367, 103d Cong., 2d Sess.

27. J.C. Penney Co. recently agreed to settle a multimillion-dollar lawsuit brought by employees claiming that the pension plan had improperly used estimates of social security benefits rather than actual figures. *Forbush v. J.C. Penney Co.*, 3–90–2719–X (N.D. Tex.).

CHAPTER 6. EATEN ALIVE (INFLATION AND PENSIONS), PAGES 63–72

1. Daniel J. Beller and David D. McCarthy, "Private Pension Benefits," in *Trends in Pensions 1992*, ed. John A. Turner and Daniel J. Beller, U.S. Department of Labor 1992, p. 251, table 10.11.

2. Beller and McCarthy, "Private Pension Benefits," p. 251, table 10.11.

3. Steven G. Allen et al., "Post-Retirement Benefits Increases in the 1980s," in *Trends in Pensions 1992*, p. 331, table 13.1.

4. Bureau of Labor Statistics, U.S. Department of Labor, *Employee Benefits in Medium and Large Private Establishments*, 1991, May 1993, p. 84.

5. Bureau of Labor Statistics, *Employee Benefits*, p. 99, table 96.

6. Bureau of Labor Statistics, *Employee Benefits*, p. 84.

7. Beller and McCarthy, "Private Pension Benefits," p. 224.

8. See, e.g., Spencer Rich, "Being 'Eaten Alive' by Inflation, Private Pensioners Complain," *Washington Post*, July 5, 1979.

9. Rich, "Being 'Eaten Alive' "; Donald S. Grubbs, Jr., "Pensions and Inflation," *Journal of Pension Planning & Compliance*, vol. 18, 1992, p. 22.

10. Alicia H. Munnell and Joseph B. Grolnic, "Should the U.S. Government Issue Index Bonds," *New England Economic Review*, September/October 1986, p. 3.

11. Grubbs, "Pensions and Inflation," p. 23.

12. John Turner, *Pension Policy for a Mobile Labor Force* (Kalamazoo, Michigan: W. E. Upjohn Institute, 1993), p. 125.

13. Fran Hawthorne, "Why Designer Pensions Are in Fashion," *Institutional Investor*, June 1992, p. 123. Notes Hawthorne, "Almost always, the reason given for adopting the new plan is that it's a better deal for employees — easier to understand, quicker to vest. And for younger workers, that's generally true. But that means that

older workers can get short shrift. Moreover, some companies use the changeover as a chance simply to cut back benefits. Too many employees may thus find themselves with a fancy new pension plan that's really just a smaller prize inside a prettier box" (p. 124).

14. When this approach was first adopted in Great Britain in 1985, it applied only to pension benefits earned after the law went effect. In 1990, it was applied to all benefits earned by an employee. Turner, *Pension Policy*, pp. 184–85.

15. Larry Ozanne and David Lindeman, *Tax Policy for Pensions and Other Retirement Savings*, Congressional Budget Office, 1987, pp. 116–18.

16. Turner, *Pension Policy*, p. 187.

CHAPTER 7. A PIECE OF THE PIE (RULES FOR DIVORCE AND DEATH), PAGES 73–82

1. Barbara P. Noble, "Old Age Is No Place for Sissies," *New York Times*, February 6, 1994.

2. Marjory Pentecost, statement at press briefing on "Pension Reform and Income Security for Divorced Older Women," May 20, 1993. The pension plans of religious organizations are not required to comply with private pension laws. However, most church plans have adopted similar rules.

3. William H. Crown et al., *The Economic Status of Divorced Older Women*, Policy Center on Aging, Brandeis University, 1993, p. 15, table 2.

4. In 1988, one-third of all elderly unmarried women relied on social security for at least 90 percent of their income. Anne E. Moss, *Women, Pensions and Divorce: Small Reforms That Could Make a Big Difference*, American Association of Retired Persons, 1993, p. ix.

5. Subcommittee on Retirement Income and Employment, House Select Committee on Aging, *Report: How Well Do Women Fare Under the Nation's Retirement Policies?* 102d Cong., 2d Sess., March 26, 1992, p. 20 (using 1990 census data).

6. *Economic Equity Act and Related Tax and Pension Reform: Hearings Before the House Ways and Means Committee*, 98th Cong., 1st Sess., October 25, 1983 (statement of Millicent Goode).

7. *Congressional Symposium on Women and Retirement: Hearings Before the Subcommittee on Retirement Income and Employment of the House Select Committee on Aging*, 102d Cong., 2d Sess., September 24, 1992, p. 59 (statement of Vicki Gottlich).

8. *How Will Today's Women Fare in Yesterday's Traditional Retirement System? Hearings Before the Subcommittee on Retirement Income and Employment of the House Select Committee on Aging*, 102d Cong., 2d Sess., March 26, 1992, p. 131 (statement of Rita Cevasco).

9. See Anne E. Moss, "Women's Pension Reform: Congress Inches Toward Equity," *Journal of Law Reform* (University of Michigan) vol. 19, no. 1 (Fall 1985), p. 169. The joint and survivor's annuity reduces the benefit to the couple while he lives an average of 15 to 20 percent, depending on their ages.

10. *Living in the Shadows: Older Women and the Roots of Poverty: Hearings Before the Subcommittee on Retirement Income and Employment of the House Select Committee on Aging*, 102d Cong., 2d Sess., May 15, 1992, pp. 63–64 (statement of Mary Souza).

11. *Economic Equity Act and Related Tax and Pension Reform* (statement of Ruth Godbold).

12. *Economic Equity Act and Related Tax and Pension Reform* (statement of Patricia Tice).

13. Either the survivor would get a two-thirds benefit, which would cost about the same as the present arrangement, or the spouse would get 100 percent of the benefit after the employee died, which would result in a lower initial benefit. *Congressional Symposium on Women and Retirement,* pp. 64–65 (statement of Vicki Gottlich).

14. See Anne E. Moss, *Your Pension Rights at Divorce: What Women Need to Know* (revised edition), Pension Rights Center, 1995.

CHAPTER 8. THE PENSION PIGGY BANK (RULES FOR THE IN-VESTMENT OF PENSION MONEY), PAGES 83–94

1. Pension and Welfare Benefits Administration, U.S. Department of Labor, 1994 (unpublished statistics).

2. Pension and Welfare Benefits Administration, 1994 (unpublished statistics).

3. Frank Greve, "Heat Is on U.S. Pension Watchdog," *Philadelphia Inquirer,* February 2, 1992. The Department of Labor recently installed a computer system to alert the investigatory staff to possible irregularities. This should speed up the review process.

4. Terri Thompson, "Watchdogging Your Pension," *U.S. News & World Report,* July 30, 1990, p. 64.

5. Calculated from Pension and Welfare Benefits Administration, U.S. Department of Labor, "Abstract of 1991 Form 5500 Annual Reports," *Private Pension Plan Bulletin* 3 (Summer 1994), p. 15, table A9.

6. Calculated from Pension and Welfare Benefits Administration, "Abstract of 1991 Form 5500 Annual Reports," p. 4, table A1; p.8, table A4.

7. Calculated from Pension and Welfare Benefits Administration, "Abstract of 1991 Form 5500 Annual Reports," p. 15, table A9.

8. Calculated from Pension and Welfare Benefits Administration, "Abstract of 1991 Form 5500 Annual Reports," p. 18, table A12.

9. Beth Kobliner, "Avoiding a Pension Plan Rip-off," *Money,* November 1991, p. 96.

10. Douglas Frantz and Robert L. Jackson, "Pension Plans Looted as Safeguards Weaken," *Los Angeles Times,* October 29, 1989.

11. Ronald Goldstock, *Corruption and Racketeering in the New York City Construction Industry,* October 1989.

12. Eugene Methvin, "Who's Plundering Union Pension Funds?" *Reader's Digest,* May 1990.

13. Douglas Frantz, "Pension Fraud Regulators Run on 'Different Tracks' and a Big Case Folds," *Los Angeles Times,* October 29, 1989.

CHAPTER 9. NOWHERE TO TURN (ENFORCING PENSION RIGHTS), PAGES 95–106

1. James Bennet, "Retirees Often Face Barriers in Fight for Pension Benefits," *New York Times,* November 7, 1992.

2. Frank Greve, "Heat Is on U.S. Pension Watchdog," *Philadelphia Inquirer,* February 2, 1992 (quoting Alan Lebowitz, deputy assistant secretary of labor).

3. Even in circuits where attorneys' fees are granted, they may not be awarded for work done by lawyers before they file a lawsuit. This can mean that most of the time spent on a case is not paid for.

4. In *Firestone Tire & Rubber Co. v. Bruch,* 489 U.S. 101 (1989), the U.S. Supreme Court ruled that if the pension plan gives authority to the plan trustees to decide disputed benefit claims, the courts will ordinarily defer to the decision made by the trustees. As a result of that case, most plans now provide for such discretion in order to avoid less favorable review of plan decisions by the courts.

5. 473 U.S. 134 (1985).

6. 113 S. Ct. 2063 (1993).

7. For years, people who were receiving their pensions as annuities from a life insurance company could not sue their plan trustees for acting improperly because they were no longer considered plan members. They now have standing to sue in court thanks to the Pension Annuitants Protection Act of 1994. Public Law No. 103–401.

8. An increasing number of courts are ruling that plan officials who make deliberately misleading statements can be sued by plan members who lose benefits because they reasonably relied on the statements. However, if a company officer who is not involved in running the plan makes a pension promise, the workers are ordinarily out of luck.

9. *Reichman v. Bonsignore, Brignati & Mazotta, P.C.,* 818 F.2d 278 (2d Cir. 1987).

10. *McLendon v. Continental Can Co.,* 908 F.2d 1171 (3d Cir. 1990).

CHAPTER 10. THE PENSION SAFETY NET (UNDERFUNDED PENSION PLANS), PAGES 107–120

1. Pension Benefit Guaranty Corporation, *Annual Report 1993,* March 1994, p. 1.

2. Thomas Geoghegan, *Which Side Are You On?* (New York: Farrar, Straus and Giroux, 1992), p. 87.

3. Multiemployer plans have different rules. For example, if a multiemployer plan were to become insolvent, benefit guarantees would be limited to $16.25 per month multiplied by years of credited service. No multiemployer plans have become insolvent since this limit was put into place in 1980.

4. Laura Jereski, "Fix What Needs Fixing," *Forbes,* February 1, 1993, p. 60.

5. Pension Benefit Guaranty Corporation, *Annual Report 1993,* p. 1.

6. Severely underfunded plans can be required to speed up their funding for new benefits.

7. Prior to 1988, plans could receive waivers of contributions from the IRS five times in a 15-year period, and they had 15 years to repay the waived contributions. The Omnibus Budget Reconciliation Act of 1987 restricted the number of waivers to three in a 15-year period, and pension plans now have only five years to repay the waived contributions. The IRS must notify the PBGC and allow comment on waiver requests that would increase the total amounts to $1 million or more.

8. U.S. General Accounting Office, *Pension Plans: Hidden Liabilities Increase Claims Against Government Insurance Program,* December 30, 1992.

9. A GAO report reviewed 40 plans with an estimated liability of $123 million. Fiduciary violations had occurred in 11 plans, with total liabilities of some $9.2 million. Most of the plans had fewer than 100 participants. U.S. General Accounting Office, *Pension Plans: Fiduciary Violations in Terminated Unfunded Plans*, May 1991.

10. Pension Benefit Guaranty Corporation, *Pension Benefit Guaranty Corporation News*, November 19, 1994.

11. See David A. Vise, "Going After the Pension Gaps," *Washington Post*, November 23, 1993.

12. Larry Light, "Pension Power," *Business Week*, November 6, 1989, p. 157. In fact, ERISA specifically states that taxpayers are not liable for the PBGC's obligations (unlike the Federal Deposit Insurance Corporation). The PBGC can only borrow up to $100 million from the U.S. Treasury. 29 U.S.C. Sec. 4002(g)(2) and 4005(c).

13. Paul Jackson, "The Pension Benefit Guaranty Corporation: An Elephant Surrounded by Blind Men," *Contingencies*, January/February 1993, p. 30.

14. "Slate Urges Congress to Work with White House on Reform Bill," *BNA Pension & Benefits Reporter* vol. 21 (March 7, 1994), p. 506.

15. Retirement Protection Act of 1994, public law no. 103–465.

CHAPTER 11. RAIDING THE COOKIE JAR (OVERFUNDED PENSION PLANS), PAGES 121–134

1. "NBC News Summer Showcase: The Pension Cookie Jar," broadcast August 2, 1988.

2. "The Pension Cookie Jar."

3. Bartlett Naylor, "Reversion Scorecard," *Corporate Governance Bulletin*, (Armonk: M.E. Sharpe, May/June 1989).

4. Janice Castro, "Is Your Pension Safe?" *Time*, June 3, 1991, p. 42.

5. *Hearings Before the ERISA Task Force on Terminations of the ERISA Advisory Council of the U.S. Department of Labor*, March 14, 1986 (statement of Percy Penley).

6. Wayne E. Green, "Employees Battle Firms for Pension-Plan Surpluses," *Wall Street Journal*, June 4, 1990.

7. Julie Kosterlitz, "That's My Money," *National Journal*, February 25, 1989, p. 455.

8. The Defense Department took the position that any surplus resulting from the termination of a pension plan reverted to the government, since the money in the plan originally came from taxpayers.

9. "The Pension Cookie Jar."

10. *Hearings Before the ERISA Task Force on Terminations of the ERISA Advisory Council* (statement of Arthur Wilson).

11. Randall Smith, "Texaco Seeks U.S. Approval to Remove $250 Million from Getty Pension Fund," *Wall Street Journal*, January 28, 1985.

12. U.S. General Accounting Office, *Recapturing Tax Benefits Contained in Asset Reversions*, November 1989.

13. Larry Light, "Pension Power," *Business Week*, November 6, 1989, p. 155.

14. *Hearings Before the Subcommittee on Retirement Income and Employment of the House Select Committee on Aging*, 102d Cong., 1st Sess., 1991 (statement of Jeffrey Lewis).

15. *Hearings Before the Subcommittee on Retirement Income and Employment*, p. 3 (statement of Joseph F. Delfico).

16. Tom Schlesinger, *Working Without a Net: Legal, Legislative, and Regulatory Developments Affecting Pension Annuity Protection*, report, Southern Finance Project prepared for the American Association of Retired Persons, February 1994.

PART III. THE PENSION STAKES

INTRODUCTION: THE LARGEST LUMP OF MONEY IN THE WORLD, PAGES 137–138

1. This was the title of a July 27, 1985, "NBC News White Paper" on pension investments produced by former NBC News president Reuven Frank and Janet Janjigian. Corporate earnings put back into company operations are a larger amount, but unlike pension funds, they are not a "single" source of capital.

2. Board of Governors of the Federal Reserve System, *Flow of Funds Accounts: Flows and Outstandings, Third Quarter 1993*, December 1994, p. 96, tables L.121 and L.123 ($3.5 trillion in the third quarter of 1993).

3. New York Stock Exchange, Inc., *Fact Book: 1993 Data*, April 1994, p. 89.

4. John B. Shoven, *Return on Investment: Pensions Are How America Saves*, Association of Private Pension and Welfare Plans, September 1991, pp. 26, 29. Professor Shoven, now dean of Stanford's School of Humanities and Sciences, explains that this is because "the real value of pension assets went up by more than did the real value of the nation's wealth."

5. Pension and Welfare Benefits Administration, U.S. Department of Labor, "Abstract of 1990 Form 5500 Annual Reports," *Private Pension Plan Bulletin*, vol. 2, Summer 1993. Private retirement plan assets, not including pension assets held by life insurance companies, grew from $564 billion in 1980 to $1.7 trillion in 1990. p. 75, table E7. Investment income for private retirement plans with 100 or more participants was $53 billion in 1990. pp. 41–42, table C9.

6. Robert Kuttner, "Uncle Bob's All-Purpose Tonic," *New Republic*, September 12, 1988, p. 25.

CHAPTER 12. THE PENSION FUND WAS JUST SITTING THERE (HOW PENSION POWER AFFECTS PEOPLE), PAGES 139–154

1. *A.C.T.W.U. v. Murdock*, 861 F.2d 1406 (9th Cir. 1988).

2. The Cannon Mills story had a sequel. In 1988, 13,000 Cannon Mills retirees were told that their pensions were being cut by 30 percent. The reason: David Murdock had bought their annuities from Executive Life Insurance Company of California, which had collapsed. Like other corporate raiders, Murdock had acquired Cannon Mills in part with financing by junk bonds issued by the insurance company's corporate parent, First Executive Company. At the urging of the ACTWU, Senator Terry Sanford announced a hearing on the plight of the retirees in Kannapolis. Huge press attention ensued. "CBS Sunday" announced that it planned to feature the hearing. Shortly before the hearing, David Murdock called a

press conference to say that he would pay the 30 percent the retirees had lost in pension benefits.

4. Randy Barber and Teresa Ghilarducci, "Pension Funds, Capital Markets, and the Economic Future," in *Transforming the U.S. Financial System: Equity and Efficiency for the 21st Century*, ed. Gary A. Dymski et al., 1994, p. 290.

4. This is not a new problem. In a book written for the Twentieth Century Fund more than 30 years ago, Professor Paul Harbrecht expressed concern about the problems likely to arise from giving control over such large amounts of money to trustees who, as a practical matter, have little accountability to the workers and retirees who are the beneficial owners of the money. Paul Harbrecht, *Pension Funds and Economic Power*, Twentieth Century Fund, New York, 1959, pp. 283–85.

5. Robert A. G. Monks, "The Role of Pension Plans in Corporate Governance," presented at ALI-ABA Pension Policy Invitational Conference, October 25–26, 1991, pp. 5–7. John Brooks, *Conflicts of Interest: Corporate Pension Fund Asset Management*, Twentieth Century Fund, 1975.

6. *Donovan v. Bierworth*, 680 F.2d 263, 271 (2d Cir. 1982).

7. James E. Heard and Howard D. Sherman, Investor Responsibility Research Center, *Conflicts of Interest in the Proxy Voting System*, 1987, p. 25.

8. Robert A. G. Monks and Nell Minow, *Power and Accountability* (New York: HarperCollins, 1991), p. 193.

9. Peter Drucker, *Post-Capitalist Society* (New York: Harper Business, 1993), p. 80.

10. Nancy Perry, "Who Runs Your Company Anyway?" *Fortune*, September 12, 1988, p. 142.

11. A study by the General Accounting Office found that the pension funds of four large companies it surveyed invested between 0.4 percent and 5.7 percent of their assets in leveraged buyout funds. *Utilization of Pension Plan Assets in Leveraged Buyouts and Related Transactions: Hearings Before the House Subcommittee on Oversight of the House Committee on Ways and Means*, 101st Cong., 2d Sess., 1989, p. 3 (statement of Joseph P. Delfico, director of income security issues, Human Resources Division, U.S. General Accounting Office).

12. "Largest Pension Funds," *Pensions & Investments*, January 24, 1994, p. 64.

13. David D. McCarthy and John A. Turner, "Stock Turnover in Private Pension Portfolios," in *Trends in Pensions 1992*, ed. John A. Turner and Daniel J. Beller, U.S. Department of Labor, 1992, pp. 543, 546. The study notes that for the largest plans — those with over $300 million in assets — 41 percent had turnover rates in excess of 100 percent. The study measured turnover by the average of purchases and sales of common stock divided by the average of beginning and year-end amounts of common stock.

14. McCarthy and Turner, "Stock Turnover," p. 550, table 22.1.

15. Carolyn Kay Brancato, Columbia Institutional Investor Project, Columbia Center for Law and Economic Studies, *Report to the Board of Advisors, Pension Fund Turnover and Trading Patterns: A Pilot Study*, January 18, 1991. The Financial Executives Institute surveyed the 36 members of its investment committee who, collectively, manage $250 billion in pension assets. The survey found that the defined benefit plans actively managed by FEI members held an average of 48 percent of the same stocks at the end of 1988 as they had held at the beginning, a 52 percent turnover rate. Overall, stock in all kinds of plans was held for an average of just 2.5

years. Committee on Investment of Employee Benefit Assets, Financial Executives Institute, *Survey of Pension Fund Investment Practices*, 1989, p. 3.

16. New York Stock Exchange, Inc., *Fact Book: Data for 1993*, April 1994, p. 17.

17. The Financial Executives Institute survey reported that members of the pension investment committee generally allowed investment managers a full market cycle (three to five years) to prove their mettle. In 1989, 7.4 percent of FEI members' investment managers were terminated. On average, managers lasted 7.5 years. According to Greenwich Associates, of the 1,106 large corporate funds included in its 1993 survey, 30 percent reported firing an investment manager in each of the three preceding years. Greenwich Associates, *Big Job Gets Bigger*, 1993, p. v.

18. For the period 1981–87, the rate of return for plans with low turnover rates was 13.1 percent. The rate of return for those with high turnover rates was 12.7 percent. McCarthy and Turner, "Stock Turnover," p. 548. A Wilshire Associates study over 7.5 years that surveyed 222 actively managed accounts representing $40 billion in equities as of June, 30, 1986, concluded that "the net management effect is zero." Monks and Minow, *Power and Accountability*, p. 252.

19. Paul Bluestein, "Brady Rips 'Short-Term' Mentality," *Washington Post*, February 23, 1990. Hilary Stout and David Wessel, "Brady Blasts Pension Funds for Taking Short-Term View, Suggests Alternatives," *Wall Street Journal*, February 23, 1990.

20. Monks and Minow, *Power and Accountability*, pp. 254–256. See also Louis Lowenstein, *What's Wrong with Wall Street* (New York: Addison-Wesley, 1988). See Jayne Elizabeth Zanglein, "Who's Minding Your Business," *Hofstra Labor Law Journal*, Fall 1992, pp. 29–37.

21. David M. Walker, "The Increasing Role of Pension Plans in the Capital Markets and Corporate Governance Matters," presented at Conference on the Fiduciary Responsibilities of Institutional Investors, June 14, 1990, p. 9. *BNA Pension Reporter* vol. 16, February 6, 1989, p. 215.

22. "Labor Department Letter on Proxy Voting by Plan Fiduciaries," *BNA Pension Reporter* vol. 15, February 29, 1988, p. 391.

23. The Senate Subcommittee on Government Oversight recommended that all controversial proxy voting decisions by pension funds be undertaken by independent third parties. Subcommittee on Government Oversight, Senate Committee on Governmental Affairs, *Report: The Department of Labor's Enforcement of ERISA*, 99th Cong., 2d Sess., 1986, p. 68. As an alternative to companies' giving control of proxy votes to outside firms, Monks and Minow propose creating entities within companies that are completely independent of the corporate structure. *Power and Accountability*, p. 196.

24. Memorandum ("Department of Labor ERISA Enforcement Proposal") from Kathleen M. Harrington, assistant secretary of labor, to interested staff, March 20, 1990. The withdrawal of the proposal may have been the result of protests by the trustees of very large pension funds that they had so many investment managers that it would have been difficult to find out how a stock was voted on a particular issue. For example, GM has 70 different managers who vote stock held by GM pension plans. Starting in 1991, however, several firms set up proxy services that can quickly and inexpensively provide this information to plan trustees. Since 1990, California, which has the largest of all public pension funds, requires the disclosure of proxy votes to participants. "Increased Disclosure by Fiduciaries Mandated in State Law Effective Jan. 1," *BNA Pension Reporter* vol. 17, January 22, 1990, p. 189.

25. Long-term Investment, Competitiveness and Corporate Takeover Reform Act of 1992, S. 2160, 102d Cong., 2d Sess.

26. Barber and Ghilarducci, "Pension Funds," pp. 306–8.

27. The Financial Executives Institute reported that the percentage of its members' funds with at least some of their common stock holdings in index funds almost doubled between 1984 and 1989. In 1984, 14 of the 36 funds had some portion of their U.S. common stock invested in index funds. In 1989, the number of funds was 27. Committee on Investment of Employee Benefit Assets, Financial Executives Institute.

28. Susan Pulliam, "Campbell Soup Fund to Take Activist Role," *Wall Street Journal*, July 15, 1993. In 1994, the Labor Department issued an interpretative bulletin providing guidance to plan trustees on their responsibilities with respect to corporate governance issues. Interpretive Bulletin 94-2, 59 *Federal Register* 38860, July 29, 1994.

29. Leslie Scism, " 'Relationship Investing' Shows Strains," *Wall Street Journal*, December 8, 1993; Leslie Wayne, "Exporting Shareholder Activism," *New York Times*, July 16, 1993; James Sterngold, "Japanese Companies Rebuff Mighty U.S. Pension Funds," *New York Times*, January 30, 1993.

30. Robert A. G. Monks, "Give Shareholders Some Real Stock," *New York Times*, May 27, 1990; Nell Minow, "Do Your Duty, Retirement Managers," *New York Times*, January 30, 1994. See also Leslie Wayne, "Have Shareholder Activists Lost Their Edge?" *New York Times*, January 30, 1994 (commenting on the successes of relationship investing).

31. An additional 3 percent of the assets were in mutual fund shares, 13 percent in corporate bonds, 27 percent in government bonds, and 1.6 percent in mortgages. Board of Governors of the Federal Reserve System, *Flow of Funds Accounts: Flows and Outsmovings, Third Quarter, 1993*, p. 96, table L.123.

32. These funds were 10.1 percent invested in international stocks, 47.8 percent in common stocks, and 29 percent in bonds. Greenwich Associates, *Big Jobs*, p. 32.

33. Walker, "Increasing Role," p. 10.

34. Carolyn Kay Brancato, Columbia Institutional Investor Project, Columbia Center for Law and Economic Studies, *The Pivotal Role of Institutional Investors in Capital Markets: A Summary of Economic Research at the Columbia Institutional Investor Project*, June 14, 1990 (revised July 18, 1990), table 12.

35. As former Labor Department administrator Ian Lanoff observes, there is nothing wrong with investing workers' and retirees' pension money in socially beneficial projects as long as the investments are prudent, show a high return, and have low risk. Lanoff is responsible for the Labor Department's view that if the interests of present and future pensioners are protected, a pension fund manager with a choice of two investments with equal rates of return and levels of risk can choose the investment that will promote jobs for plan members, reduce day-to-day living expenses of pensioners, or enhance their community.

36. Olena Berg, "Putting Pensions to Work," *USA Today*, November 29, 1993.

37. Teresa Ghilarducci, *Labor's Capital: The Economics and Politics of Private Pensions* (Cambridge: MIT Press, 1993), p. 124. Job-creation efforts by construction industry pension funds include those of the Bricklayer and Laborer Union pension fund, which buys federally insured certificates of deposit from a bank, which in turn

finances construction loans for union-built low-price housing, and the Sheet Metal Workers pension fund, which owns a stake in an asbestos-removal contractor that provides jobs for union members. In 1994, the Labor Department issued an interpretive bulletin clarifying that private pension plans may invest in ETIs. Interpretive Bulletin 94-1, 59 *Federal Register* 326060, June 23, 1994.

38. Investment returns for the Housing Investment Trust for the one-year period ending on March 31, 1993, was 7.83 percent (8.66 percent over a three-year period). The Community Investment Demonstration Program is Section 8 of the HUD Demonstration Act of 1993. HUD will provide more than $500 million to this program in 1995. "Federal Officials Promote ETIs as Vehicle to Rebuild the Economy," *BNA Pension & Benefits Reporter* vol. 21, February 14, 1994, p. 368.

39. In *Putting People First*, then presidential candidate Bill Clinton outlined a proposal for a Rebuild America Fund with a $20 billion annual federal investment that would be leveraged by other sources, including pension fund contributions. Bill Clinton, *Putting People First* (New York: Times Books, 1992). See also Felix G. Rohatyn, "Self-Defeating Myths About America," *Washington Post*, July 6, 1992.

40. Commission to Promote Investment in America's Infrastructure, U.S. Department of Transportation, *Financing the Future*, 1993, p. 1. The corporation would, among other things, have authority to issue guaranteed securities offering competitive rates of return.

41. AFL-CIO, *Pensions in Changing Capital Markets*, 1993, p. 57.

42. The AFL-CIO's Housing Investment Trust has invested in the construction of nursing homes, including nursing homes specializing in care for elderly patients with Alzheimer's and related diseases, other nursing homes in Philadelphia, assisted-living complexes for low-income elderly individuals, and senior citizens' housing projects. Barber and Ghilarducci have put forward the concept of "life cycle" portfolio analysis under which, in addition to considering rate of return and risk, trustees would be explicitly permitted to "consider the needs and interests of participants as a whole, not just as potential recipients of a pension check." Barber and Ghilarducci, "Pension Funds," pp. 308–9.

43. College Retirement Equities Fund, *Prospectus: Individual, Group, and Tax-Deferred Variable Annuities*, 1993, p. 16.

44. The Employee Pension Rights Act of 1989 (H.R. 2264), 101st Cong., 2d Sess.

45. Actuary Donald S. Grubbs, Jr., citing these reasons and others for opposing the Visclosky legislation, proposed that all plans be required to have independent trustees, such as bank trustees, no-load mutual funds, and insurance companies. *Hearings Before the House Committee on Small Business*, 101st Cong., 2d Sess., 1990 (statement of Donald S. Grubbs, Jr.). In 1986, Australia passed legislation requiring all pension funds established in the future with 200 or more participants to be governed by either an independent trustee or a body controlled by an equal number of representatives of the employer and employees. The government reportedly plans to extend this law to all plans in the future. For a detailed discussion of the Visclosky proposal, see CRS Research Team, Congressional Research Service, *Joint Pension Trusteeship: An Analysis of the Visclosky Proposal*, 1990.

46. *Hearings Before the House Committee on Small Business* (statement of Prof. Roy Schotland).

CHAPTER 13. THE PENSION PLAYERS (HOW PENSION RULES ARE MADE), PAGES 155–164

1. *Retirement: Whose Responsibility Is It?* video by State Street Bank, 1993.

2. Joel Chernoff, "Metzenbaum Yanks His ERISA Liability Measure," *Pensions & Investments*, June 28, 1993.

3. Paul Yakoboski and Sarah Boyce, *Pension Coverage and Participation Growth: A New Look at Primary and Supplemental Plans*, Employee Benefit Research Institute Issue Brief No. 144, December 1993, p. 5, table 2.

4. On another occasion, EBRI responded to newspaper articles highlighting the shift away from defined benefit plans with a report pointing out that the number of workers in large defined benefit plans had remained constant since the enactment of ERISA—27 million in 1975 and 27 million in 1989. Celia Silverman, *Pension Evolution in a Changing Economy*, Employee Benefit Research Institute Special Report and Issue Brief No. 141, September, 1993, p. 8. Not mentioned was the fact that the workforce had grown substantially during this period—by 26 million— with the result that the proportion of workers participating in plans had actually declined by 25 percent.

Similarly, when concern was expressed in Congress that the tax subsidy for private pensions disproportionately benefits better-off segments of the population, EBRI published papers asserting that "86.7 percent of participants had earnings below $50,000." Dallas Salisbury, *Pension Tax Expenditures—Are They Worth the Cost?*, Employee Benefit Research Institute Issue Brief No. 134, February, 1993, p. 1. Celia Silverman and Paul Yakoboski, "Public and Private Pensions Today: An Overview of the System," in *Pension Funding & Taxation: Implications for Tomorrow*, ed. Dallas Salisbury and Nora Super Jones, 1994, p. 7. Even sophisticated readers concluded from these statements that "pensions primarily benefit those with incomes of less than $50,000 a year." Michael J. Clowes, "A Symposia of Pension Fund Issues," *Pensions & Investments*, April 4, 1994; Deloitte & Touche, "New Look at Pension Coverage and Participation Growth," *Deloitte & Touche Review*, January 24, 1994. Few took the time to note that 92 percent of the workforce earns less than $50,000 a year, which is why there are so many more participants in this group. Even if 100 percent of the 8 percent of the workforce earning more than $50,000 participated in plans, they would represent a very small proportion of all participants.

5. In late 1994, a report by Lewin-VHI, Inc., commissioned by the American Association of Retired Persons, came up with an even more positive assessment of the pension system, asserting that in 1990 half of all persons aged 65 to 84 received pensions, and that their median benefit was $6,600. It went on to predict that by the year 2030, more than four-fifths of persons in this age group will receive pensions, with a median benefit of $6,900 a year. David L. Kennell and Kevin A. Coleman, *Baby Boomer Pension Benefits: Will They Be Adequate for the Future?* The study arrived at these remarkably encouraging figures by counting as "persons" receiving benefits not only retirees who are getting pensions but also their husbands and wives who are not receiving benefits. Thus the study counted a retiree receiving a pension of $6,600 and a homemaker without a pension as two pension recipients.

To determine the median pension of aged persons, the study added together the benefits of the husband and wife. If the husband received $6,600 and the homemaker wife nothing, the benefit was counted as $6,600. However, if both spouses earned pensions, the amounts were combined: If the husband's pension was $6,600 and the wife's pension was $4,200, the benefit was counted as $10,800, and that amount was used to calculate the median benefit of all aged persons.

When it came to making the year 2030 projections, the authors incorporated concededly "optimistic" assumptions, particularly about the likely future participation of lower-income workers in 401(k) savings plans. For example, the study projects that one-fourth of the workers in a typical 401(k) plan who are earning less than $13,750 a year will contribute the maximum amount allowed by the plan (8 percent of pay is suggested), as will one-half of those earning between $13,750 and $24,000.

6. *Economic Equity Act and Related Tax and Pension Reform: Hearings Before the House Ways and Means Committee*, 98th Cong., 1st Sess., 1983 (statement of Geraldine Compton).

7. Retirement Equity Act of 1984, Public Law No. 98-397.

8. Unpublished estimate, Joint Committee on Taxation, 1995. The tax breaks for pensions are greatest for people with the highest incomes, those who defer the taxes for the longest periods, and those who earn the highest interest rates. See Daniel I. Halperin, "Special Tax Treatment for Employer-Based Retirement Programs: Is It 'Still' Viable As a Means of Increasing Retirement Income? Should It Continue?" *Tax Law Review*, vol. 49. No. 1, 1993. Southern Finance Project director Tom Schlesinger notes that data in an Employee Benefit Research Institute publication indicates that "the wealthiest one-fifth of households received two-thirds of the total benefit from the tax advantaged treatment of the pension funds." (See Dallas Salisbury, *Pension Tax Expenditures—Are They Worth the Cost?*, p. 14, table 7).

9. Joint Committee on Taxation, *Estimates of Federal Tax Expenditures for Fiscal 1995–1999*, Committe on Ways and Means, U.S. House of Representatives, and Committee on Finance, U.S. Senate, November 9, 1994.

10. The Unemployment Compensation. Similarly, in the Omnibus Budget Reconciliation Act of 1993, Public Law 103–66, Congress limited to $150,000 the amount of salary that can be taken into account in figuring tax deductions for pension benefits. The ceiling had previously been $235,840. This legislation had the dual objectives of reducing the taxes lost when companies take deductions for large pensions for company owners and officers, and requiring employers who continue to pay big benefits to their executives to contribute a higher percentage of pay for their rank-and-file workers.

11. The Commission on Retirement Policy Act of 1994 (S. 2308).

PART IV. PEOPLE WITHOUT PENSIONS

INTRODUCTION: DO IT YOURSELF!, PAGES 167–170

1. Economic Recovery Tax Act of 1981, Public Law No. 97-34.

2. Nancy Ross, "New Tax Rules Raise Critical Choices," *Washington Post*, November 8, 1981.

3. Presidential Task Force on Regulatory Relief, "Small Business Regulations and Paperwork Requirements to Be Reviewed for the Presidential Task Force on

Regulatory Relief," *Reagan Administration Achievements in Regulatory Relief: A Progress Report*, August 1982, attachment 2, p. 3.

4. Curtis Vosti, "401(k) 'Clarification' a Crossroads," *Pensions & Investments*, October 28, 1991.

5. Spencer Rich, "401(k) Savings Plans Defended at Hill Hearing," *Washington Post*, September 6, 1985.

6. Individuals with incomes over $25,000 a year ($40,000 for married couples) who were already covered by pension plans could no longer take deductions for IRA contributions, but they could still set them up and defer taxes on their investment earnings. The limit on 401(k) contributions was set at $7,000 a year for employee contributions and a maximum of $30,000 or 25 percent of pay for total employer and employee contributions. (The $7,000 employee contribution limit is indexed for inflation. In 1995, it is $9,240.)

7. Pension and Welfare Benefits Administration, U.S. Department of Labor, "Abstract of 1991 Form 5500 Annual Reports," *Private Pension Plan Bulletin* vol. 3, Summer 1994, p. 41, table B17.

8. Pension and Welfare Benefits Administration, U.S. Department of Labor et al., *Pension and Health Benefits of American Workers: New Findings from the April 1993 Current Population Survey*, May 1994, p. 2.

9. Calculated from Pension and Welfare Benefits Administration, *Pension and Health Benefits of American Workers*, p. A-2, Table A2; p. B-1, Table B1.

CHAPTER 14. POTS OF GOLD? (THE NEW SAVINGS PLANS), PAGES 171–182

1. Jane Bryant Quinn, *Making the Most of Your Money* (New York: Simon & Schuster 1991), p. 747.

2. Steven D. Kaye, "A Revolution in Retirement Planning," *U.S. News & World Report*, June 14, 1993, p. 88.

3. Another term for these plans is cash or deferred arrangements, because employees can choose to take the money in cash or defer it (and the taxes otherwise payable on it) by putting it in the plan. The limit for employee contributions to 403(b) plans is $9,500 a year.

4. Pension and Welfare Benefits Administration, U.S. Department of Labor et al., *Pension and Health Benefits of American Workers: New Findings from the April 1993 Current Population Survey*, May 1994, p. C-16, table C10.

5. Bureau of Labor Statistics, U.S. Department of Labor, *Employee Benefits in Medium and Large Private Establishments, 1991*, May 1993, p. 104.

6. Calculated from Pension and Welfare Benefits Administration, "Abstract of 1991 Form 5500 Annual Reports," *Private Pension Plan Bulletin* vol. 3 Summer 1994, p. 42, table B18; Pension and Welfare Benefits Administration, findings from 1991 Form 5500 annual reports (unpublished).

7. Internal Revenue Service, "Determination Letters Issued for Employee Benefit Plans, October 1991–September 1992," IRS News Release No. 92-107, November 18, 1992; Internal Revenue Service, "Determination Letters Issued for Employee Benefit Plans, October 1992–September 1993," IRS News Release No. 94-7, January 31, 1994.

8. Richard Ippolito, Pension Benefit Guaranty Corporation, *Pension Plan*

Choice, December 1990, p. 1. Leslie Wayne, "Pension Changes Raising Concerns," *New York Times*, August 29, 1994.

9. Leslie Eaton, "A Cloudy Sunset: A Grim Surprise Awaits Future Retirees," *Barron's*, July 12, 1993. Fran Hawthorne, "Thought About Your Pension? You Will," *New York Times*, August 27, 1994.

10. Christine Philip, "Employers Pass on Costs," *Pensions & Investments*, September 5, 1994. A recent study by MassMutual Pension Management revealed that while participants paid all or a portion of the plan expenses in 28 percent of the companies surveyed in 1990, in 1993, the number had risen to 43 percent. Mass-Mutual Pension Management, *401(k) Survey Report*, 1993, p. 5.

11. David Kirkpatrick, "Will You Be Able to Retire?" *Fortune*, July 31, 1988.

12. Jacklyn Fierman, "How Secure Is Your Nest Egg?" *Fortune*, August 12, 1991, p. 50.

13. Melynda D. Wilcox, "Why New Rules Worry the Founder of 401(k)s," *Kiplinger's Personal Finance Magazine*, December 1993, p. 130.

14. Calculated from Pension and Welfare Benefits Administration, *Pension and Health Benefits of American Workers*, p. D-5, table D5, (includes lump sum payments from pension and profit sharing and other non-401(k) plans).

15. Fran Hawthorne, "The Search for a New Retirement Paradigm," *Institutional Investor*, January 1994, p. 53. The withholding law is the Unemployment Compensation Act of 1992, Public Law no. 102-318.

16. Hewitt Associates, *401(k) Plan Hot Topics 1993*, p. 22.

17. Jerry Morgan, "Have We Created a Monster?" *Newsday*, June 27, 1993.

18. Robert A. Rosenblatt, "It Takes a Strong Stomach to Get the Most Out of Your 401(k) Plan," *Los Angeles Times*, January 23, 1994. See Deborah Rankin, *Investing on Your Own: A Commonsense Way to Make Your Money Grow* (Yonkers: Consumer Reports Books, 1994) p. 34.

19. Pension and Welfare Benefits Administration, "Abstract of 1991 Form 5500 Annual Reports," p. 36, table B13.

20. Morgan, "Have We Created a Monster?"

21. Bureau of the Census, U.S. Department of Commerce, Survey of Income and Program Participation, 1991, table E (unpublished data).

22. Pension and Welfare Benefits Administration, *Pension and Health Benefits of American Workers*, p. C-12, table C7. The median income of men who are in both a traditional pension plan and a 401(k) is $41,600 a year.

23. Bureau of the Census, U.S. Department of Commerce, *Current Population Reports Median Income of Households and Families in the U.S., 1992*, 1994, table A (unpublished data). The median income of all families is $36,812.

24. Christine Philip, "Special Report: Defined Contribution," *Pensions & Investments*, November 29, 1993, p. 19.

25. Hewitt Associates, *401(k) Plan Hot Topics*, p. 6.

26. Hewitt Associates, *401(k) Plan Hot Topics*, p. 8.

27. Albert B. Crenshaw, "New Rule Likely to Give 401(k) Retirement Savings Plans a Boost," *Washington Post*, January 10, 1993.

28. Employee Benefits Research Institute, "Pension Coverage and Participation Growth: A New Look at Primary and Supplemental Plans," *EBRI Issue Brief* 144, (December 1993), p. 18, table 9.

29. The estimated cost to the Treasury for 401(k)s over the five-year period

1986–90 was $11.6 billion. Spencer Rich, "401(k) Savings Plans Defended at Hill Hearing," *Washington Post*, September 6, 1985.

30. Julie Kosterlitz, "Pension Zigzag," *National Journal*, March 21, 1992, p. 688.

31. Hewitt Associates, *401(k) Plan Hot Topics*, p. 13.

32. The Conference Board, *Encouraging Employee Self-Management in Financial and Career Planning*, 1991, pp. 7–8.

33. Eric M. Engen, William G. Gale, and John Karl Scholtz, "Do Saving Incentives Work?" *Brookings Papers on Economic Activity*, Spring 1994.

34. Ellen E. Schultz, "Raiding Pension Money Now May Leave You Without Piggy Bank for Retirement," *Wall Street Journal*, April 7, 1993.

35. The Pension Portability Act of 1987 (H.R. 1961). Profit Sharing Council of America, Press Release, "PSCA Recommends Simplified Qualified-Plan Designs to Encourage Small Businesses to Sponsor Retirement Programs," May 1994.

36. Pension and Welfare Benefits Administration, *Pension and Health Benefits of American Workers*, p. A-2, table A2.

37. The Labor Department has discovered "a growing problem involving small, ailing companies misusing worker contributions" to 401(k)s. Kathy M. Kristof, "Troubled Firms Seen Misusing Pension Funds," *Los Angeles Times*, January 11, 1994.

CHAPTER 15. A FOUR-LETTER WORD (NO PLAN AT ALL), PAGES 183–192

1. Patricia Saiki, statement at press conference, June 18, 1991.

2. An estimated 82.7 percent of the 7.3 million U.S. private for-profit firms did not provide retirement plans for any of their workers in 1990. David L. Kennell et al., Lewin-ICF, *Retirement Plan Coverage in Small and Large Firms: Final Report*, June 1992, p. III.24 (prepared for Office of Advocacy, U.S. Small Business Administration).

3. More than nine out of ten businesses in the country are small: 94.4 percent of firms have fewer than 25 employees. They employ 27.6 percent of all private sector workers. Kennell, *Retirement Plan Coverage*, fig. III-3.

4. Only 0.2 percent of firms have 500 or more employees, but they employ 45.6 percent of all workers. Kennell, *Retirement Plan Coverage*, fig. III-3.

5. Current population survey data for all private sector workers show that in 1988, "75 percent of manufacturing workers had a pension plan available compared to 40 percent of workers in retail trade." The same data show that a plan was offered to 89 percent of union members versus 55 percent of nonunion workers. William J. Wiatrowski, "Factors Affecting Retirement Income," *Monthy Labor Review*, March 1993, p. 26.

6. Bureau of the Census, U.S. Department of Commerce, Survey of Income and Program Participation, 1991, table 1 (unpublished data) (does not include workers under age 25).

7. Kennell, *Retirement Plan Coverage*, table III-12. Employers' economic concerns included, "Company's income is too uncertain or variable, firm has merged or shut down a plant, the company is a partnership and owners have other jobs with retirement plans, or the company is a self-employed person with no employees."

Although the regulations were not the reason employers without plans gave for not having them, the rules were the principal reason employers gave for terminating plans between 1986 and 1990. Two-thirds of very small firms that did not replace their terminated plans with other plans cited the regulations as the primary reason for the termination. Of the companies with more than 500 employees that did not replace their plans, 34.4 percent cited the rules as the reason.

8. The uniform percentage of pay is required by the IRS Model SEP, Form 5305-SEP. Employers can also set up non-model SEPs through financial institutions, to which they can contribute twice as much on earnings above the social security wage base as below.

9. The form (IRS Model SEP Form 5305-SEP) also includes questions and answers explaining how SEPs work.

10. David Kirkpatrick, "Will You Be Able to Retire?" *Fortune*, July 31, 1989.

11. In firms with fewer than 25 employees that had defined benefit or defined contribution plans available, 22.7 percent of workers had SEPs. Kennell, *Retirement Plan Coverage*, tables III-29 and III-30. Twenty-six percent of the smallest firms with primary defined contribution plans available had SEPs; 39.6 percent had profit sharing plans or ESOPs; and 29.5 percent had money purchase or thrift savings plans. Kennell, p. III.66. No distinction is made here between SEPs and salary reduction SEPs. Salary reduction SEPs are tax-sheltered savings plans that can be set up by for-profit companies with fewer than 25 eligible employees if half of the employees contribute. Employers ordinarily do not contribute to salary reduction SEPs.

12. Employers can also set up prototype plans. These are more complicated plans that have been approved by the Internal Revenue Service. Mutual funds, banks, consultants, and others offer these plans, which are simple to set up. They do, however, have disclosure requirements so that workers can know the rules (on who may be left out of the plan and which groups of employees may be favored under the plan's benefit formulas). Also, if the employer retains control over fund assets, there are financial reporting requirements so that participants (and the government) can monitor the investment of their money. In some cases, the costs for servicing these plans can be substantial.

13. The other factors that would induce employers to set up plans were workforce changes such as lower turnover or more full-time employees (7.1 percent), greater demand by employees or unions (6.8 percent),lower setup or administrative costs (4.8 percent), and less costly or burdensome federal laws or regulations (4.6 percent). Kennell, *Retirement Plan Coverage*, table III-15.

14. The annual social security benefit for retired workers is approximately $8,376 in 1995. Office of the Actuary, Social Security Administration, 1994 (unpublished estimate). A full-time worker earning the minimum wage receives $8,840 a year (assuming a national minimum wage of $4.25 per hour).

15. Iris Lav, Cindy Mann and Pauline Abernathy, *The Contract With America Proposal: Assessing the Long-Term Impact*, Center on Budget and Policy Priorities, November 4, 1994, p. 24. "In 1995, more than 70 percent of taxpayers with earnings will be eligible for an up-front tax deduction for IRA contributions." In 1993, nearly 92 million taxpayers reported income from salaries and wages out of a total of 107 million taxpayers; taxpayers include couples filing a joint return. Michael E. Weber,

"Individual Income Tax Returns, 1993: Early Tax Estimates," *Statistics of Income Bulletin*, Internal Revenue Service, Fall, 1994, p. 22, table 2.

16. Michael E. Weber, *Statistics of Income Bulletin*, p. 25, table 3.

17. John R. Woods, "Pension Coverage Among the Baby Boomers: Initial Findings from a 1993 Survey," *Social Security Bulletin*, vol. 57, No. 3, Fall 1994, table 1, p. 15, an unpublished estimate. Fifty-eight percent of workers who reported to contributing to an IRA in 1992 also said they were participating in their employer's retirement plan. (Six percent of private sector workers contributed to IRAs; 56 percent were also in another plan.) An earlier survey of all workers over age 25 found that 77 percent of those who reported having IRA accounts work for employers that offer other retirement plans. Bureau of the Census, *Survey of Income and Program Participation*, unpublished data, table D.

18. Pension and Welfare Benefits Administration, U.S. Department of Labor, et al., *Pension and Health Benefits of American Workers: New Findings from the April 1993 Current Population Survey*, May 1994, p. E-2, table E2.

19. Bureau of the Census, *Survey of Income and Program Participation*, unpublished estimate. The median income of people with IRAs who are also participating in other plans is more than $44,550; those with no plans have median incomes of $15,000.

20. See William G. Gale and John Karl Scholz, "IRAs and Household Saving," *American Economic Review*, December 1994. The revenue loss for IRAs is estimated to be $8.4 billion in 1995. Joint Committee on Taxation, *Estimates of Federal Tax Expenditures for Fiscal Years 1995–1999*, 1994, p. 18, table 1 (prepared for the House Committee on Ways and Means and the Senate Committee on Finance).

21. For those without homes, the median personal savings amount (liquid financial assets) was $800. Congressional Budget Office, *Baby Boomers in Retirement: An Early Perspective*, September 1993, p. 70, table C-7 (tabulations using the 1989 Survey of Consumer Finances). Most older persons receive little income from savings and other assets. In 1992, 22 percent of all "aged units" received less than $250 a year in income from savings. The median income from assets for all units age 65 or older was $1,719. (Aged units are households that have at least one person over age 65.) Susan Grad, Social Security Administration, *Income of the Population 55 or Older, 1992*, May 1994, p. 87, table V.D.1.

22. Congressional Budget Office, *Baby Boomers*, p. 70, table C-7.

23. Congressional Budget Office, *Baby Boomers*, p. 68, table C-5 (figure for nonhousing worth includes savings and tangible assets such as automobiles). In 1993, half of all people over 65 received less than $10,808 a year in income from all sources. (Bureau of the Census, *Income, Poverty, and Valuations of Noncash Benefits: 1993*, U.S. Department of Commerce, unpublished data.)

24. Bureau of the Census, U.S. Department of Commerce, excerpt from *Income, Poverty, and Valuation of Noncash Benefits: 1993, 1994*, table C.

25. Bureau of the Census, U.S. Department of Commerce, *Income, Poverty, and Health Insurance: 1993*, October 1994, p. 303, table A-2.

26. The Villers Foundation, *On the Other Side of Easy Street: Myths & Facts About the Economics of Old Age*, 1987, pp. 12–14.

27. Bureau of Labor Statistics, U.S. Department of Labor, *Employer Costs for Employee Compensation*, March 1993, p. 4 (includes all private employers whether or

not they provide retirement benefits). A Chamber of Commerce survey reports that in 1992, employer costs for retirement programs accounted for 6.1 percent of payroll. U.S. Chamber Research Center, *Employee Benefits: Survey Data from Benefit Year 1992*, 1993, p. 23, table 12 (includes defined benefit pension plan contributions; employer defined contribution plan payments; profit sharing, stock bonus, and employee stock ownership plans; pension plan premiums under insurance and annuity contracts; and administrative and other costs).

28. A proposal along these lines was introduced by former Representative Alan Wheat. H.R. 4534, 103d Cong., 2d Sess., 1994.

PART V. WHAT IS TO BE DONE?

CHAPTER 16. MAKING THE OLD WAY WORK (REFORM PROPOSALS WITHIN A VOLUNTARY SYSTEM), PAGES 199–204

1. Citizens' Commission on Pension Policy, June 8, 1993 (statement of Paul Edwards).

2. "Special Report," *BNA Pension & Benefits Reporter* vol. 21 June 6, 1994, pp. 1119–20.

3. When an industry is dominated by nontraditional workers, Gordon believes that it may be necessary to limit employers' choice of plans to occupational-based ones. Due to the continuing changes in the economy, he believes that this approach would lead to the widespread adoption of occupational plans and the phasing out of the employment-based system.

4. S. 2235, 93d Cong., 1st Sess., 1973.

5. The bill envisioned that the funds would operate like defined contribution pension plans, with individual accounts for participants. Contributions would be tax deductible (up to specified limits) and immediately vested. The amounts of contributions, but not investment earnings, would be guaranteed. Workers would be permitted to retire at any age, but only once. The money accumulated in their accounts, plus projected earnings on those amounts, would then be used to pay lifetime monthly benefits to retirees and their surviving spouses. Once payment began, the annuities would be guaranteed.

CHAPTER 17. NEW DIRECTIONS (REFORM PROPOSALS FOR A MANDATORY SYSTEM), PAGES 205–216

1. Public Law. No. 89-73, Section 101(1).

2. Teresa Ghilarducci, *Labor's Capital: The Economics and Politics of Private Pensions* (Cambridge: MIT Press, 1993). Professor Ghilarducci took a leave of absence from Notre Dame in September 1994 to serve as assistant director of the Employee Benefits Division at the AFL-CIO in Washington, D.C.

3. President's Commission on Pension Policy, *Coming of Age: Toward a National Retirement Income Policy*, February 26, 1981. See Donald S. Grubbs, Jr., "Solving the Coverage Problem Under Private Pension Plans," *BNA Pension and Benefits Reporter*, Special Supplement, December 1994, p. 5–27.

4. All minimum universal pension proposals are similar in their reliance on

mandatory contributions to a pension system that will supplement the existing social security system. They differ from one another in two main respects: first, the control of investments — whether it lies mainly with a clearinghouse arrangement run by public boards, with employers through private plans, or with financial institutions; and second, the treatment of pension contributions above the minimum — whether they will be limited and whether they will receive tax breaks.

5. S. 3184, 102d Cong., 2d Sess., 1992.

6. H.R. 2390, 102d Cong., 1st Sess.

7. Professor Guarrera teaches at the California State University at Northridge.

8. American Society of Pension Actuaries National Retirement Income Policy Committee, *National Retirement Income Policy: Executive Summary and Research Papers*, 1994.

9. These contributions would be either amounts sufficient to produce a defined benefit of one-third of 1 percent of their workers' final pay *or* a defined contribution amount ranging from 2 percent of current pay for younger employees up to 4 percent for older employees.

10. ASPA Committee, *National Retirement Income Policy*, p. 73.

11. Sidney Margolius, "The Cost of Retirement, and 2 Beers a Week," *Washington Star*, March 18, 1978.

12. John Sherlock, "Retirement Costs in the U.S.," *USA Today*, September 15, 1982. Inflation-adjusted 1994 amounts were: New York City, $18,033; Chicago, $15,124; Atlanta, $14,764; Los Angeles, $15,884. The Reagan administration eliminated the retired couples' budget in 1982. The official explanation was that the market baskets used in the budgets were outdated and it would be too costly to reconstruct them. Some advocates for the elderly suspected that the action was motivated by a concern that the budgets too dramatically exposed the inadequacy of U.S. retirement income programs at a time when the administration was proposing to cut them back.

13. Board of Trustees of the Federal Old-Age and Survivors Insurance and Disability Trust Funds, *1994 Annual Report of the Board of Trustees of the Federal Old-Age and Survivors Insurance and Disability Trust Funds*, April 11, 1994.

14. Merton C. Bernstein and Joan B. Bernstein, *Social Security: The System That Works* (New York: Basic Books, 1988), pp. 232–9.

15. Payments would be in a joint and survivor form for married participants. Also, retirees would be allowed to take 20 percent of their accounts as a lump sum, with the remaining 80 percent payable as an annuity. Vineeta Anand, "Mandatory System Gives Benefits to All," *Pensions & Investments*, August 22, 1994.

16. William G. Gale and Robert E. Litan, "Saving Our Way Out of the Deficit Dilemma," *Brookings Review*, Fall 1993, pp. 6–11. See also Robert E. Litan, "Force-Feeding Our Piggy Banks," *Washington Post*, May 30, 1993. Gale and Litan's proposal is similar to that outlined by Leon Irish, except that there would be no tax breaks for contributions on earnings. Only people earning $20,000 or more would be required to save.

17. Matt Moffett, "Latin American Model for Financial Reform," *Wall Street Journal*, August 22, 1994.

18. Estelle James and Dimitri Vittas, "Mandatory Savings Schemes: Are They an Answer to the Old Age Security Problems?" presented at Securing Employer

Based Pensions: An International Perspective, symposium of the Pension Research Council, Wharton School of the University of Pennsylvania, May 5–6, 1994. Chile requires all workers to purchase disability insurance and provides public assistance for those outside the system.

19. World Bank, *Averting the Old Age Crisis: Policies to Protect the Old and Promote Growth* (New York: Oxford University Press, 1994).

Appendix A

Federal Government Agencies

U.S. DEPARTMENT OF LABOR

Pension and Welfare Benefits Administration
200 Constitution Avenue, NW
Washington, DC 20210
(202) 219-8233

Division of Technical Assistance and Inquiries
(202) 219-8776

Public Disclosure Room
(202) 219-8771

Office of the Inspector General
(202) 219-7296

PENSION AND WELFARE BENEFITS ADMINISTRATION FIELD OFFICES

790 E. Colorado Boulevard
Pasadena, CA 91101
(818) 583-7862

71 Stevenson Street, Suite 915
P.O. Box 190250
San Francisco, CA 94119
(415) 744-6700

One Bowdoin Square, 7th floor
Boston, MA 02144
(617) 424-4950

231 W. Lafayette Street, Room 619
Detroit, MI 48226
(313) 226-7450

1730 K Street NW, Suite 556
Washington, D.C. 20006
(202) 254-7013

111 NW 183rd Street, Suite 504
Miami, FL 33169
(305) 651-6464

1371 Peachtree Street, NE, Room
205
Atlanta, GA 30367
(404) 347-4090

410 S. State Street, Suite 841
Chicago, IL 60605
(312) 353-0900

1885 Dixie Highway, Suite 210
Fort Wright, KY 41011
(606) 578-4680

1111 Third Avenue, Room 860
Seattle, WA 98101
(206) 553-4244

911 Walnut, Room 1700
Kansas City, MO 64106
(816) 426-5131

815 Olive Street, Room 338
St. Louis, MO 63101
(314) 539-2691

1633 Broadway, Room 226
New York, NY 10019
(212) 399-5191

Gateway Building
3535 Market Street, Room M300
Philadelphia, PA 19104
(215) 596-1134

525 S. Griffin Street, Room 707
Dallas, TX 75202
(214) 767-6831

INTERNAL REVENUE SERVICE

Employee Plans Technical and Actuarial Division
1111 Constitution Avenue, NW, Room 6526
Washington, DC 20224
(202) 622-6074 or 6075
(1:30–4:30 P.M. eastern time, Monday–Thursday)

KEY DISTRICT OFFICES —
EMPLOYEE PLANS
EXEMPT ORGANIZATIONS

CENTRAL REGION
EP/EO Division
Internal Revenue Service
550 Main Street
Cincinnati, OH 45202
(513) 684-3751

NORTH ATLANTIC REGION
EP/EO Division
Internal Revenue Service
10 MetroTech Center
625 Fulton Street
Brooklyn, NY 11201
(718) 488-2010

MID-ATLANTIC REGION
EP/EO Division
Internal Revenue Service
31 Hopkins Plaza
Baltimore, MD 21201
(410) 962-3290

MIDWEST REGION
EP/EO Division
Internal Revenue Service
P.O. Box A3290, DPN-28-4
Chicago, IL 60609
(312) 886-4700

SOUTHWEST REGION
EP/EO Division
Internal Revenue Service
4900 DAL
1100 Commerce St.
Dallas, TX 75242
(214) 767-1490

SOUTHEAST REGION
EP/EO Division
Internal Revenue Service
Stop 500-D, Room 1503
401 W. Peachtree Street, NW
Atlanta, GA 30365
(404) 331-6949

WESTERN REGION
EP/EO Division
Internal Revenue Service
300 N. Los Angeles, Room 5101
Los Angeles, CA 90012
(213) 894-3748

PENSION BENEFIT GUARANTY CORPORATION

1200 K Street, NW
Washington, DC 20005
(202) 326-4040

Case Operations and Compliance Department
(202) 326-4000

Participant Services Division
(202) 326-4090

Problem Resolution Officer
(202) 326-4014

Freedom of Information Act Offices
(202) 326-4040

SOCIAL SECURITY ADMINISTRATION

Room 4J5 West High Rise
6401 Security Boulevard
Baltimore, MD 21235
(800) 772-1213

U.S. ADMINISTRATION ON AGING

330 Independence Avenue, SW
Washington, DC 20201
(202) 619-0724

U.S. CONGRESS

U.S. Capitol Switchboard
Washington, DC 20515

SENATE COMMITTEES

Committee on Labor and Human Resources
835 Senate Hart Office Building
Washington, DC 20510
(202) 224-6770

Committee on Finance
205 Senate Dirksen Office Building
Washington, DC 20510
(202) 224-4515

Special Committee on Aging
G-31 Dirksen Senate Office Building
Washington, DC 20510
(202) 224-5364

HOUSE OF REPRESENTATIVES COMMITTEES

Committee on Economic and Educational Opportunities
2181 Rayburn House Office Building
Washington, DC 20515

Subcommittee on Oversight
Committee on Ways and Means
1102 Longworth House Office Building
Washington, DC 20515
(202) 225-3625

Appendix B:

Private Organizations

AFL-CIO
Department of Employee Benefits
815 16th Street, NW
Washington, DC 20006
(202) 647-5202

American Association of Retired Persons
Pension Equity Project
601 E Street, NW, Room A5520
Washington, DC 20049
(202) 434-2060

Citizens' Commission on Pension Policy
56 Treetop Avenue
Springfield, MA 01118
(413) 796-1710

National Council of Senior Citizens
1331 F Street, NW, 5th floor
Washington, DC 20004
(202) 347-8800

Older Women's League
666 11th Street, NW, Suite 700
Washington, DC 20001
(202) 783-6686

Pension Rights Center
918 16th Street, NW, Suite 704
Washington, DC 20006
(202) 296-3776

Appendix C:

Pension Information and Counseling Demonstration Projects

Pima Council on Aging
Pension Project
5055 E. Broadway, #104
Tucson, AZ 85711
(602) 790-7262 (serves Pima
  County)

California Advocates for Nursing
  Home Reform Pension Project
1610 Bush Street
San Francisco, CA 94109
(415) 474-5171 (Bay Area)
(800) 474-1116 (elsewhere in
  California)

Gerontology Institute
University of Massachusetts–
  Boston
Pension Assistance Project
100 Morrissey Street

Boston, MA 02125
(617) 287-7311 (Boston)
(800) 882-2003 (elsewhere in
  Massachusetts)

Area Agency on Aging
1B Pension Information Assistance
  Project
400 Franklin Center #4
29100 Northwestern Highway
Southfield, MI 48034
(810) 948-1640 (Serves Oakland
  and Macomb Counties)

Upper Peninsula Pension
  Information Assistance Project
Area Agency on Aging
P.O. Box 606
Escanaba, MI 49829
(906) 786-4701 (Upper Peninsula)

Minnesota Senior Federation
Metro Region Pension Rights
  Project
1885 University Avenue West,
  Suite 190
St. Paul, MN 55104
(612) 645-0261 (Twin Cities)
(800) 365-8765 (elsewhere in
  Minnesota)

Older Women's League Pension
  Project
c/o Aging Consult Inc.
10425 Old Olive Street, Suite 7
Creve Coeur, MO 63141
(314) 997-1811 (Serves St. Louis
  City and St. Louis County)

Legal Services for the Elderly
Pension Hotline
New York, NY 10036
(212) 997-7714 (New York City)
(800) 414-7714 (elsewhere in New
  York State)

Note: These projects were established under grants from the U.S. Admin-istration on Aging (AoA) that end in 1995. It is likely that new grants will be awarded to some or all of these projects and/or to new projects in other parts of the country. For information about the AoA Pension Information and Counseling Demonstration Program call (202) 619-1058.

Appendix D:

Legal Assistance

LEGAL ASSISTANCE PROGRAMS

Legal Aid Foundation of Los
   Angeles
Employment Law Office
1636 W. Eighth Street, Suite 313
Los Angeles, CA 90017
(213) 389-3581

Legal Assistance to the Elderly
1453 Mission Street
San Francisco, CA 94103
(415) 861-4444

Legal Hotline for Older Americans

Arizona (except Tucson) ....(800) 231-5441
Arizona (Tucson) ....(602) 623-5137
District of Columbia ....(202) 434-2170
Florida (except Dade County) ....(800) 252-5997
Florida (Dade County) ....(305) 576-5997
Maine (except Augusta) ....(800) 750-5353

Maine (Augusta)....................................(207) 623-1797
Michigan (except Lansing).........................(800) 347-5297
Michigan (Lansing)................................(517) 372-5959
New Mexico (except Albuquerque)...................(800) 876-6657
New Mexico (Albuquerque)..........................(505) 842-6252
Ohio (except Hamilton County) ....(800) 488-6070
Ohio (Hamilton County)............................(513) 621-8721
Pennsylvania (except Allegheny County) ....(800) 262-5297
Pennsylvania (Allegheny County) ....(412) 262-5297
Texas (except Austin).............................(800) 622-2520
Texas (Austin) ....(800) 477-3950

LAWYER REFERRAL PROGRAMS

National Academy of Elder Law
  Attorneys, Inc.
655 North Alvernon Way, Suite
  108
Tucson, AZ 85711
(602) 881-4005

National Center for Employee
  Stock Ownership (ESOPs)
1201 Martin Luther King Jr. Way,
  2nd floor
Oakland, CA 94612
(510) 272-9461

National Employment Lawyers
  Association
600 Harrison Street, Suite 535
San Francisco, CA 94107
(415) 227-4655

National Pension Assistance
  Project
918 16th Street, NW, Suite 704
Washington, DC 20006
(202) 296-3776

National Senior Citizens Law
  Center
1815 H Street, NW Suite 700
Washington, DC 20006
(202) 887-5280

Northeast Ohio Legal Services
700 Metropolitan Tower Building
Youngstown, OH 44503
(216) 744-3196

Appendix E:

Publications

U. S. DEPARTMENT OF LABOR PUBLICATIONS

Division of Public Affairs
Pension and Welfare Benefits Administration
200 Constitution Avenue, NW, Room N-5651
Washington, DC 20210
(202) 219-8921

How to Obtain Employee Benefit Documents from the Labor Department (free)

Consumer Information Center
P.O. Box 100
Pueblo, CO 81002

What You Should Know About the Pension Law (50¢)
How to File a Claim for Your Benefits (free)

U.S. Government Printing Office
Superintendent of Documents
Washington, DC 20402

Simplified Employee Pensions: What Small Businesses Need to Know
($1, order number 045-000-00256-0)

INTERNAL REVENUE SERVICE PUBLICATIONS

All the following publications are free. Call (800) 829-3676 to order.

Individual Retirement Arrangements (Publication 590)
Retirement Plans for Self-Employed Persons (Publication 560)
Tax Sheltered Annuity Programs for Employees of Public Schools and Certain Tax-Exempt Organizations (Publication 571)
Looking Out for #2: A Married Couple's Guide to Understanding Your Benefit Choices at Retirement from a Defined Contribution Plan (Publication 1565)
Looking Out for #2: A Married Couple's Guide to Understanding Your Benefit Choices at Retirement from a Defined Benefit Plan (Publication 1566)

PENSION BENEFIT GUARANTY CORPORATION PUBLICATIONS

Pension Benefit Guaranty Corporation
1200 K Street, NW
Washington, DC 20005

Your Guaranteed Pension (free)

U.S. Government Printing Office
Superintendent of Documents
Washington, DC 20402

Your Pension ($1, order number: GPO Serial #068-000-00003-3)

AMERICAN ASSOCIATION OF RETIRED PERSONS PUBLICATIONS

AARP Fulfillment
601 E Street, NW
Washington, DC 20049

A Guide to Understanding Your Pension Plan (free; order number D13533)
A Woman's Guide to Pension Rights (free; order number D12558)
Women, Pensions & Divorce (Small Reforms That Could Make a Big Difference) (free; order number D14956)

Appendix E:

Publications

U. S. DEPARTMENT OF LABOR PUBLICATIONS

Division of Public Affairs
Pension and Welfare Benefits Administration
200 Constitution Avenue, NW, Room N-5651
Washington, DC 20210
(202) 219-8921

How to Obtain Employee Benefit Documents from the Labor Department (free)

Consumer Information Center
P.O. Box 100
Pueblo, CO 81002

What You Should Know About the Pension Law (50¢)
How to File a Claim for Your Benefits (free)

U.S. Government Printing Office
Superintendent of Documents
Washington, DC 20402

Simplified Employee Pensions: What Small Businesses Need to Know
($1, order number 045-000-00256-0)

INTERNAL REVENUE SERVICE PUBLICATIONS

All the following publications are free. Call (800) 829-3676 to order.

Individual Retirement Arrangements (Publication 590)
Retirement Plans for Self-Employed Persons (Publication 560)
Tax Sheltered Annuity Programs for Employees of Public Schools and Certain Tax-Exempt Organizations (Publication 571)
Looking Out for #2: A Married Couple's Guide to Understanding Your Benefit Choices at Retirement from a Defined Contribution Plan (Publication 1565)
Looking Out for #2: A Married Couple's Guide to Understanding Your Benefit Choices at Retirement from a Defined Benefit Plan (Publication 1566)

PENSION BENEFIT GUARANTY CORPORATION PUBLICATIONS

Pension Benefit Guaranty Corporation
1200 K Street, NW
Washington, DC 20005

Your Guaranteed Pension (free)

U.S. Government Printing Office
Superintendent of Documents
Washington, DC 20402

Your Pension ($1, order number: GPO Serial #068-000-00003-3)

AMERICAN ASSOCIATION OF RETIRED PERSONS PUBLICATIONS

AARP Fulfillment
601 E Street, NW
Washington, DC 20049

A Guide to Understanding Your Pension Plan (free; order number D13533)
A Woman's Guide to Pension Rights (free; order number D12558)
Women, Pensions & Divorce (Small Reforms That Could Make a Big Difference) (free; order number D14956)

OLDER WOMEN'S LEAGUE PUBLICATIONS

Older Women's League
666 11th Street, NW, Suite 700
Washington, DC 20001

Women and Pensions ($6)

PENSION RIGHTS CENTER PUBLICATIONS

Pension Rights Center
918 16th Street, NW, Suite 704
Washington, DC 20006

Can You Count on Getting a Pension? Vesting Rules ($3.00)
Donde Buscar Ayuda Cuando Hay Un Problema De Pension ($8.50)
National Pension Assistance Project Lawyers Directory ($8.50)
Protecting Your Pension Money ($8.00)
SEPS: The Pension Plan (Almost) Nobody Knows About ($3.50)
Where to Look for Help with a Pension Problem ($8.50)
Your Pension Rights at Divorce: What Women Need to Know ($23.95)

Appendix F:

Government Statistical Resources

BUREAU OF THE CENSUS

Income Branch
HHES Division, Room 307-1
Iverson Mall
Washington, DC 20233-8500
(301) 763-8576

DEPARTMENT OF LABOR

Office of Research and Economic
    Analysis
Pension and Welfare Benefits
    Administration
200 Constitution Avenue, NW,
    Room N-5718
Washington, DC 20210
(202) 219-5752

Bureau of Labor Statistics
2 Massachusetts Avenue, NE
Washington, DC 20212
(202) 606-5900

INTERNAL REVENUE SERVICE

Statistics of Income Division
P.O. Box 2608
Washington, DC 20013
(202) 874-0410

SOCIAL SECURITY ADMINISTRATION

Office of Research and Statistics
4301 Connecticut Avenue, NW
Washington, DC 20008
(202) 282-7126

INDEX

ABOUT THE AUTHORS

Karen Ferguson is director of the Pension Rights Center. A lawyer and widely recognized pension rights advocate, she testifies frequently before Congress, is regularly quoted in the press, and often appears on radio and television talk shows to discuss pension issues. Before starting the Center in 1976, she worked as a lawyer for a law firm and the federal government, a consultant to public interest organizations, and an advisor to a large pension fund. She is a graduate of Bryn Mawr College and Harvard Law School, and the recipient of a Wonder Woman Foundation Award.

Kate Blackwell, coauthor with Ralph Nader of the 1973 *You and Your Pension,* is a freelance writer living in Washington, D.C. Her published works include short stories, travel pieces, book reviews, and two nonfiction books. She also teaches writing. A graduate of Wellesley College, with an M.A. in English from the University of North Carolina at Chapel Hill, she was a 1994 Fellow at the Virginia Center for the Creative Arts and is a member of the District of Columbia Bar's Board on Professional Responsibility.

The Pension Rights Center is a nonprofit public interest group that protects and promotes the pension rights of workers, retirees, and their families. For nearly two decades, the Center has been at the forefront of efforts to reform the nation's pension laws and inform the public on pension issues. The Center's National Pension Assistance Project operates a nationwide lawyer referral service. Its Women's Pension Project targets inequities in pension policies affecting women. Millions of retirees, widows, and divorced women can now count on getting pensions as a result of the Center's advocacy, education, and legal assistance activities over the years.